Midnight Basketball

Midnight Basketball

Race, Sports, and Neoliberal Social Policy

DOUGLAS HARTMANN

The University of Chicago Press
Chicago and London

Douglas Hartmann is professor of sociology at the University of Minnesota.

The University of Chicago Press, Chicago 60637
The University of Chicago Press, Ltd., London
© 2016 by The University of Chicago
All rights reserved. Published 2016.
Printed in the United States of America

25 24 23 22 21 20 19 18 17 16   1 2 3 4 5

ISBN-13: 978-0-226-37484-0 (cloth)
ISBN-13: 978-0-226-37498-7 (paper)
ISBN-13: 978-0-226-37503-8 (e-book)
DOI: 10.7208/chicago/9780226375038.001.0001

Library of Congress Cataloging-in-Publication Data

Names: Hartmann, Douglas, author.
Title: Midnight basketball : race, sports, and neoliberal social policy / Douglas
    Hartmann.
Description: Chicago ; London : University of Chicago Press, 2016. | ©2016 |
    Includes bibliographical references and index.
Identifiers: LCCN 2015039622 | ISBN 9780226374840 (cloth : alkaline paper) |
    ISBN 9780226374987 (paperback : alkaline paper) | ISBN 9780226375038
    (e-book)
Subjects:: LCSH: Recreation and juvenile delinquency—United States. | Crime
    prevention—Social aspects—United States. | Youth league basketball—
    United States. | Urban youth—Government policy—United States.
Classification: LCC HV7432 .H37 2016 | DDC 362.7/7896073—dc23 LC
    record available at http://lccn.loc.gov/2015039622

This book is for my parents,
Robert T. and Esther T. Hartmann

CONTENTS

PREFACE

The notion that sport is an effective tool for risk prevention, intervention, and even social mobility for otherwise marginalized, disadvantaged young people—especially for boys and young men of color—abounds. You hear it espoused by sports enthusiasts and youth sport organizations. It appears in corporate advertising campaigns and on school websites, and it is championed by youth programs ranging from those at your local club or recreation department to multimillion dollar, multinational United Nations development initiatives.

The idea that sport is a powerful and positive developmental force is, of course, an old one, almost as old as the origins of modern sport itself. But this belief appears today in the early twenty-first century in the United States and all over the world in many forms and under quite different conditions. Among the most prominent and important new trends in the sport-for-marginalized-youth playbook are programs oriented not so much toward education and development as toward control—that is, programs designed not to provide opportunities for young people to be empowered and encouraged as they grow up, but rather to change their behaviors and attitudes and divert them from pathways and behaviors that are believed to be dangerous or somehow problematic. With "crime prevention" or "risk reduction" as the watchwords, it is what some have called "the social problems industry" in youth sports and recreation; I myself tend to think of sport in this guise as "intervention."

This book is about the program or policy innovation that I believe did more than any other to bring this latest generation of sport-based social intervention into being: the late-night, basketball-based crime prevention programs that emerged in the late 1980s and early 1990s in dozens of American cities, the programs that came to be known as midnight basketball. It is a history of the midnight basketball idea, a cultural and institutional analysis of why midnight basketball programs were at first so popular and then so controversial, and a study of how such programs evolved, and were implemented and experienced, and expanded on in the decade that followed.

Midnight basketball is not, as will become clear below, a perfect microcosm, or ideal type, of all sport-based social intervention programs for youth and young adults. But the innovation was extremely well known and widely copied early on, and the struggles these programs faced in the late 1990s and early 2000s provided lessons and cautionary tales that helped shape programs today in a multitude of ways, some of which current funders and supporters of the whole set of sport-based social intervention programs may not even realize. Its most distinctive qualities—the older target age of participants, its explicit police presence and containment rationale, its late-night, inner-city, basketball-only characteristics and, most of all, its public prominence and deeply racialized character—expose and reveal, I believe, the underlying cultural tensions and institutional realities that inform, define, and shape this entire field of sport-based social policy and practice in the neoliberal era. Put differently, midnight basketball embodies the greatest possibilities of neoliberal sport-based intervention as well as reveals its dangers and potential downfalls. Ultimately, in fact, I will argue that midnight basketball provides a unique lens onto the culture of sport and race in America and neoliberal social policy broadly conceived.

I didn't necessarily realize all these angles and implications when I first got started working in and around a few local midnight basketball programs almost twenty years ago, or even when I made the commitment to turn my interest and experience in midnight basketball into a full-fledged, social scientific research project a decade after that. But I did have a certain kind of faith or intuition—solidified by my reading of the great French sociologist Pierre Bourdieu's call for more research on sport ([1982] 1988) and more grounded, case-based research (1998), and Howie Becker's (1998) delightful *Tricks of the Trade*—that what made midnight basketball interesting and intriguing to me had a certain, much broader cultural significance and theoretical import. I don't know whether my research on midnight basketball as rendered in this book can live up to all that. It certainly took longer than I expected to even get to this point. But hopefully that vision and ambition provides a sense of how seriously I have taken this project, as well as conveys what I'm hoping it can contribute to scholarly research, public understanding, and public policy practice related to youth sports, race, social intervention, and neoliberal public policy in the contemporary world.

ACKNOWLEDGMENTS

All research and writing is, to one degree or another, conducted in dialogue with others, and thus requires an author like myself to acknowledge and thank all those who have provided inspiration, assistance, and support along the way. For a project that had as many moving parts as this one, and has taken as long to come to fruition, that list is long, and I apologize in advance for anyone whom I have overlooked.

First on this list of individuals to recognize are those who offered encouragement, counsel, and insight when this project wasn't even really yet a project—my senior colleagues at the University of Minnesota Ron Aminzade, Candace Kruttschnitt (now at Toronto), and Jeylan Mortimer, as well as early career mentors Steve Cornell, George Lipsitz, Hugh "Bud" Mehan, and Dave Roediger.

Next are all the students, both graduate and undergraduate, at Minnesota who helped at various points and with different tasks. Darren Wheelock signed on as my first research assistant when I didn't really know what I was doing and has stayed with me even as the project took numerous (and often unexpected) twists and turns. As undergraduates years ago, John Gipson and Randon Gardley were the core players on the fieldwork team who helped with all the interviewing and fieldwork detailed in the ethnographic chapters of the book. Kyle Green, Christina Kwauk, Alex Manning, Mike Massoglia, John Sullivan, Antoni Tang, and Melissa Weiner were among the best collaborators and coauthors I could ever ask for, even if the papers we did together weren't as well circulated or directly cited as they might have deserved. Other great graduate students—many of whom are now well into their own careers—who provided stimulation, support, and real help on this particular project were Amy August, Joyce Bell, Amy Blackstone, Tiffany Davis, Danielle Docka-Filipeck, Sara Dorrow, Murat Ergin, Emily Houghton, Thomas C. Johnson, Heather McLaughlin, Wendy Moore, Libby Sharrow, and Marcia Williams. Undergraduates who made specific contributions include Alex Casey, Ben Fiest, Molly Goin, Tiffany Mak, Chris Phelps, Roman Postle and, last but certainly not least (since he shouldered the fact-checking, formatting, and indexing in the home stretch), Jason Robey.

Comments, questions, criticisms, and suggestions from numerous audiences have played a major role in shaping this work. I have benefited from especially engaged and inspiring audiences at a slew of Minnesota venues: the African American Research Collective, the Life Course Center, the Departments of Sociology and American Studies, the Tucker Center, and the Center for the Study of Individuals in Society in the Psychology Department. I also received wonderful, provocative feedback from presentations at Augsburg College, Brandeis University, Bryn Mawr College, Concordia University, Morehead, the University of Illinois (Urbana-Champaign and Chicago), and the annual meetings of the American Sociological Association, the North American Society for Sport Management (NASSM), and the North American Society for the Study of Sport (NASSS) as well as at a Harvard Color Lines Conference organized long ago by my one-time undergraduate employer Gary Orfield.

Folks in my home department who offered particularly helpful remarks, or directed me to literatures or ideas I otherwise would not have encountered, include Liz Boyle, Michael Goldman, Teresa Gowan, Ann Meier, Josh Page, David Pellow, Joachim Savelsberg, Robin Stryker (now at Arizona), and Rob Warren. Extra thank-yous go to Penny Edgell, Joe Gerteis, Teresa Swartz, and Chris Uggen who were unfailing in their friendship and support of this project even as its extended germination delayed my collaborations with each of them. Additional generous colleagues in other Minnesota departments have been Rose Brewer, Jo Ann Buysse, Rod Ferguson (now at UIC), Walt Jacobs (now at SJSU), Mary Jo Kane, Nicole LaVoi, Josephine Lee, Rich Lee, Larry May, Keith Mayes, Toben Nelson, Jennifer Pierce, Alex Rothman, Mark Snyder, Joe Soss (several times over!), Catherine Squires, and John Wright.

Scholars around the country who helped move the project along in one way or another at key moments include Jo Mills Braddock, Scott Brooks, Susan Brownell, Michael Burawoy, Ben Carrington, Laurence Chalip, Jay Coakley, C. L. Cole, John Crompton, Michael Giardina, Richard Guilianotti, Keith Harrison, David Karin, Bruce Kidd, Richard King, Samantha King, Charles Lemert, Andrew Lindner, Reuben May, Doug McAdam, Mary McDonald, Mike Messner, Robert Schinke, Loïc Wacquant, Bob Washington, Mary Waters, and Peter Witt. Special commendations also go to C. L. Cole and

Dan Cook for having the faith to publish the first piece that came out of this project in article form.

I must also offer my gratitude for the editors and presses who saw fit to publish articles and chapters related to this project as it developed. Several chapters draw on previously published works quite directly. The argument, analysis, and framing that is presented in chapters 2 and 3 found its first form in "Notes on Midnight Basketball and the Cultural Politics of Recreation, Race, and At-Risk Urban Youth" (*Journal of Sport and Social Issues* 25 [2001]: 339–72). Chapter 4 incorporates material drawn from research I originally conducted and published with Brooks Depro as "Re-Thinking Sports-Based Community Crime Prevention: A Preliminary Analysis of the Relationships between Midnight Basketball and Urban Crime Rates" (*Journal of Sport and Social Issues* 30 [2006]: 180–96). Chapter 5 is based on the methods, findings, and analysis first published with Darren Wheelock as "Midnight Basketball and the 1994 Crime Bill Debates: The Operation of a Racial Code" (*Sociological Quarterly* 48 [2007]: 315–42). And chapter 6 is informed by and reproduces some passages from "Rethinking Community-Based Crime Prevention through Sports" (pp. 73–88 in *Sport for Development, Peace, and Social Justice*, edited by Robert Schinke and Stephanie J. Hanrahan [Morgantown: West Virginia University Press / Fitness Information Technologies, 2012]). Permission from Sage, Wiley, and West Virginia University Press/FIT, respectively, to use and adapt these works for this book is gratefully acknowledged.

Douglas Mitchell once again served as my editor at the University of Chicago Press, and this book would not exist without his patience and professionalism. I also deeply appreciate the production assistance provided by Tim McGovern and Kyle Adam Wagner at crucial stages in the process, and Kelly Finefrock-Creed's close reading and attention to detail reminded me again of all that is special about the U of C and its press. Pauline Swartz supplied invaluable archival and informational assistance in the research phases of the project, and Letta Page did her usual brilliant job of helping to clean and smooth the prose as chapters took shape. I should also note that funding from the Life Course Center and the Center for Urban and Regional Affairs at the University of Minnesota helped with the initial launch of this project, and a Sabbatical Supplement from the university allowed me to shape all the various pieces into a relatively coherent whole in the home stretch.

Without getting too sentimental, I also want to give a shout-out to the family I share my daily life with—my wife, Teresa, who not only puts up with my sometimes crazy ideas and work habits but actually enables and encourages them, and my children, Benjamin and Emma. I can only hope to have the positive and profound influence on them and their lives that my parents have had on me and mine. Often critical but never cynical, my dad helped seed my love of sports and taught me that it is not whether you win or lose, but rather how and why, and with and for whom, you play the game that really matters. And my mother's love and support has been unconditional. Even though their politics may be somewhat different from mine, I know that my parents' lifelong commitment, in both principle and practice, to fairness, encouragement, and support for all not only inspired this project, but it also represents the higher ideals to which we can and should all aspire. This book is dedicated to them for those reasons. And I don't want to forget John MacAloon and the late Larry Hawkins, from my early academic days in Chicago. I've thanked them both before for the various contributions they made to my career and whole way of thinking, but this project may actually be a better, more direct reflection of the lessons both taught me than anything that has come before it.

Finally, I need to recognize and thank all those people in various basketball-based programs who talked to me and allowed me to be part of their lives and worlds over the course of this research. Some of you will see your names in the pages that follow, or at least pseudonyms. Others will not—either because there's just too many of you to acknowledge or because such acknowledgements would have been awkward or inappropriate. But please know that while I can't name or remember each one of you, my goal with this book has been to honor your involvement in this work, and your commitment to the communities you live in and the ongoing project of using sport to make the world a better place.

ONE

Introduction:
At the Intersection of Sports, Race, and Risk

Midnight basketball may not have been invented in Chicago, but the City of the Big Shoulders, home of Michael Jordan and the Bulls, is where midnight basketball first came to national prominence. It is also where I first began to think seriously about the audacious notion that having young men in shorts run around in the wee hours of the night trying to throw a leather ball through a metal hoop constituted meaningful social policy.

In the winter of 1990, the Chicago Housing Authority (CHA)—with a matching grant of $50,000 from the Department of Housing and Urban Development (HUD) under the direction of Jack Kemp, the former congressman whose initial claim to fame was as quarterback for the Buffalo Bills—organized leagues in two of its notoriously troubled housing projects (Rockwell Gardens and Henry Horner Homes) for purposes of urban social intervention and change. Even before the first game was held, the Chicago midnight basketball experiment was a public relations coup. The initiative was followed closely in the local media and praised on editorial pages. Prominent local leaders—former Chicago Bulls coach and NBC basketball commentator Doug Collins among them—were identified as "league owners" (a donation over $2,000 made anyone an owner), local sports celebrities including the legendary Jordan himself were signed up to make appearances at games, and the *Chicago Sun-Times* agreed to publish league statistics, standings, and schedules in its sports section. Opening night at Malcolm X College was attended by the mayor, HUD secretary and presidential cabinet member Kemp, and other luminaries, and halftime featured a performance by the Jesse White Tumbling Team (known for its performances at Bulls games). Within weeks, the program had been featured on ABC's *Good Morning America*, in one of NBC's national NBA broadcasts, and in dozens of newspapers and magazines across the country. Not long after,

President George H. W. Bush would identify midnight basketball as one of the signature programs of his Points of Light Foundation.

I wasn't right there, but I did have a small, backstage connection with midnight basketball in Chicago. It had come somewhat by happenstance in the summer of 1989, well before I thought of midnight basketball as an object of research—or of myself as a social scientist, for that matter. I was a recent college graduate living on Chicago's South Side, and I had taken a part-time position as a staff assistant for a highly respected high school educator, community leader, and youth sports advocate named Larry Hawkins. A one-time Harlem Globetrotter, Hawkins was the first African American coach of an all-black team to win the state championship in Illinois, a feat accomplished in 1964, the year *after* his most famous player—Connie Hawkins, no relation—graduated. In the wake of the so-called Martin Luther King riots of the late sixties, Hawkins had quit his job as a public school teacher and coach to launch a series of highly regarded sport-based community outreach and education programs for the University of Chicago (Hartmann 2003b). My new boss, it turned out, had ties with the new league's "commissioner," a city administrator named Gil Walker, and had been tapped to serve as an official consultant on the CHA initiative. As a staffer for Hawkins, I was tasked with reviewing CHA plans for the program, participating in staff discussions about the project, and eventually preparing a memo summarizing our analysis and recommendations.

Given the federal funding, the media attention, and the charismatic personalities involved, it was heady stuff. Truth be told, however, my boss wasn't entirely sold on the midnight basketball concept. Trained in the YMCA social work tradition, Hawkins was generally interested in earlier, longer term, and more extensive interventions in and especially through sport. He was also troubled by midnight basketball's lack of solid, well-developed educational elements or a serious jobs training component. (For my part, I recall being alternately puzzled and appalled by the emphasis on personal grooming—regular haircuts, proper attire, and even, if memory serves, the provision of free manicures.) Nevertheless, all of us in Hawkins's shop were impressed by the media coverage, both local and national, devoted to the initiative. We came to see that midnight basketball was on the cutting edge of a whole new generation of sport-based social programs, projects, and initiatives.

Motivated in part by the popularity of midnight basketball, in fact, Hawkins redoubled his efforts to champion sport-based programming for education and social intervention among mostly minority inner-city kids nationwide. Under the auspices of the Institute for Athletics and Education, the advocacy organization he had created in the 1970s, Hawkins organized a series of regional and national conferences, experimented with model programs for elementary school youth, and worked with high school coaches, both local and national, in training, test preparation, counseling, and grassroots sports advocacy. I remained involved with these efforts for the next couple of years, going to conferences in places ranging from Newark to Los Angeles, and did what I could to follow the development of midnight basketball along the way. At one point while in graduate school, I even found myself working with the sociologist Hugh Mehan in southeast San Diego, California, on an evaluation of a midnight basketball program (which included the making of a small, student-produced documentary) run by a nonprofit, religiously based outreach organization called High Five America. But for the most part, my interest in midnight basketball remained an after-hours side project, more advocacy than research. This was because by the middle of the 1990s, I had settled into a different project that combined my interests in sports and race: a dissertation study of the origins and impacts of the 1968 African American Olympic protest movement, the activism most famously associated with Tommie Smith's and John Carlos's iconic, clenched-fist victory stand demonstration.

The idea of taking on midnight basketball as a formal object of a scholarly study didn't really take shape for me until much later in the decade, *after* I had finished the first draft of a full-length book on the 1968 Olympic activism (Hartmann 2003a) and began reading what other scholars were writing about the emerging relationships among race, sports, and crime in contemporary American culture. What piqued my curiosity at that time (at least as I remember it now—who really knows how such things come to pass?) was midnight basketball's unique juxtaposition of the positive and negative perceptions of African American men that then dominated the American public imagination.

African American Men in the Post–Civil Rights American Culture

To many late twentieth- and early twenty-first-century observers (scholarly and otherwise), African American men appeared in the national culture and consciousness in one of two seemingly opposite forms: either as spectacular, superstar athletes or as violent, superpredator criminals, gangbangers, dropouts, and drug pushers. For most Americans, this juxtaposition was little more than a terrible and unfortunate irony, one of those strange quirks of a media-dominated society obsessed with entertainment, celebrity, and all the latest excesses. For a select handful of sport specialists and race critics, however, it was much, much more. For scholars like C. L. Cole, David Andrews,

Earl Smith, and Harry Edwards (on the sport front), or Eric Michael Dyson, David Theo Goldberg, bell hooks, Kobena Mercer, or Robin Kelley (from the race side),[1] the incongruous, ostensibly opposed representations of African American men actually revealed an underlying and indeed structuring logic—the cultural logic of race. More specifically, these social analysts and cultural commentators helped show that the fear of African American violence was intimately linked with the fascination with African American athleticism—and both were rooted in (and thus reproductive of) stereotypical perceptions of black culture and family life. In this cultural imaginary, in other words, crime represented the capitulation to the risks and dangers of the street, while sports embodied its most visible, socially sanctioned alternative.

Once these connections became clear, sport researchers began to document and analyze this racial dyad in earnest. Some focused on the marketing of "deviant" or somehow subversive African American athletes such as Charles Barkley, Dennis Rodman, Mike Tyson, or, slightly later, Allen Iverson (cf. Cashmore 2005; LaFrance and Rail 2001; Boyd 2003, 1997; Cole and Andrews 1996; T. Brown 2005). Some dug out the romanticized imagery underpinning the phenomenal success of the PBS documentary *Hoop Dreams* (Cole and King 1998), while others (Cole and Denny 1994; D. L. Andrews 1996) demonstrated how quickly and decisively the public discourse about star African American athletes such as Jordan or Magic Johnson shifted from celebration to condemnation once certain problems in their personal lives (gambling for Jordan, HIV infection for Johnson) became public. Yet other groups of scholars explored the media obsession with distinguishing "good" and "bad" black athletes (B. Wilson 1997); the public fixation on violence, crime, and mayhem among African American male athletes (Lapchick 2003; Berry and Smith 2000; Benedict 1998; Edwards 2000); or the "policing" of racially marked behaviors such as end zone dances in athletic arenas or the establishment of formal codes of conduct and sportsmanship by athletic leagues and officials (V. L. Andrews 1998, 1996; see also G. Hughes 2004; Cunningham 2009). And this isn't even to mention the work by scholars in other, related fields on the downward spiral of one-time NFL superstar and celebrity pitchman O. J. Simpson (Crenshaw 1997; L. Johnson and Roediger 2000; Lipsitz 1998, chaps. 5 and 6; Reed 1997; Williams 2001) or the traumatic case of Len Bias, the basketball star who died of a cocaine overdose the night he was drafted (#1 overall) by the Boston Celtics (Reeves and Campbell 1994).

As chronicled by Dan Baum (1996, 225), Tip O'Neill, the longtime Speaker of the House, called an emergency session for chairs of committees related to crime precisely because of this last incident. "Write me some goddamned legislation," O'Neill demanded of his aides and associates. "All anybody up in Boston is talking about is Len Bias. The papers are screaming for blood. We need to get out in front of this now. This week. Today. The Republicans beat us to it in 1984 and I don't want it to happen again."[2] Could there have been a clearer signal and precursor of the otherwise unappreciated power and import of sport and race linkages in criminal justice policy and public life more generally?

I found this work remarkable—sophisticated, relevant, and critical, clearly among the most vibrant and impressive bodies of research and writing by sport scholars that had ever been produced. Playing off of the assumption that sport is a uniquely powerful (if sometimes contradictory and often deeply contested) venue for race-making in contemporary American culture, this body of work served as an important corrective to popular, overly optimistic images and ideologies about race and sport. It showed that, contrary to their ostensibly positive and progressive appearances, sporting representations and practices were contained within stereotypical images of African American men—images that stripped black athletes of their agency and humanity on the one hand and reinscribed and naturalized racial difference on the other. I also became convinced that this sport-based sociology was on the cutting edge of contemporary critical race theory taken as a whole. In fact, I thought this work invited readers to see how deeply rooted racism and prejudice actually were (and are) in contemporary American culture, and to understand how they are conveyed not only through negative attitudes (as conventional sociological assumptions and methods would have it) but also through images, identities, discourses, and even ideals that are deeply romanticized. This sports-based scholarship had important contributions to make in terms of how racial formations and inequities are rationalized and legitimated in the post–civil rights United States. Perhaps it is not surprising that this work and many of these authors paved the way for much critical theoretical work in sport studies as well as broader explorations of sports' connection to color blindness, whiteness, and the normalization of mainstream, middle-class norms and values more generally (see, for examples, Leonard 2011, 2004; Carrington 2010, 1998).[3] And as I read and reflected, I kept coming back, time and again, to midnight basketball.

The core concept and underlying logic of midnight basketball played off both the positive and negative stereotypes of black men in the media and popular culture. More specifically and precisely, midnight basketball put the valorized images linking African American men and sport (basketball, in particular) in direct service of the problems or perceived pathologies of this population, combining these seemingly opposed racial images and cultural ideals into a single, synthetic solution. In the context of this vibrant body of work and the continuing societal interest in African American athletes, I found this unique combination more intellectually fascinating than ever and began to see a study of midnight basketball as an opportunity to take the study of these linkages among sport, race, and risk in some new directions.

For example, according to sport policy researchers Laurence Chalip and Arthur Johnson (1996), midnight basketball marked "the first time [in American history that] the [federal] legislature . . . seriously considered the possibility that sport could be incorporated into the domestic agenda" (426). Chalip and Johnson may have overstated the case a bit, but I took their point about the unique political and public policy status of midnight basketball in American legislative history seriously. I began to wonder why midnight basketball had received such unprecedented treatment, and what this said about the status and broader significance (or lack thereof) of sport and sport policy in contemporary American culture, politics, and policy.

Taking these questions about the broader impact and social significance of midnight basketball up another notch or two was the political controversy that surrounded the initiative during the 1994 crime bill debates. What had happened, in a nutshell, is this: Democrats, in classic Bill Clinton fashion, put forward the idea of including some new (if limited) federal funding for midnight basketball and other related sports programs under the crime prevention titles in the $33 billion omnibus bill. As the legislation neared ratification, self-styled conservative politicians and pundits—led by radio talk show host Rush Limbaugh, then at the zenith of his popularity—began to lambast midnight basketball as an example of everything they saw wrong with the crime bill and with Democratic approaches to crime prevention more generally. Once these criticisms took hold, Republicans mobilized multifaceted attacks that held up the bill's passage for several weeks and (arguably) led to the elimination of several billion dollars of prevention-oriented funding.

It was, in retrospect, impossible not to be struck by how much national attention midnight basketball received. I also puzzled over why conservative legislators and pundits suddenly attacked a program that had been a signature piece for a sitting Republican president only two short years before. What provoked this dramatic about-face? And perhaps more importantly, why had this small, experimental sport-based program come to play such a prominent and seemingly consequential role in the legislative process? At a projected cost of about $50 million, midnight basketball was, after all, a proverbial drop in the bucket, barely a tenth of a percentage point, a mere fraction of a fraction of the $33 billion bill. Although I couldn't prove it at the time, I became convinced that Republicans had used midnight basketball in much the same way they had mobilized the "Willie Horton" image during the 1988 presidential campaign: as a thinly veiled threat, a racial code intended to undermine support for the legislation and remake crime a partisan wedge issue (Mendelberg 2001, 1997).

Since midnight basketball served as the symbolic centerpiece of the legislative proceedings that produced the largest and most far-reaching criminal justice reforms in our nation's history (and whose basic policy framework is still in place today), I believed that a study of the program wouldn't just be about sport and sport policy, but could help us better understand the place of sport (and sport policy) in the public sphere—that is, its symbolic role in politics and the legitimation of public policy, what is often called the cultural politics of sport. Eventually, in fact, I came to realize that a study of midnight basketball was actually about transformations and changes in all manner of social policy—criminal justice, social welfare, urban development—in the post–civil rights, neoliberal era. Both because of its own social structure as well as the broader public attention that surrounded it, midnight basketball was, in other words, not only a product of these larger policy shifts. It was also a lens through which I could focus and refine my understanding of the nature of neoliberal social policy in the contemporary United States—its ideological and organizational structures, its racial dimensions, its conflation of punishment and prevention/paternalism and penology in a single disciplinary logic, and its popularization and promotion. In short, I came to believe that a study of midnight basketball would not just be about midnight basketball; it would also be about race and sport and risk prevention and neoliberal social policy most broadly conceived.

While it was easy to get swept up in these ideas about broad symbolic significance and policy impacts, there were concrete programmatic and policy dimensions here as well. Although decades of scholarly research made me skeptical about popular ideologies characterizing sport as a means for the development, socialization, and mobility of youth and young people, I didn't think of midnight basketball as an entirely misguided programming initiative. I didn't see supporters as political opportunists or policy pimps. Fascinated with sport's historic claims to youth development and social intervention, I came to believe that studying actual midnight basketball programs like those in Chicago and San Diego provided an opportunity to reexamine how sport could be used for social intervention and change—or what was coming to be called "risk prevention" (Foster and Spencer 2011; see also

P. Kelly 2000)—in the lives of young African American men. In other words, I started thinking that a study of midnight basketball had the potential to help explore the ways in which and the extent to which sport-based social programs and public policy could turn otherwise troubling racial images and stereotypes to productive use.

The "craft par excellence of the researcher," the great French sociologist Pierre Bourdieu said in his foundational "Program for a Sociology of Sport," is "investing a theoretical problem of far-reaching implications in an empirical object that is well-constructed and controllable with the means at hand" ([1982] 1988, 156). So it was for me, at least in theory, with midnight basketball. With all these different questions and analytic tentacles, midnight basketball was starting to look like a perfect case to study, a contained, concrete empirical phenomenon pregnant with broad meaning and social significance.

This book is, then, an attempt to make good on these ideas, this possibility and promise. It is an extensive, multifaceted case study of midnight basketball, the late-night basketball leagues that dozens of American cities organized in the last decade of the twentieth century for purposes of social intervention, risk reduction, and/or crime prevention (one's choice of terms, as we shall see, is complicated). It explains where this idiosyncratic policy innovation came from, how it became so popular at so many levels, the political controversies that surrounded it, and the programs and reforms that were eventually consolidated. The latter chapters of the book use ethnographic fieldwork to delve into the actual, on-the-ground experiences of operating and participating in basketball-based social programming, and the opportunities for intervention, resistance, and change presented therein. Overall, the book is also an attempt to use the case of midnight basketball to reveal and deepen our understanding of the broader social context and environment of neoliberalism, the dynamics of race and sport in contemporary society, the characteristics of neoliberal social policy, and the evolution, contributions, and limits of sport-based social intervention.

The Narrative and Analysis That Follows

This case study of midnight basketball, as I detail more fully in the methodological appendix, is what I have come to think of as an "emergent" case study. It is based on over a decade's worth of research and a number of journal articles, book chapters, conference presentations, and research reports. It is written largely in the first person in order to convey my own idiosyncratic understandings and interpretations of midnight basketball—its

structure and meaning, its social context, and its broader cultural and theoretical significance—as well as to capture the research methods and data
from which these understandings derive. The chapters do not, however, follow the actual logic and unfolding of the research project itself. Instead, the
book offers a more or less linear narrative that traces the history of the midnight basketball phenomenon, from its origin in the late 1980s and early
1990s, to its controversial explosion onto the national scene in the middle
of the decade, to the more scaled-back, programmatic reforms it settled into
as the new millennium emerged.

The next two chapters use original archival materials and oral history
interviews—situated in dialogue with the salient scholarly literatures on
sports history, the culture of race in post–civil rights America, and contemporary neoliberal social policy—as a means to describe and explain the
origins of midnight basketball as initially conceived in the late 1980s and
early 1990s. Chapter 2 provides the more concrete, immediate history of
where this program came from and an analysis of what made it so widely
popular, at least initially. It is in this context that midnight basketball's racial
roots and contours begin to emerge and take shape. Chapter 3 then extends
and deepens this analysis by locating midnight basketball in the broader
context of sport's long-standing (and self-satisfied) interventionist ideals
and romanticized racial ideology, late twentieth-century transformations in
neoliberal American social policy, and current American racial politics and
discourse.

Inspired by the work of culturally oriented sport sociologists such as
David Andrews, Ben Carrington, and C. L. Cole as well as that of critical
race theories and scholarship more generally, I explore the racialized and
gendered underpinnings of these dynamics in detail. This broad cultural
and historical context puts in relief the ideologies and cultural assumptions
about *both* the social value of sport *and* the perceived problems of urban
youth—the risks they face, and the risks they pose—that made sports-based
crime prevention programs such as midnight basketball so appealing to
political leaders and media elites across the political spectrum and that help
explain the power and enduring appeal of the race-sport-crime nexus. Social
context here is key. Indeed, the argument and analysis built up in these
chapters is that midnight basketball was a distinct and affordable synthesis
of liberal and conservative approaches to the perceived problems of crime
and violence among "at-risk" youth and urban young men (and to social
intervention more generally).

Chapters 4 and 5 situate the early years of midnight basketball in broader,
more explicit political terrain by focusing on the cultural functioning of

media coverage and public discourse on midnight basketball with respect to neoliberal politics and social policy. Here, my analytic focus is somewhat inverted from the previous chapters so as to argue that midnight basketball not only reflected the broad contours of American neoliberal social policy but also played a role in shaping certain aspects of neoliberal policy and thought. Put a bit differently, these chapters not only advance the narrative of the midnight basketball story, but they also expand the scope and significance of that story such that midnight basketball helps enrich and enlarge our understanding of neoliberal social policy as well as the often underappreciated political significance of sport and sport policy in the broader political landscape.

In chapter 4 I look at midnight basketball's symbolic and ideological functions within the context of neoliberal social political transformations. My central claim is that midnight basketball galvanized the contours of neoliberal social policy in a specifically racial way and then helped legitimate, or provide an ideological rationale for, such policies and approaches. Midnight basketball, in this context, is best understood as a prototype of and indeed commercial for the neoliberal social policy regime we now live under.

Ultimately, of course, midnight basketball did not offer a workable coalition or stable synthesis—at least not politically. Chapter 5 explains the breakdown of the initial neoliberal consensus about midnight basketball as it played out in the 1994 crime bill debates. It details the political and cultural roots of this collapse, its broader political consequences, and its impacts on and implications for law and public policy. Specifically, I explain why the tensions between conservative and liberal approaches to crime and violence (represented here by the visions of Rush Limbaugh and Bob Dole against those of Bill Clinton) became acute in the context of the crime bill debates, and I demonstrate how conservatives used midnight basketball's connections to both *race* and *play* to problematize and trivialize (respectively) the prevention-oriented components of the crime bill. Never again has midnight basketball occupied such a prominent place in the national imagination. At the same time, the outcomes of these debates over midnight basketball established the conditions within which it—and all manner of youth sport policy and sport-based social intervention—was reenvisioned and reformed, and would be implemented ever after.

The book shifts gears at this point, turning away from the national political context and questions about broad symbolic functioning back toward a more grounded, ethnographic examination of midnight basketball as mode of targeted social outreach and intervention in the aftermath of the 1994 crime bill controversies. Chapter 6 documents the rethinking and reform of sport-based social programming that took shape in the later part of the 1990s, the post–crime bill period. It details the consolidation of a more liberal, prevention-oriented coalition in support of midnight basketball and the subsequent emergence of a new, more mature understanding of the role of sport in social intervention and risk prevention. Here I draw on both archival work and my own ethnographic research and program experience. The vision, theory, and practice of midnight basketball that ultimately takes shape in these years, I argue, provides the conceptual foundation that animates and informs the best of our sport-based intervention practices and policies for youth and young people today.

Chapters 7 and 8 provide an illustrative insider account of a basketball-based prevention program located in Minneapolis, Minnesota. Written with Darren Wheelock and based on some fifteen months of fieldwork, chapter 7 focuses on the objectives, implementation, and day-to-day operation of an actual late-night basketball program in the Twin Cities. It wasn't exactly the experience we envisioned. This chapter documents the deep and unexpected tensions among the program administrators and grassroots organizers we encountered. Focusing on the resources and power differences that were crucial to the outcome of these grassroots, community-based struggles, we describe how they played out, thus providing an analysis of the tensions and contradictions within the liberal-preventionist coalition concerning both the social value of sport and the needs of urban youth and young men of color. Chapter 8 continues this field study by drawing out the lessons and implications of our observations and involvement with respect to some of the larger questions of racial politics and neoliberal policy. This chapter also considers the meaning of and motivation for basketball-based risk prevention programs from the point of view of program participants and members of the African American community more broadly.

One of the central findings of chapter 8 is that young men of color who participate in these programs have very little interest in the social interventionist objectives that motivate their funders and administrators. Instead, they participate for reasons of health, fitness, recreation, and leisure and, to a lesser extent, in hopes of personal mobility and attainment through sport. And for other members of the African American community, midnight basketball functions as a symbol of a more proactive, community-based vision of social policy, state intervention, and public safety. This chapter highlights the features of the urban landscape and cultural environment that make these views reasonable for those who hold them. It also presents findings that suggest that locally based programs like midnight basketball may have broader, community-level impacts that have not been previously understood. Taken together, the main thrust of chapters 6–8 is not to advocate for a particular policy approach but rather to demonstrate how midnight basketball in general and the Minnesota variation on the theme illustrate the possibilities and challenges of sport-based intervention in the neoliberal era.

Overarching Aims and Ambitions

Hopefully, it is clear that each of these chapters, or at least many of the sections within these chapters, has a methodology and integrity of its own—which is to say, data and an underlying research design matched to the empirical question or questions each was initially undertaken to answer. As distinctive pieces of social research, each is also in dialogue with and tries to contribute to various scholarly issues and substantive bodies of work. For example, the chapters 2 and 3 on the origins and appeal of midnight basketball draw on research on the history of sport as a social intervention, and then, in dialogue with critical social and race theories, they try to suggest how this notion has been transformed in theory and application in the neoliberal era. Similarly, chapters 4 and 5, which focus on the broader symbolic and ideological functions of midnight basketball, both build off of and are intended to contribute to arguments about the broader cultural significance and political power of sport in contemporary culture. The more ethnographic, field-based chapters 6, 7, and 8, for their part, are oriented much more toward sport policy and programming, working from questions of theoretical foundations and design to issues of implementation, effectiveness, and experience.

Still, the real point and ultimate objective of this project—of the book itself—is not the pieces but the *whole*, the synthesis of the parts. In producing all these different pieces of research, organizing them together, and writing them into a book, my goal has been to use the case of midnight basketball to help us better understand the interactions of race, sport, risk, and social policy in the contemporary United States.

The payoff of such a broad, synthetic—*sociological*—approach defies easy summation or categorization. At one level, the objective is to advance a specific interpretation of and set of arguments about the uniquely popular and idiosyncratic cultural phenomenon known as midnight basketball. Formulated as a thesis, my argument is that midnight basketball is the product of a historic set of ideas about the relationships among sport, young people of color, and social intervention that are given new life and form in the context of the neoliberal transformations of American social policy that coalesced in the late twentieth and early twenty-first centuries. The corollary of this core claim would be that, understood in this fashion, midnight basketball can also deepen our appreciation of certain key dimensions of the culture of race and racism in America and neoliberal social policy as well as help us more fully grasp the opportunities for and limitations on sport-based social intervention more generally conceived.

On another level, this broad, holistic orientation is meant to leverage the immediate interest and intrigue that surrounds a sporting phenomenon like midnight basketball to engage readers and audiences (perhaps like yourself) in thinking seriously and critically about social issues they (or you) might not otherwise be inclined to take up. I am thinking of, for example, the function of racial stereotypes in contemporary American politics and policies, or the variability and consequence of cultural conceptions of risk, or even the peculiar, troubled character of neoliberal social policy itself. Hopefully, the narrative and analysis that follows introduces these themes, and then dives into the complexities of such contemporary structures, digs deep into cultural common sense, strikes a critical stance toward the choices and values embedded in existing cultural conceptions and neoliberal public policy regimes, and spells out some of the costs and consequences thereof.

This bigger-than-just-sport orientation is connected with another larger ambition: that of modeling a more expansive and interdisciplinary brand of sport scholarship. My goal in this sense is not just to better analyze and understand the sporting phenomenon known as midnight basketball, or even to reveal it as a microcosm of more general social patterns and forces (important as both projects are). More than this, my goal is to show the necessity, value, and larger payoffs of situating sports phenomena in broader social context. In the tradition of C. L. R. James's magisterial *Beyond a Boundary* (1963), the point is to signal and contribute to a brand of sport scholarship which insists that the study of sport cannot be conducted in a vacuum or silo. It must be bigger, drawing out connections and consequences well beyond the confines of the world of sport itself. The result of situating sport in its broader social contexts is not just a better understanding of sport but research that brings the study of sport more into mainstream social science and closer to the core of understanding contemporary culture and social life.

Somewhat ironically, such an approach must necessarily be as precise and specific as possible about what is culturally unique about the structure and function of sport itself—its role in society, what it is about sport that marks its cultural significance and societal impact as truly distinctive. The characteristics that mark and define sport as a unique and powerful (or, uniquely powerful) social force are varied, diverse, and paradoxical. Most sport scholars start, either intuitively or self-consciously, with the basic material facts involving the large number of people who participate in sport in one way or another as well as the depth and sheer amounts of energy and resources so many invest in their participation. These two character- istics alone—the number of people involved in sport and the tremendous passion they have for it—are sufficient, in my view, to justify treating sport as an important social phenomenon and devoting serious and systematic analytical attention to it. But they are just a start. As these chapters unfold, I hope to highlight several other features that mark sport as distinct from popular cultural domains such as television, film, music, media, or gaming.

In the first place, I want to call attention to the deep, passionate beliefs about the moral value and social virtue of sport held by so many sports par- ticipants, promoters, and fans, especially with respect to racial progress and change. These are the convictions that sport constitutes a serious, special, or even sacred social practice and cultural space. Secondly is sport's playful side, and the fact that in spite of the grand moral claims of sports idealists, many—perhaps even most—Americans see sport as a diversion or distrac- tion, perhaps a guilty pleasure, but certainly not something that should be taken too seriously. Following Clifford Geertz, I will call this the "deep play" of sport. Finally, there are the longstanding norms about the separation of sport and politics—the perceived need to keep these two often intercon- nected domains of life isolated and distinct, neither one impacting or cor- rupting the other (MacAloon 1987).

I take the political, ludic, and moralistic aspects of sport as cultural struc- tures that shape and determined many of the social dynamics that play out in and around sport in contemporary culture, and, as such, as keys to many of the questions, puzzles, ironies, and intrigues that shape this narrative. They help explain, just to give one example, what made midnight basketball so amazingly and unexpectedly popular as an approach to social interven- tion, even in a culture that is typically disdainful of state sport policy. And they also help us understand how and why such a small and idiosyncratic policy initiative played such a powerful role in shaping both federal criminal justice policy and social service regimes in cities all across the country. I have a good deal more to say about these defining if sometimes conflicting char- acteristics as I identify them in the chapters that follow.

While this study of midnight basketball depends on, and is intended to further develop, an analysis of the distinctive cultural status of sport, I want to be sure that this emphasis doesn't overshadow or obscure the other distinctive analytic aspect of the project—namely, the racial angles and am- bitions that I alluded to at the beginning of the chapter. In fact, not only do I want to make sure the racial focus isn't forgotten or rendered secondary; I want to suggest that the unique cultural status of sport may actually parallel and even heighten the racial dimensions of the project.

The parallels, overlaps, and reinforcing cultural characteristics of sport and race are perhaps not obvious at first glance. The cultural status of race could appear, in certain ways, the opposite of sport: serious and controversial, not playful and light, difficult to discuss, race is more likely to be avoided in polite conversation and public discourse than to be the subject of constant, everyday conversation and political banter, more likely to promote controversy and conflict than to serve as a distraction or diversion (see, for discussions, Bonilla-Silva 2010; Bobo and Charles 2009; Eliasoph 1999; Crenshaw 1997). Yet I would argue that sport and race are animated by similar cultural features and peculiarities. Like many otherwise disavowed popular pursuits, race, in our contemporary post–civil rights, postracial moment, is both hypervisible and invisible, everywhere around us and yet difficult to acknowledge in a society that hopes to be color-blind, race-neutral, or postracial. More than this, in spite of the many problems race presents for us, race, not unlike sport, represents some of our greatest hopes and grandest ideals—the celebration of difference, the possibilities of multicultural mobility and opportunity in liberal democratic culture, or what Joyce Bell and I (2007) have described as the "happy talk" of racial diversity in contemporary American culture (see also Berrey 2015; Burke 2012). Indeed, I believe that the unique cultural characteristics of sport feed into the problems of race in contemporary culture—how the dynamics of race and racism are reproduced and perpetuated even when we try to embrace racial fairness and justice. What may be most revealing and intriguing is how race and sport really operate together in contemporary, post–civil rights American culture.

I highlight and expand on the unique, multifaceted structure, dynamics, and impacts of sport and race in the pages that follow. In a certain sense, in fact, this entire project can be read as much as a study in the interactions of sport and race in contemporary American culture and neoliberal social policy as it is a study about a specific sport-based social intervention. But I don't want to get ahead of myself or my narrative and analysis. After all, none of these claims—those about the deep, embedded social significance of sport and race, on their own terms and especially when taken together—really mean much in the absence of actual empirical research that demonstrates the import and significance of what is going on out there, in front of us all even if some of us do not see or choose not to see it. And so it is time to stop talking about what the book is about (or what I want it to be about) and get on with the project. You, the reader, can then decide for yourself the extent to which I have made good on these various objectives, promises, and potentials.

TWO

The Midnight Innovation

Certain ideas, events, and experiments seem to come out of nowhere—and when they do, it can be hard to figure out if they are inspired or insane, acts of creative genius or misguided attempts at innovation (or something even more devious or deceptive). In my experience, midnight basketball elicits all these reactions from folks hearing about it for the first time. Some find the claim that lives can be improved and crime reduced simply by having young men play basketball in the midnight hour to be preposterous. Others find the notion intriguing if a bit unlikely, and some of those folks believe it to be ingenious, or even inspired. But whatever their evaluation, almost everyone believes the notion is as original as it is unexpected.

The sociological response in such cases, especially when the phenomenon comes to broader visibility and influence as midnight basketball did, is to take a step back and try to figure out where the idea came from and what made it appealing in the first place—in short, to locate the historical roots and social conditions of the innovation. Like historians, we sociologists realize that although an idea like midnight basketball may seem unprecedented, it has to come from somewhere. We realize that there are always both historical precursors and a preexisting social context, a set of enabling institutional structures and cultural pathways that allows new ideas and institutional innovations to be recognized as reasonable and potentially valuable. And it is in this context that we can best understand the appeal of apparently brand-new initiatives and what all this hubbub might tell us about the social world of which they are part and parcel.

This chapter and the next describe the origins of midnight basketball and the social, cultural, and historical contexts that help account for its popularity and appeal. It is an exercise that requires us to look into the archives of midnight basketball's inception and then the history and literature on sport policy and sport-based social intervention in the United States, late twentieth-century transformations of social services in the American welfare state, and the complexities of race and racial politics in the post–civil rights era that provide the social and historical context within which midnight basketball took shape. Ultimately, the story will be as much about broader transformations in public policy, big ideas like risk society, and what Joe Soss, Richard Fording, and Sanford Schram (2011) have called "neoliberal paternalism" as it is about sport history, racial culture, and midnight basketball itself. And it all starts with the inventor of midnight basketball, the mellifluously named town manager G. Van Standifer.

Beginnings, in the Midnight Hour

I introduced this book by saying that midnight basketball first came to national attention (not to mention my own personal awareness) when the Chicago Housing Authority (CHA) partnered with the Department of Housing and Urban Development (HUD) to launch leagues in two of its most troubled residential communities in 1990. This is true, but far from the whole story. As I learned almost immediately upon doing background research on the initiative in Chicago back in the 1990s, midnight basketball was not a Windy City original. The CHA had actually borrowed the concept from G. Van Standifer, a retired systems analyst and former administrator from a place just outside of Washington, DC, in Prince George's County, Maryland, called Glenarden. In the mid-1980s, Standifer became convinced that one of the keys to the problems of poor, inner-city young men was the absence of safe, constructive activities between the hours of 10:00 p.m. and 2:00 a.m. His solution was to organize a basketball league that would operate in his community during these "high crime" hours. Standifer's program was intriguingly simple. First piloted in 1986, the league operated only during the summer and had three core components: first, that young men between the ages of seventeen and twenty-one were targeted for recruitment; second, that no game could begin before ten at night; and third, that two uniformed police officers had to be present and visible at each game.

By all reports, the Glenarden program was a remarkably vibrant and successful basketball league. A full schedule of games was offered with a regular season and playoffs. Teams were composed of players who had tried out and placed via an actual draft. There were coaches, uniforms, fully outfitted referees, and even spectators in the stands and fans who followed the league's results and weekly standings. Within a few short years, Standifer's midnight basketball program established itself as a stable, viable presence on the public service grid. In other words, midnight basketball had become "a thing."

Though I never witnessed games in Maryland, I've seen enough basketball-based sports intervention programs over the years to have a pretty good handle on the atmosphere and level of play. Teams are usually composed of young men who played a lot of basketball on high school teams, at recreation centers, and in traveling leagues when they were younger. The play is intense and competitive, well beyond your typical pickup game.[1] Basketball novices or weak players would not find a place on most midnight teams or courts. What's more, the leagues offer a fairly rugged (though some would say ragged), physical brand of basketball that has its own appeal. One year in the Minneapolis program I describe in chapters 7 and 8, for example, the coach of a precollege, AAU traveling team entered his squad of seventeen-year-old stars in the midnight league in order to "toughen them up" and expose them to a more mature, "hard-nosed" style of play. At least in these early years, it wasn't unusual to see a community college coach or two at games, checking out the action or scouting a player or two, and in most leagues, an all-star game functioned as a kind of showcase for these local scouts and recruiters. Suffice it to say, the basketball played in these late-night leagues was a lot like the off-season, out-of-school basketball circuits that have been described by Scott Brooks (2009) and Reuben May (2008) in their vivid ethnographies of the high-end, high school–aged basketball in the black communities in Pennsylvania and Georgia, respectively.

That being said, the level of play wasn't what distinguished midnight basketball in the public imagination or social policy circles. Launched in the final years of the Reagan-era war on drugs, what distinguished Standifer's midnight basketball then—and makes it the topic of our investigation now—were its claims to be able to control lawlessness and reduce risk, its crime-fighting capacity. As a social program, midnight basketball's purported deterrent effects were remarkable, awe-inducing, almost jaw-dropping. With endorsement and backing from local law enforcement officials, Standifer claimed his program contributed to a 30 percent reduction in late-night crime in Glenarden in its first three years of operation. A Maryland County Corrections chief told *Chicago Sun-Times* reporters, "I haven't seen one single one of these basketball players back in my jail" since the program began (December 5, 1989).

While I was dubious about the purported crime-fighting capacities of the program (rightly, it would turn out), there was no denying that these were impressive claims, lending empirical support to the intrigue and intrinsic appeal of Standifer's basic model. Indeed, city officials in Chicago resolved to develop a pilot program of their own after seeing a story about the effectiveness of the Maryland program in the *New York Times* (Carter 1998). And after the Chicago program aligned with this Maryland operation, things really took off. Standifer launched Midnight Basketball Leagues Inc., the organization that eventually became the National Association of Midnight Basketball Inc. NAMB experienced dramatic growth in the early 1990s. Within two short years, the association had sanctioned some thirty-eight affiliates or "chapters" nationwide—including those in Chicago and San Diego. Each chapter, according to the parent organization, was a "non-profit, community-based organization adhering to formal training, rules and regulations" based on the original, three-point Standifer model.[2] Over the course of several years, the national association was written up in dozens of stories nationwide and featured on *60 Minutes*, ESPN, ABC's *World News Tonight*, CNN, and a wide variety of other broadcasts. In the wake of all this publicity, in the spring of 1991, President Bush designated Standifer and his program one of his official "thousand points of light" (#124, to be exact), and start-up grants for late-night basketball leagues were included in Section 520 of the Cranston-Gonzalez National Affordable Housing Act passed in the final months of the Bush administration (*Washington Post*, April 13, 1991).

Tip of the Iceberg

Impressive and intriguing in itself, midnight basketball was on the leading edge of a much larger trend of using sport for purposes of social intervention and risk prevention. Standifer's midnight model spawned countless, nonsanctioned variations and knockoffs all across the United States. Dozens of basketball-based programs—some new initiatives, others more established, preexisting programs—came to adopt the late-night designation and trumpet impressive claims about the deterrent impact and crime-fighting abilities of sport-based youth intervention programs. And the idea of using sports as a tool for reducing risk, preventing crime, and improving lives was not just limited to late night or basketball.

A whole host of sports-and-recreation-based programs with activities ranging from biking and soccer to golf and the martial arts began to adopt similar language, principles, and funding strategies. In a 1994 report titled "Beyond 'Fun and Games': Emerging Roles of Public Recreation" (Tindall 1995), the National Recreation and Park Association profiled 19 representative programs operated by its local affiliates and dealing with a wide variety of social problems and public concerns. The NRPA touted this collection of programs—which ranged from disease prevention and public health to day care, juvenile delinquency, and teenage pregnancy to gangs, drugs, and violence to education and economic revitalization—for "bringing new dimensions to public recreation as human service" (86). Reliable estimates were never compiled, but if you consider that in 1997 the journal *Parks and Recreation* identified some 621 programs focused specifically on reaching "at-risk" youth (Witt and Crompton 1996a), and multiply that by the number of participants these programs served and then add in the number of participants in comparable formal and informal projects implemented by organizations such as the YMCA, Boys and Girls Clubs, Police Athletic Leagues, schools and community centers, and other such institutions all across the country, the scale and scope of this emerging industry becomes almost impossible to ignore. In the early years of this project, my research assistants and I were able to identify over 100 such programs serving thousands of young people in the Twin Cities metropolitan area alone. It is an analysis that we and other researchers (see Clark 2003) repeated on several occasions throughout the first decade of the new millennium, always with similar results, and I daresay it could have been replicated in every major metropolitan area of the country across the period.

In an early and still useful treatment, Robert Pitter and David Andrews (1997) described the emerging phenomenon that midnight basketball was a part of as the "social problems industry" in urban sport and recreation provision. This framing was eye-opening and analytically formative for me. The realization that midnight basketball was actually part of a much larger trend in the world of youth and recreational sport toward sport as a form of risk prevention and social intervention[3] was one of the first and most basic insights (or discoveries) I came upon when I decided to research midnight basketball more systematically. In fact, it is important to see midnight basketball as a window onto the whole concept of sport-based social intervention as it was beginning to be played out in late twentieth-century American culture (as well as in many other of the so-called developed nations of the world; see, for examples, L. Kelly 2013; Coalter 2007; Giulianotti 2011; Nichols 2004).

Pitter and Andrews (1997, 93) characterized midnight basketball as the "catalyst and template" for the entire movement of sport-based social intervention. I was then (as I am now) a bit ambivalent about this formulation. On the one hand, midnight basketball clearly provided inspiration and a model for many of these initiatives all over the country. On the other hand, midnight basketball was far from a perfect or even typical representative of all problems-based, interventionist-oriented youth sports initiatives. Few social problems–oriented sport initiatives were/are as racially marked and gender-targeted as midnight basketball. Also, the police presence and security emphasis was always far more pronounced in midnight basketball than in any other sports-based interventions, and most such programming was aimed at much younger populations (now even more so) and took place much earlier in the day (often after school).

On the more positive side, these various instantiations were obviously all linked together, and I believe that the features which marked midnight basketball actually brought the unique qualities and characteristics of this larger problems-based youth sports movement into focus. They helped me get to the center of core images, ideals, ideologies, and issues built into and swirling around all such initiatives (Hartmann 2001) as well as the opportunities for intervention and change therein (Hartmann 2012b, 2006). I still believe this is true, and hope that subsequent chapters will provide further insight into both best practices for sport-based, social change initiatives and their broader social significance and political function. In the rest of this chapter, however, I will reverse the analytic logic, using Pitter and Andrews's social problems industry analysis to begin to unpack the mysterious prominence and appeal of basketball in the midnight hour.

Sports for the Underserved

According to Robert Pitter and David Andrews, the emerging social problems industry in urban sports is best understood in the context of the social organization of sport in the United States (conceived as a whole system of institutions and facilities providing opportunities for competitive and recreational physical activity, especially for youth and young people). More specifically, they saw sports-based social outreach and intervention programs like midnight basketball as a way to provide access to sports and physical recreation for otherwise underserved communities, focusing especially on poor youth and young people of color living in urban, inner-city neighborhoods. Participatory sport provision, in short, was the key to their vision and analysis.

Pitter and Andrews's analysis was informed by John Wilson's (1994) important history of how public sports, parks, and recreation have been funded and organized in the United States. Wilson's understanding of the American sport system begins from the absence of publicly supported, state-directed sport provision for the masses and the concomitant domination of market- and consumption-based modes of sport access and delivery. These forces have combined, especially since the 1960s, to produce a "two tiered" or "two stream" system wherein "people who have the access to the disposable income and free time necessary to consume these services" have their sport and recreation needs served, while "the poor [and otherwise disadvantaged] are left with a shrinking pool of public . . . and private services, none of which they can afford" (Pitter and Andrews 1997, 86).[4] Poor and disadvantaged populations haven't had to rely exclusively on market-based resources for financing sport and recreation activities at any point in time; rather they have long been served by a relatively large if decentralized system of public sport provision operated and financed through private, philanthropic organizations, local parks and recreation departments, community centers, and (perhaps most importantly) schools. This patchwork quilt of agencies, facilities, and programs is where innovations like midnight basketball fit into Pitter and Andrews's scheme. Like other social problems–based sporting initiatives, midnight basketball leagues emerged by taking advantage of resources and funding niches that were not sport specific but targeted to variously disadvantaged youth and their communities. League operators located these funding opportunities and developed sports-based programs around them. Indeed, Pitter and Andrews succinctly describe the social problems approach as a "new style of bringing sport and recreation to America's underserved youth" (86).

This characterization of the social problems industry as a mode of sport provision for essentially disadvantaged and underserved populations is a very useful frame for beginning to make sense of midnight basketball. After all, whatever other, larger objectives and ideals may be embedded in or projected onto these leagues, midnight basketball was, in a very basic and obvious way, a sports program, a competitive athletic operation. Midnight basketball leagues were usually run and operated by folks who loved sports. One of the core, unspoken elements or beliefs built into the initiative, as Standifer (who was not himself a sports aficionado per se) first conceived it, was that basketball would bring poor, inner-city youth and young men of color in the door—hard-to-reach individuals would come to play ball. Without sports provision and the interest in and demand for basketball among young African American men, in other words, there wouldn't have been any such programs or any of the much-trumpeted positive effects.

The supply side of this equation was also important. Beginning in the late 1980s and early 1990s, sports practitioners, especially in depressed or disadvantaged communities, began to realize that if they were going to sustain (if not expand) their offerings, they would need to attach them to larger spending priorities and the funding climate in general. This was the point of the 1994 National Recreation and Park Association report I quoted a few pages back: the organization was trying to create new justifications and mechanisms for funding sport and recreation programs. This was also the economic climate surrounding the programs and organizations with which I came into contact when I was working with Larry Hawkins and his Chicago-based Institute for Athletics and Education throughout the 1990s (as well as with a large percentage of the programs around the country I have studied since). Schools and other educational institutions were probably hit hardest of all by these financial pressures. Already in 1992 the Amateur Athletic Foundation of Los Angeles, the sports advocacy agency created with the windfall from the 1984 Olympic Games (and now known as "LA '84"), organized and hosted a national conference titled "The Funding Crisis in High School Athletics: Causes and Solutions."

The problem sports providers faced in the last decade of the century (and continue to face today) was not just limited funding for their programs but declining resources overall. Beginning with dramatic budget cuts to public parks and urban recreation departments in the 1970s (Shivers and Halper 1981; Ingham 1985; Crompton and Wicks 1988; Crompton and McGregor 1994) and intensifying with rising liability costs and the elimination of free "extracurricular" activities in schools in the 1980s (cf. Rauner, Stanton, and Wynn 1994; Chalip 1988), funding and support for public parks, recreation, and sport provision stagnated in the 1990s—especially for program operation and staffing. Pitter and Andrews did not emphasize this dimension, but the work of John Crompton and his colleagues (Crompton and Wicks 1988; Crompton and McGregor 1994) on public parks and recreation departments and facilities, one crucial institutional element of youth sports provision, did. By the mid-1990s, according to Crompton (1998; see also Crompton and Kaczynski 2003), parks and recreation budgets were slashed so dramatically at both state and local levels that reliance on external resources had almost doubled in the earliest years of this period (from 14 percent in 1974–75 to 24 percent in 1987–88), and the slide continued throughout the 1990s. I never found comprehensive, longitudinal data of the funding declines for public youth sport provision at the time, but it is clear that these pressures and dynamics were affecting nonprofits, community-based organizations, and school systems all over the country. In his keynote address to the 1992 Los Angeles conference on the funding crisis, for example, Bruce Durbin, executive director of the National Federation of State High School Associations, described the declines in tax-based funding for school sport as "precipitous." He and his organization spent the better part of the decade defending and reconfiguring high school sports funding.[5]

The larger point here is that cutbacks and declines in public provision forced youth sport administrators and operators to be more responsive than ever before to nontraditional funding sources. They had to get creative—and innovative programming like midnight basketball leagues and other problems-based sports initiatives provided a vehicle for them to fund sports and recreation programming for populations and communities with otherwise limited resources and facilities. To put it bluntly, then, it is not a stretch to suggest that this new "social problems" frame was adopted by sports providers simply to gain access to new funding streams.

None of this would have been particularly surprising for anyone who spent any time in or studying public policy and social service provision at the time. The Reagan-dominated 1980s were, after all, an era marked by the effort to privatize and scale back government services across a whole range of sectors and domains—"retrenchment," it was called then (Pierson 1994), "neoliberalism" more recently (Kettl 2002). There is a much larger social policy context here obviously, but before I get to that, it is important to understand that what was happening with midnight basketball and other social problems–oriented programming had a unique, sport-specific feel that was fairly consistent with the larger culture and history of youth sport policy and provision in the United States.

Sport has never been particularly high on the public policy agenda, and there has never been a real, stand-alone "right to play" or "sport for its own sake" ethos in the United States. Because of American tendencies toward laissez-faire social policy and longstanding Puritan suspicions about the purposelessness or even irrationality of play and leisure in general, the sporting establishment in this country has invariably and almost inevitably been required to justify youth sport provision—all participatory sport provision really (though not more professional, performance-oriented sport)—as a means to some larger ends. Educational institutions, for example, have long defended interscholastic athletic competition as a tool for cultivating school spirit and building character and self-discipline among youth and adolescent students (Mangan 2000). Similarly, the "play movement" of the early twentieth century was championed by Progressive Era reformers who promoted the development of parks and recreation programs as a way to socialize, assimilate, and "Americanize" the largely immigrant ethnic working classes moving to American cities (cf. Cavallo 1981; for a more general overview, see Pope 1997; Hardy and Ingham 1983). And when President Kennedy launched the President's Council on Physical Fitness in the 1960s, it was in direct response to the threat of Soviet expansionism at the height of the Cold War (Hoberman 1984, 21). Today the rallying cry has shifted to health and wellness, focusing on the prevention of smoking, drinking, and especially obesity. Think of Michelle Obama's Let's Move campaign (*New York Times*, February 10, 2010).

Suffice it to say, the United States has never had a real rhetoric for or commitment to sport for its own sake at least in terms of recreation and participation for the masses. In this sense, problems-based sports programs like midnight basketball were just another chapter in this whole history of what might be called, extrapolating from Pitter and Andrews, sport provision for other purposes.[6]

Seeing midnight basketball as part of a larger, more-or-less coordinated, grassroots effort to justify and finance sport and recreation for otherwise underserved populations also helps put in clear relief the social disparities and inequalities produced by a decentralized, market-dominated sport-delivery system. Pitter and Andrews made this point by contrasting the slow and uncertain development of problems-based sports programs like midnight basketball with the rapid take-up and proliferation of consumption-driven suburban soccer leagues in the late twentieth century, symbolized by the spectacular and unparalleled success of the American Youth Soccer Organization (AYSO). The general explanation for the participatory success of an athletic pursuit like soccer is fairly obvious and straightforward: wealthier neighborhoods and suburban communities simply had the resources, financial and otherwise, to offset funding shortfalls and cutbacks. For what it's worth, Pitter and Andrews predicted—ominously, if presciently—that the social problems–based approach would be "insufficient to sustain the provision of sport and recreation to disadvantaged communities" (1997, 96).

The discrepancies between these two different modes of youth sport delivery involve unequal access to resources, programs, and facilities, but the problems run deeper than that. They also have to do with differential treatment as well. Pitter and Andrews touched on this when they pointed out that problems-oriented sport programs are typically "bounded by strict rules, a code of conduct and mandatory workshops," whereas suburban soccer programs tend to be oriented toward participant-driven demands for recreation, physical fitness, community building, and fun as well as toward athletic achievement. In fact, they even speculated that these different modes of treatment "may be exacerbating the social and racial division[s] responsible for the very conditions the [problems-based] initiatives are trying to improve" (1997, 93).[7]

These comparisons and contrasts are of the utmost importance and are precisely where the racial (and gender) dimensions of this project began to take on additional significance and meaning. Think, for example, of how middle-class, mostly white boys and girls are equally served and often even play sports together at early ages, and more importantly how they are allowed and even encouraged to play in different ways and for different reasons. In the whiter, more middle-class suburban soccer communities, fun and fitness typically rule the day for youth athletics; in city sports, discipline and structure seem to predominate. However, we shouldn't get too far ahead of ourselves.

Powerful and important as it may be, Pitter and Andrews's emphasis on sport and recreation provision is just a starting point for analysis and interpretation. It doesn't really provide the context and analytical leverage by which to develop these critical insights fully. For one thing, such a sport-centered orientation can't explain why coaches and administrators—presumably interested only in securing support for underfunded programs—would adopt such radically different styles of running sports programs and dealing with program participants. Secondly and even more fundamentally, while conceptualizing midnight basketball in terms of its meanings and implications for sport provision may help us understand why sports providers found it expedient to adopt a social problems rhetoric and rationale to secure a slice of scarce program resources, it cannot account for why public policy makers were inclined to shift funding from other domains to sports-and-recreation-based programs in the first place. This is crucial because the last thing that program funders, editorial writers, and citizen supporters had on their minds when they endorsed sport-based programs like midnight basketball was youth sports provision.

More than Fun and Games

When I began working in the media archives and historical records on midnight basketball, one of the first things that jumped out at me were the catchy sports metaphors and tropes that editors used to introduce midnight basketball to the public. In their initial stories and editorials on the initiative, for example, the *Chicago Tribune* and *Chicago Sun-Times* used some of the following phrases and headlines: "Midnight Basketball Idea Scores," "Chicago Housing Authority deserves a trophy," "Nice move, Mr. Lane," and "Slam dunk at the city's public housing projects."[8] These headlines were sometimes followed by lighthearted copy and commentary. "Who knows?" one *Chicago Tribune* editorial mused, "Tomorrow's Michael Jordan or Dr. J may be warming up in the CHA today" (December 5, 1989).

It doesn't take a sport scholar to realize the athletic angle was key to the intrigue, appeal, and claims to originality of the entire midnight basketball experiment. Sport is fun and interesting, and as such, it provided a lighter, more upbeat approach to the otherwise discouraging news that was coming out of inner-city neighborhoods at the time. But this first glance and initial impression were also kind of deceptive. Playful framing and a lighthearted touch in the news media quickly turned—often in the space of a single story or news cycle—to a somber, even stoic tone that downplayed or even denied the sport-specific aspects of midnight basketball.

In one of the earliest profiles introducing Standifer's fledgling Maryland midnight basketball concept, for example, the *Washington Post* assured its readers on August 18, 1988, that "there are more serious things than basketball going on here." The sporting aspect of the program was, according to the *Post*, "just one part of a living clinic . . . in the omnipresent war on drugs." When the *New York Times* picked up the story a few months later, its treatment also downplayed athletics. With a delightfully revealing twist of tropes and tones, the *Times*'s headline read on February 13, 1989: "In a Late-Night Sport, the Game is Fighting Crime." These stories, I should note, didn't run in the sports pages, but in the main news sections of both papers.

This editorial emphasis and general cultural orientation were in keeping with the initial framing and financing of the midnight basketball concept by organizers themselves. When the Chicago Housing Authority proposed its variation on the midnight basketball concept to HUD officers in the fall of 1989, for example, grant writers packaged the program as a "positive alternative to gangs and hanging out on street corners for high risk young adults," and described it as both an "integral part of a much larger anti-drug strategy" and a "proactive step . . . in deter[ring] gang activity." Neither sport provision nor recreation (nor, for that matter, physical fitness and health) was mentioned anywhere in its cover letter or the ten-page (single-spaced) proposal outlining the details of the plan.[9] I have only been able to find one reference to sport, recreation, or physical fitness in all the documents I have assembled on these original initiatives. That reference came in the media packet originally compiled and released by Standifer's league as it tried to expand, but still, the sport rationale was only one of a dozen reasons midnight basketball programs were touted as effective—and the document was still somewhat ambiguous even on that point: "The mandatory use of all players in each game and required man-to-man defense insures a high degree of participation and physical activity." Even here, physical activity seemed to be as much about occupying the time and energy of young men as it was about providing them with legitimate athletic opportunities.[10]

The rhetorical dampening of the sports-specific aspects of the program carried through in the funding and support used to implement these programs.

Early midnight basketball initiatives were typically funded and operated by public agencies and private organizations whose officials had little or no immediate connections to or even interest in athletics. Recall that Standifer was neither a coach nor an athletic administrator but a retired computer systems analyst and a town manager. Legend holds that Standifer got interested in basketball only after he concluded that it was the "activity of choice" for young men in his community. In the first couple of seasons of Standifer's league, the coaches came not from parks and recreation departments or typical basketball circles but from the Maryland State Department of Corrections and the US Marshals Service. Even more intriguing (if not ironic), Standifer's first corporate sponsor was the Beer Institute of America (Carter 1998, 26–27).

The programs with which I was involved and in which I conducted actual fieldwork had similar stories. The officially sanctioned San Diego affiliate I worked with as a graduate student in the early 1990s was run by High Five America, an evangelical Christian group (not unlike the more well-known Fellowship of Christian Athletes), best known for putting on antidrug and antialcohol rallies at high school assemblies and college campuses around the country. As program director Rle Nichols told the *San Diego Union Tribune* (March 3, 1994), High Five leaders have "lived the life of those the program is aimed at. [They] know the score." High Five viewed its basketball work as part of its commitment to charity as derived from its beliefs and responsibilities. Its organizers, coaches, and officials obviously loved sports and knew a lot about basketball, but a larger mission and calling moved them to invest their time, talent, and energy into late-night, inner-city leagues. According to Nichols, "We're talking about saving a lot of lives here. I've always had kind of an inclination to see young kids who aren't getting breaks at home. Doing it through sports is not a good way. Doing it through sports is a great way."[11]

The Minnesota-based Stay Alive basketball program that is the focus of chapters 7 and 8 was funded by the Minneapolis Department of Health and Family Support (DHFS) as part of an initiative on violence prevention that began following a summer with an extremely high number of homicides in majority-minority neighborhoods and communities (Barnes-Josiah, Ansari, and Kress 1996). Its planners weren't interested in basketball any more than they were interested in waterskiing or figure skating. Indeed, so few had any basketball experience or expertise that they actually had to go out and recruit staffers with experience in the athletic arena to make the program happen—a process that created a whole host of challenges on its own (which I will detail later). Rather, they simply saw in basketball an opportunity for social outreach and intervention. As one city official told me in October 1999 regarding his decision to dedicate a significant chunk of money toward a basketball-based program: "I don't care about basketball at all—and neither does the mayor or the city council. That's why we've got a parks and rec[reation] department. I only care about finding programs that decrease the rates of violence and crime in our neighborhoods. That's what this program is all about: violence prevention. If it is just about basketball, we shouldn't be funding it—and if that's what this program turns out to be, I'll stop funding it in a second. I'll cut off the dollars myself."

So, too, on the national level. When federal funding was first allocated for midnight basketball in the early 1990s, it was not through the most obvious, sport-oriented agencies or programs—such as the President's Council on Physical Fitness or the grassroots sports development arm of the United States Olympic Committee. It wasn't even through any of the various nongovernmental agencies and organizations that are part of the decentralized American sport delivery system—the National Recreation and Park Association, for example, or the NCAA (the organization the federal government turned to in the late 1960s when it wanted to set up athletically oriented "cooling off" centers in the wake of the urban riots of the period [Hartmann 2003a, 227–31]). Rather, it came through the Department of Housing and Urban Development (granted, an agency that was at the time headed by a former professional football star).

The point is *not* that the midnight basketball initiative was about *more than* basketball. The point is that for most administrators, public officials, funders, and observers, midnight basketball was about *anything but* basketball. Basketball was merely a means to some other, larger end. In this context, we can now appreciate how the CHA must have been pleased, if not entirely surprised, to see the *Chicago Tribune* on December 5, 1989, rate the idea a "slam dunk," but then go on to opine on its main editorial page that the initiative was "not just fun and games." Rather, the newspaper saw midnight basketball as part of an "innovative" set of ideas to "break the cycle of crime, poverty and dependence that plagues life in public housing." In naming midnight basketball one of his official "thousand points of light," President Bush could not have made the point clearer or more concise: quoted in the *Washington Post* on April 13, 1991, the president insisted, "The last thing midnight basketball is about is basketball."

Targeting Black Youth and Young Men

The nonsport or even antisport framing of midnight basketball is obviously part and parcel of the curious "deep play" paradox of American sport. In a country and culture otherwise obsessed with sport, Americans rarely allow themselves—either as a people or in public policy—to see athletic competition or physical activity as an end in itself, especially for youth and young people (MacAloon 1998). And this is even less the case for those who are seen as somehow marginal, vulnerable, or disadvantaged. Indeed, one of the great ironies of American sport culture is how many young people participate in athletics and how many do so at elite levels, even though the United States is one of the few countries in the world without a real national sports policy or even a cabinet-level sports administrator. The United States Olympic Committee represents the extent to which any federal agency has been designated with grassroots sports development—though the USOC, as Laurence Chalip (1988) anticipated, is far more oriented toward the identification of potential elite-level athletes and then channeling them into elite-level, high-performance sport than toward the provision of sport for the masses.[12] Familiar though it may be, this rhetoric and rationale requires an analysis that gets out of or goes beyond the usual, sport-centric analytic comfort zone—one that focuses less on the sport itself and more on the broader social context and sport's role therein.

If midnight basketball wasn't about basketball, what *was* it about? What were the "real" ends it was intended to accomplish? I found myself asking these questions over and over in the early days of this project. And as I examined the broader social problems and public policy emphases of the period, the answers weren't immediately obvious. The *Washington Post* thought midnight basketball was part of the ongoing "war on drugs." The *New York Times* believed it was about crime fighting in general. When the CHA proposed league sponsorship to HUD, it described the goals of midnight basketball as a combination of the two: for CHA, it was about deterring gang activities and supporting a larger antidrug strategy. In Minneapolis, late-night basketball was part of a youth violence prevention initiative created in the wake of a spike in the homicide rate in the late 1990s (thus the title "Stay Alive") and funded through the city's Department of Health and Family Support.

For their part, the agencies and organizers I worked with in Chicago and around the nation throughout the nineties didn't care one way or the other whether their grant proposals and funding discussions focused on drugs, crime, violence, gangs, or conflict resolution. They would simply tailor or rewrite proposals, position papers, and personal pitches depending on the particular interests of the foundation or funding agency they were appealing to at the moment—better yet, they'd throw all these problems and noble goals into the mix.

As a young, idealistic staffer working in and with sports-based educational outreach organizations before I started studying them, I found this almost willful embrace of multiple and sometimes contradictory problem frames and policy approaches very uncomfortable. I was sometimes left feeling confused, or duplicitous, or both. As time went on, it became clear that there was good reason for my discomfort: some of these frames (crime control and delinquency, for example) took precedence over others (drug abuse prevention or poverty alleviation), and there were real costs and consequences depending on which of these framings of the various "problems" that a program like midnight basketball was intended to "solve" was emphasized or adopted. However, I also came to realize that expert organizers and practitioners like Standifer and my former boss Larry Hawkins adopted this semantic ambiguity not because they didn't care about the larger social ends toward which their sports-based programs were oriented. Nor was it because they lacked an understanding of the distinctiveness of specific problems and the alternative ways to frame them. (Nor, for that matter, were they unaware of racial stereotypes and preconceptions built into these frames.) Rather, these organizers embraced multiple frames because they saw *all* these problems as intimately interconnected and inseparable, both in terms of fundraising and institutional support and in terms of programming and social policy.[13] In other words, when it came to programming and social policy, it didn't matter what you *called* these interventions, or what social problems you said you were targeting—what mattered were the resources you could secure and what you did with them.

Recalling this broad, flexible orientation proved very useful as I thought through my questions about the larger ends and ultimate objectives of midnight basketball as a policy innovation. The upshot is that I realized that, instead of getting sidetracked right from the beginning in an analysis about which of these social concerns was actually more fundamental or pressing, the more appropriate course of action was to focus on what these various characterizations of midnight basketball shared (besides basketball, of course)—and that was the desire to reach a very specific population that was considered acutely "at risk" and hard to reach: poor, inner-city youth and young men of color, African American men in particular. Midnight basketball, that is to say, was targeted not to a specific social *problem* but to a specific social *group*. What I realized, in short, was that the target group *was* the problem midnight basketball was intended to address.

This "epiphany"—that is, my realization that midnight basketball was aimed specifically at young, urban African American men (or at least a particular conception of this group) rather than any particular problem they faced—was not, in and of itself, particularly original or earthshattering; at times, in retrospect, it seems so obvious that my belated recognition is almost comical or embarrassing. After all, the links among black men, sport, and crime had been well established by others (in addition to the references cited in chapter 1, see Hargreaves 1986), and my own personal interest in African American young men was what marked midnight basketball as an intriguing research project in the first place. Moreover, the social problems of the African American community, especially in poor, urban areas, had been prominent in public policy agendas (not to mention politics) at least since the 1960s—and early in the 1990s, evidence was beginning to gather that suggested the situation for African American young men was getting worse, not better.

Poverty and unemployment, welfare dependence, drug abuse and addiction, crime, and violence in African American communities were all at levels the University of Chicago sociologist William Julius Wilson, the most acclaimed and influential public scholar on the matter, described in *The Truly Disadvantaged* (1987) as having reached "catastrophic proportion" (see also Wacquant and Wilson 1989). And in public housing projects like those in Chicago where midnight basketball came to national prominence, the problems were acute. According to one of Wilson's collaborators, Sudhir Venkatesh (2000), 90 percent of CHA residents were unemployed and on welfare in the late 1980s, 75 percent lived in female-headed households, and project neighborhoods had the highest crime rates in the city. Young African American men in these settings presented a particularly vexing challenge. They were conspicuous not only by their *involvement* in delinquent activities and criminal behaviors but also in their *absence* from family life and child-rearing, education, legitimate employment, and public life. Put differently, not only were policy makers and demographers at a loss to try to help young black men, but they often couldn't find them in the first place. And when they could be located, research into the lifeworlds these young African American men inhabited and the worldviews they espoused yielded sobering and disturbing portraits.

Many young black men, according to Elijah Anderson, inner-city ethnographer and author of renowned books such as *Streetwise* (2013) and *Code of the Street* (2000), had succumbed to the pressures of "the street," or what he also called "the fast life." This lifestyle was marked by the conspicuous consumption of cell phones, fancy cars, and stylish, often sports-oriented clothing and shoes as well as drug dealing, theft, other petty crimes, and illegal employment. Even "decent" youth and young men in these communities felt compelled to mimic aspects of street life to either secure social status or simply stay safe and avoid confrontation and violence. "The seeming intractability of their situation," Anderson (2000, 46) summarized, ". . . has engendered deep-seated bitterness and anger in many of the most desperate and poorest blacks, especially young people."

Obvious as it may be in retrospect, locking in on the fact that midnight basketball was targeted toward African American youth and young men—realizing that the public interest in midnight basketball was not about sport, or even about any specific social problem, but rather about a specific population and its purported constellation of challenges—helped focus my research and a large part of my analysis and interpretation as I moved forward. It sharpened my sense of some of the analytic questions that would be paramount, the puzzles that would need to be unpacked. It became an organizing principle and focus for the project that unfolded. But it was just a start.

Complications and Complexities

Having clarified my understanding of the basic motivations and emphases of midnight basketball initiatives, I must also admit that there was a lot more going on here than I realized at first. One of the complications had to do with the framing or emerging conceptualization of African American men and their problems. If African American men were seen as the problem to be addressed, their problems tended to be seen and understood in very particular and, from a critical-sociological vantage point, problematic kind of way.

Research from sociologists like William Julius Wilson and Robert Sampson (Sampson and Wilson 1995) and others[14] confirmed that high rates of crime and social dislocation among African Americans were the result of interconnected, societal-level processes of deindustrialization and job loss, the concentration of poverty, and social isolation. However, public thinking about African American poverty and inequality, as it had at least since the 1960s, tended to explain these problems with reference to deeply racialized and gendered discussions of the breakdown of black families and the perceived pathology of African American urban culture. In other words, the explanation and public understanding of the challenges and problems faced by African American young men tended to put the blame on their culture, their lifestyle, and their choices—a "tangle of pathology" in the now famous (or infamous) language of the 1965 Moynihan report on African American inequality. Missing from this discussion and framing were the structural conditions that were key to the struggles of all African American men: poverty and lack of employment, poor schools and inadequate social supports, and (perhaps most of all) prejudice and discrimination in the culture as a whole.[15]

Extending from this problematic framing—and even more to the point for midnight basketball—were ambiguities and confusions about the concepts of risk, at risk, risk prevention, and risk reduction used to justify and organize social intervention in urban, African American communities. In sociology, the idea of risk and social life is mostly associated with the work of Anthony Giddens and especially Ulrich Beck's (1999, 1992) whole notion of a "risk society." In this view, modern industrial society is marked by levels of order, stability, growth, and productivity that were inconceivable in more traditional, preindustrial times. Ironically, however, this new order produces its own set of problems—environmental degradation, nuclear proliferation, rising social inequality, pockets of dislocation, extreme hunger, poverty, and poor health. Both at a social and an individual level what emerges then is an obsession with systems—social safety nets, insurance, and so on—that can protect against such collectively constructed "risks." And one of the real risks of our complex, interwoven society is that it enriches and enhances life chances and life quality for many but leaves others vulnerable and isolated. Enter, here, the young African American men who were the focus of this project and research—"at-risk" youth.

In our better, more compassionate visions, we might say that the "risk" these young men face is that they can't reach their fullest potential as citizens, workers, human beings—that without the proper social supports, they stand a great risk of being left behind. Often, however, the risk concept that was (and is) employed in the public discourse with respect to young, African American men is just another stereotyping, stigmatizing label (Acland 1995; Franklin 1998; Swadener and Lubeck 1995), one that constructs these young men as somehow deviant or deficient, and thus prone to violence, crime, disorder, and mayhem. As Soss and Kindervater (unpublished ms., n.d.) have recently put it: "The at-risk concept can be expanded, narrowed, or tailored to fit almost any governing context: healthcare, education, criminal justice, welfare, employment, suicide prevention, teen pregnancy, substance abuse, etc. . . . Assembled together, these risk discourses guide and legitimate targeted and precise governmental interventions." What's more, this framing constructs and conveys an inverted, almost diametrically opposed vision where "risk" comes to refer to the supposed threat that these young men pose to others in the society. This perceived risk may be either in terms of being an immediate threat to safety and order or being a larger threat to public order and to the stability and viability of public programs and services of the welfare state if they fail to develop into active, engaged, productive citizens and workers. Here, Mary Douglas's version of the "risk society" may be more useful, highlighting as it does the racialized ways in which modern social arrangements construct certain groups as problematic (see, again, Acland 1995). And either way, when applied to African American youth and young men, "risk" refers not to young people being "at risk" in their own lives and unlikely to reach their full potential. Instead, it is all about producing problems and disorder for "the rest of us," and thus helps contextualize and explain the obsession with public policies related to containment and social control, prisons and policing for young black men.[16]

A third dimension of the complexities involved in the initial midnight basketball innovation involved the curious racial rhetoric and rationale that surrounded the programs—more specifically, the ways in which race *was* and *was not* talked about. On one level, it is obvious that the program was targeted to African American men. Indeed, this is exactly why the sport of choice for the initiative was basketball rather than any other competitive athletic pursuit. The connections between basketball and blackness go back to the history of the sport—from the emergence of traveling all-star teams like the Harlem Globetrotters or the Renaissance Rens and the early embrace (at least in American terms) of interracial teams and integrated play to the sport's explosion on urban playgrounds in the 1960s and 1970s (Caponi-Tabery 2002). They have to do with the popularity of the game in the black community as well as the way in which African Americans dominate the sport at the elite level both in the United States and all around the world today. Many of these notions were constructed and consolidated in the popular imagination in the 1970s with the publication of best sellers such as Pete Axthelm's *The City Game: Basketball from the Garden to the Playgrounds* (1970) and Rick Telander's *Heaven Is a Playground* (1976) as well as Nelson George's famous cultural treatments. And in recent years, writers and scholars such as Todd Boyd (2003) and John Wideman (2001) have offered up powerful and provocative commentaries that capture the power of the sport as experienced and understood within the African American community itself (for sociological treatments and critiques, see Boyd and Shropshire 2000; McLaughlin 2008). And the racial meaning and significance of basketball stem from the deep and intimate affinity between basketball's most essential athletic qualities (its fast pace and improvisational nature, its unique combination of individual athleticism and team chemistry, the sheer energy and high emotional engagement it requires) and distinctive aesthetic characteristics that have been associated with and claimed for African American culture, music, and style. Indeed, it seems no exaggeration when David Andrews and Michael Silk (2010, 1626) talk about the National Basketball

Association as the embodiment of a "ghettocentric logic" that is an "instructive window into . . . racial representation," both "a problem" to manage as well as "a site for the creative mobilization of stereotypical understandings of Black spaces, experiences, and aesthetics" (see also Buffington and Fraley 2011).[17]

While I don't want to idealize or romanticize the role of basketball (or any other sport) in the construction of blackness in American culture, the connections between blackness and basketball were and are manifest. The sport of basketball has been dominated by African American players in the last third of the twentieth century and has become, for many both inside and outside the African American community, fundamental to a distinctive African American aesthetic and identity. It is, at least in the American imagination, a black practice. So if and when neoliberal social policy—which has almost certainly been overdetermined by its obsession with race and risk, especially in cities—turned to sport (or, for that matter, when sport turned to it), it seems only natural that a basketball-based program took center stage.

In spite of all of the history and context that suggests midnight basketball was specifically intended for African American youth and young men, the racial dimensions of the program—both its motivations and the social problems it was purported to address—were rarely discussed in explicit racial terms. Program proponents seemed entirely uncomfortable with identifying midnight basketball's specific racial dimensions—or, more bluntly, its targeting of young black men—especially in public venues. Reading through archival documents, mass media coverage, and public commentary of the period, I found it almost impossible to locate any references to the race of the target population, even or perhaps especially in the early years of the initiative. To the extent the obvious racial dimensions of the program were publically acknowledged, it was usually in the context of trying to set aside or transcend those social particularities. Gil Walker, the CHA sports director who imported Standifer's midnight basketball model to Chicago, was a master of this sound bite: "Come into the gym," he told Vivian Carter (1998, 38), "and all of a sudden those barriers are broken down because of basketball. Basketball transcends gang affiliation, it transcends race, it transcends economic situation—basketball transcends all of that nonsense."

At least since the post–civil rights 1980s, Americans have tended toward an abstract, ostensibly race-neutral language—which the sociologist Eduardo Bonilla-Silva (2010) and others (Lewis 2004; Carr 1997; Crenshaw 1997) have called "color-blind discourse." This discourse has held even when Americans are talking about social problems that are clearly identified with race, and even though minority communities and racial issues receive inordinate attention in politics, culture, and public policy. Whether it was about crime and violence, poverty and welfare, public schools or unemployment, African American men and their problems provoked far more anxiety than one might expect given their relative numbers in the population (see Bobo and Charles 2009). Sociologists and other scholars have written a great deal about how this peculiar attention to and avoidance of race has affected social policies and politics in domains ranging from housing and schools to jobs programs, health care, and poverty programs (Gilens 1999; Lieberman 1998; Quadagno 1994). Some have gone so far as to suggest that this racialization and racism itself help account for the exceptional underdevelopment of the American welfare state (see Manza [2000] for a turn-of-the century discussion) and have driven much of the national politics of the post–civil rights period. Suffice it to say, midnight basketball seems to have been discussed in this curious, color-blind fashion Robert Smith (1995) used to characterize racism in the post–civil rights era: "Now you see it, now you don't."

If the racial dimensions of midnight basketball presented many of the initial challenges and deeper complexities of my initial archival research, the other big set of questions that puzzled me early on were about sport, the sporting context itself. Why athletics? I kept wondering. What was it that compelled community leaders, politicians, policy makers, and the general public—many of whom, like G. Van Standifer, had no particular interest in sports, and some of whom were even rather nerdy, antisport critics—to believe that having young African American men throw balls at baskets late into the night might be good, sensible programming and social policy? This, the more I thought about it, was a really radical and kind of crazy idea, especially given the enormity of the problems this group of young men faced.

In a certain sense, all these questions and complexities about race, risk, the urban underclass, young African American men, sport, and athletics were frustrating and overwhelming once I specified and formulated them. It seemed like I was moving backward analytically, not forward. But what I also came to realize was that this all reinforced the broader social significance of midnight basketball. It made it easy to see that there was a lot more at stake in midnight basketball than sport policies or even the immediate social problems of young black men. Eventually, in fact, I came to embrace these complexities as questions to be answered rather than obstacles in my way; I realized that they also signaled and helped organize and prioritize the analytical challenges ahead. And I realized that unpacking all of this would be the key to understanding the mystery of midnight basketball on its own terms and revealing its broader political and analytic significance and consequence.

To do this required digging deeper into the ideas, ideals, and images underlying midnight basketball and the social problems industry in sport more generally. It required that I situate midnight basketball in the context of attacks on the welfare state and the emergence of neoliberal governmentality in the post–civil rights era; that I review the ways in which midnight basketball played off of sport's historic, self-celebrated reputation as a positive, progressive force for social intervention, especially for marginalized and disadvantaged youth and young men of color; and that I more carefully consider the visions of intervention and risk embedded in this program and the deeper ideologies of race, public policy, and the public good driving it. In other words, I had to make these ideological and institutional complexities and this "context" the focal point of the analysis, seeing midnight basketball as but one indicator of a set of social changes and ideological shifts that had been changing the face of American public policy and social service provision since at least the 1980s.

I turn to all this in the next chapter. But let there be no doubt: whatever else I may have to say about these images, ideas, and contexts, *and* however you, the reader, may come to understand it, the "problem" midnight basketball was meant to address had everything to do with young, urban African American men. Though few were willing or able to acknowledge it publicly, the racial character of the problems midnight basketball was truly meant to address was on the tip of every tongue, pictured in every photograph, and embedded in every conversation and exchange.

THREE

An Unlikely and Revealing Consensus

In the late 1980s and early 1990s—just about the time that midnight basketball was coming to national prominence—another late-night, basketball-based phenomenon was gaining popularity all across the United States: the season-starting, 12:01 a.m. basketball practices at colleges and universities that came to be marketed as Midnight Madness. There are some obvious parallels between midnight basketball and Midnight Madness. Both were late at night. Both attracted lots of media and public attention. And both famously featured African American young men. However, that is about as far as the parallels go. Playing off the larger American fascination with NCAA basketball and the hype of its year-end tournament—*March* Madness, it was called—*Midnight Madness* was marketed and consumed as a joyful, jovial, deliberate inversion of dominant cultural norms and values about the relationships between academics and athletics, playfulness and seriousness, sanity and insanity. It is entertainment, diversion, spectacle, and even carnival. *Midnight basketball*, in stark contrast, was serious public policy and high-minded problem solving.

Sport scholars have a fairly good understanding of what makes the collegiate version of midnight madness so engaging and entertaining, as it is just one more example of the intersections of blackness and basketball I discussed in the previous chapter (see, again, D. L. Andrews and Silk 2010; Leonard 2010, 2006). But the urban policy variation on the midnight theme is a bit more paradoxical and perplexing. Why are we so serious about basketball-based social programs in America's biggest cities and poorest neighborhoods? They are anything but entertainment. What was it that compelled community leaders, politicians, policy makers, and regular citizens—even those with no particular interest in sports—to believe that this kind of basketball at midnight made good, sensible programming and social policy? Was it a different kind of madness? The more I learned about midnight basketball and the more I looked at the evidence of its effectiveness (or lack thereof), the less convincing its proponents' claims and core ideas seemed to be. Making sense of the popularity and appeal of midnight basketball actually got harder before it got easier.

Midnight Madness?

Living, as we do, in an age of information, investigative journalism, and regulatory oversight, you might think that a policy innovation as popular and yet peculiar as midnight basketball would have been subject to a certain degree of media scrutiny and public debate. Yet it was not, at least not initially. And the fact that midnight basketball wasn't scrub-brushed and scrutinized by the media or other critics might further lead you to infer that its organizers and proponents must have assembled a good deal of evidence of its effectiveness. But they didn't, at least not really.

It doesn't take a lot of digging to discover that Standifer's oft-repeated claim that midnight basketball had reduced crime by 30 percent in its first three years of operation—a figure actually doubled by President Bush in a national ceremony honoring the initiative (*Washington Post*, April 13, 1991)—was a spurious statistical association, based on little more than the observation that his program had been in operation during the same years the crime rate in his community had dropped by this amount. The fact of the matter is that crime rates were in decline all across the country throughout the period, a fact that criminologists are still trying to explain today (cf. Uggen and McElrath 2014). Over the next few years, other basketball-based program operators and advocates offered similar claims, and a few preliminary studies and assessments appeared. A program in Milwaukee, for example, claimed responsibility for a 30 percent reduction in crime (Farrell et al. 1995), and a Phoenix project purportedly resulted in 10.4 percent fewer juvenile arrests and a 50 percent reduction in juvenile incidents reported to the police in the affected neighborhoods (McCann and Peters 1996). Impressive as these statistics sounded (see also Derezotes 1995; Wilkins 1996), the studies were not all they were cracked up to be because they were all missing the comparisons and controls a proper analysis of treatment effects requires (cf. Baldwin 2000).

Results from the ballyhooed Chicago pilot program weren't any more convincing. The official evaluation of Chicago's original pilot program assembled a good deal of evidence about the popularity of the program among participants and program stakeholders (coaches and sponsors) and suggested that favorable news coverage had positively affected public perceptions about the Chicago Housing Authority. However, the report, which was prepared by Wolanyo Kpo of Chicago State University, also detailed a number of shortcomings—among them, inadequate needs assessment, monitoring, and documentation as well as lack of formal service or training modules—and could only say that it was "too early to determine any impact of the MBL [Midnight Basketball Leagues] program on . . . crime statistics" (Kpo 1990, 2). Others in Chicago were even more skeptical. Police captains went on record saying that gang activity hadn't declined in the targeted neighborhoods. Even program director Gil Walker publicly bemoaned the fact that so few of the program participants had taken advantage of the job opportunities offered to them. "We're not naïve," Walker told the *Chicago Reporter* in May 1990. "We need a lot more than basketball . . . and have a long way to go."[1]

Other athletically oriented intervention initiatives didn't provide any more reassuring results either. The claims were often impressive: one Police Athletic League, for example, trumpeted the claim that juvenile arrests dropped 16.1 percent, and juveniles were 43.9 percent less likely to be victims; in Cincinnati, there was talk of a 31 percent reduction in crime incidence; Fort Myers, Florida, touted a 27 percent drop in crime with its STARS outreach program; Kansas City, Missouri, claimed a 25 percent reduction in crime; and Fort Worth, Texas, reported a 28 percent crime drop within a one-mile radius of the program site. But once again, as David Witt and John Crompton (1997) pointed out in an important scholarly review at the time, each of these reports lacked any scientific comparisons or controls.

In spite of its grandiose aspirations and intentions, in fact, the entire social problems industry in urban youth sports and recreation described in the previous chapter could produce almost no evidence of effectiveness for intervention, risk reduction, or crime prevention. The most comprehensive and rigorous survey of the social scientific literature on crime prevention of the period (Sherman et al. 1998) listed only one scholarly study that focused explicitly on recreation-based programs, and its findings about community-based after-school recreation programs were limited and contradictory at best (Howell 1995). In an examination of the literature on athletic boot camps, criminologist Mark Correira (1997) concluded that these programs failed to affect arrest records, recidivism rates, or probation results among participants. To the extent that such camps could claim positive impacts at all, the results seemed to be limited to participants likely to have benefited from programmatic interventions of *any* type (see Mackenzie [1993, 1990]; Mackenzie and Shaw [1990] for supporting studies). Numerous programs that included athletic and physical activities as one aspect or component of a larger integrated service or outreach effort—Boys and Girls Clubs, YMCA, and after-school programs would be typical examples—were found to have positive violence prevention effects (cf. Thurman et al. 1996; Gambone and Arbreton 1997; M. McLaughlin, Irby, and Langman 1994; Tierney and Grossman 1995; Gottfredson 1986). However, these tended not to be exclusively sport based or even to use recreation as the key to their outreach and recruitment. In other words, they were a lot different than sport-based programs like midnight basketball.

Highly visible programs and initiatives can, of course, have impacts far beyond their immediate scope—especially if they are properly conceived and well designed. But there wasn't a great deal of reason to believe that this was the case for midnight basketball. Even the most extensive basketball-based programs operated only a few nights a week for a couple of months a year, and they served no more than a couple hundred individuals. Standifer's original program in Maryland, for example, counted only 60 participants during its first year of operation (1986), and had only 84 in 1988, the year in which it was discovered by the national media. The Chicago plan, for its part, called for a total of 160 participants (Carter 1998; US Department of Housing and Urban Development 1994). While this number may have been impressive for a basketball league, it paled in comparison to the estimated 6,600 "at-risk young adults" residing in the Horner and Rockwell homes at the time, let alone alongside the 85,000 who lived in CHA housing across the city. Hundreds of thousands more young men of color who might be considered just as "at risk" didn't reside in public housing at all. Indeed, even if you accept the claims of Midnight Basketball Inc. that there were almost 40 official midnight basketball leagues by the early 1990s and grant that these leagues had a full complement of 160 players each, the maximum number of young men in official midnight basketball leagues nationwide wasn't even equal to the number of young men living in the two housing projects in which the programs were located in Chicago.

Furthermore, it wasn't actually clear that midnight was the best time frame for these programs in the first place. On the younger end of the age range for the target population (school-age teenagers), criminological research has long suggested high-crime hours are not late at night, but rather after school and in the early evening when these young people are inclined to be active yet out of normative institutional settings (Fox and Newman 1997; Snyder and Sickmund 1999). On the upper end of the age range, it wasn't difficult to imagine how a late-night basketball league would wreak havoc with anyone who held (or desired) a regular day job or had family responsibilities—in either case contributing to (rather than mitigating) the problems many believed confronted African American men and their families. Suffice it to say, the more I looked at their structure and design, the more it seemed midnight basketball leagues had about as much chance of mitigating the problems of urban youth and young men of color as Robert Pitter and David Andrews said the social problems industry had of equalizing access to sports and recreation across the country. That is to say, almost nil.

In retrospect, none of this is surprising. The relationships between social intervention and sport participation have always been somewhat tenuous and uncertain in the research literature,[2] and the rationale for the earliest midnight basketball programs was relatively unsophisticated, little more than a hodgepodge of longstanding sports slogans and ideals about the social interventionist capacities of sport. These also played off of (and were sometimes connected with) entrenched beliefs about sport providing an unparalleled avenue of opportunity and mobility, as a positive, prosocial force, for racial minorities and race relations more generally. But, again, these shortcomings and limitations were not talked about a great deal at the beginning—and certainly not discussed much by the originator of midnight basketball himself.

The closest thing to a vision that I have ever been able to document in archives and materials related to midnight basketball's initial inception was the mantra that the program provided a "safe and structured" alternative to the chaos and even destructive activities of the street. "The Alternative," in fact, served as the program's official motto and appeared on all official correspondence and stationary (US Department of Housing and Urban Development 1994). These kinds of slogans appeared prominently and regularly in the newspapers that reported on midnight basketball (and that my research team and I heard when we did interviewing and ethnography in similar programs). Midnight basketball was believed to provide a safe, stable, secure place in a community and for a population that otherwise lacked such venues. But again, organizers didn't promote this rationale widely, or really even develop it explicitly. It was simply built into the structure and operation of the program, along with some allusions to traditional sports chestnuts such as building character and better citizens, or transcending the boundaries of race and class. Indeed, the program evaluators could name at the end of its first year of operation only one real objective: that midnight basketball in Chicago provided a "constructive divergence" from "unacceptable behaviors . . . a viable and attractive alternative to street life, and the resultant potential criminal activity and drug use" (Kpo 1990, 3). Whatever its broader ideological appeal and its larger historical legacy, midnight basketball was essentially founded on a kind of "Field of Dreams" model: if you build it, they will come—and somehow, somewhat mysteriously, be the better for it.

In the face of such limitations and lack of evidence of effectiveness, it would be easy to be critical, skeptical, or cynical about midnight basketball organizers and supporters—concluding that they were completely misguided, crazy, or driven by other, broader, if more insidious interests and agendas. I eventually did learn that there was some truth to this latter theory. Early on, however, I tried to avoid such quick conclusions. It is all too easy for scholars to be critical of practices, policies, and programs in the sporting world (or any other policy domain, for that matter) when they fail to make good on their high ideals or big promises or when they exhibit stereotypes (racial or otherwise) that reproduce and reinforce existing social inequalities. More difficult—and far more important and revealing, in my view—is to understand policy initiatives and their advocates on their own terms, to give them and their programs and ideas the benefit of the doubt, situating their motivations, understandings, and ideals within the context and constraints in which those visions are most meaningful, commonsensical, and intuitive.

Midnight basketball proponents, at least the ones I had known in my own early experiences and the ones I later discovered in the archives and in the field, were neither cynical nor stupid; they were not dismissive or half-hearted. Take midnight basketball's "inventor," G. Van Standifer. Due to his untimely death in September of 1992, I was never able to meet, much less interview him.[3] But Standifer was, according to my research and interviewing, a passionate and entrepreneurial individual whose charisma, energy, and ambition were key to the ascension of the midnight basketball concept. He and other organizers were truly, genuinely convinced they were onto something powerful. They also had plenty of supporters—community leaders, political elites, and media pundits who not only embraced this rather flimsy idea, but actually extolled midnight basketball as a noble experiment and inspiring policy initiative. In a commentary on its main editorial page, the *Chicago Sun-Times* (December 3, 1989) summed up the view in four words: "Simple. Logical. Cheap. Effective." The paper asked, "Why didn't anyone think of [it] sooner?" A nonscientific poll conducted by the *Chicago Defender* (April 20, 1990), one of the nation's historic African American newspapers, found that fully 85 percent of Chicagoans surveyed approved of the program, seeing it as giving youths "opportunities to get involved in a positive and constructive activity." Even at the height of conservative attacks on midnight basketball in the debates over the 1994 crime bill, Gallup polling indicated that midnight basketball retained a 65 percent approval rating, a figure some 10 points higher than support for the compromise crime bill itself.[4]

There is something very important going on here, and something potentially revealing. Rather than dismiss for lack of evidence this enthusiasm and support, I decided it would be better to try to understand the appeal of midnight basketball on its own terms and in the context within which it was so positively produced and perceived. And so I returned to thinking through midnight basketball's appeal for key supporters, public policy and opinion leaders like Housing and Urban Development (HUD) secretary Jack Kemp. And I began in time-honored sociological fashion by situating their enthusiastic embrace in the broader context of politics and public policy—the neoliberal transformations that were reshaping the whole American social service landscape in the late twentieth century.

The Broader Social Policy Context

Like other sport researchers, I made a lot of the impact that the embrace of market-based approaches and the retrenchment of the welfare state was having on youth sport and recreation provision when I first started researching midnight basketball and the whole evolution of sport-based social intervention in late twentieth-century America. However, as I contemplated the twin facts that the athletic aspects of the program were woefully undertheorized *and* that midnight basketball was popular in spite of its sports emphasis (not because of it), I realized I needed to go further. I needed to see how transformations in social service provision had a much broader impact and significance, not just on sport policy but on social policy in far more general terms.

The late 1980s and early 1990s were, after all, a period in which funding for all sorts of social service programs—education, job training, welfare, and health care, not just sports, parks, and public recreation—was being cut back, curtailed, retrenched. I am referring here to the cuts to the various social programs that constituted the American welfare state as ushered in under President Ronald Reagan's "new federalism" in the 1980s (Wacquant 2009, 2008b; see also Danziger and Gottschalk 1993; Gans 1995; Katz 1989; Pierson 1994; Korpi and Palme 1998). These cuts hit hardest in the nation's cities, home to the young African American men targeted by midnight basketball and all sports-based intervention initiatives. Between 1982 and 1987, to give one particularly pertinent example, the nation's public housing budget was cut by 87 percent. At one point, according to Sudhir Venkatesh (2000, 116), it got so bad in Chicago that the Housing Authority's request for money to bring its housing up to minimum standards actually exceeded the Department of Housing and Urban Development's nation-wide budget for all such repairs! The impact of budgetary cutbacks was, moreover, exacerbated in urban areas which had already seen major portions of their jobs and industrial tax bases leave for suburbs, the American Southwest, and overseas.

Such cutbacks and institutional shifts left community organizers, social workers, and urban policy makers—anyone, really, with any inclination to help alleviate the problems of poor, African American men (or any members of the urban underclass)—with few options. Therefore, any social policy initiative had to be, first and foremost, inexpensive—or, as the *Chicago Sun-Times* (December 3, 1989) described midnight basketball, "cheap." By the end of the twentieth century, in other words, the challenge for urban social policy makers wasn't just how to do more with less; it was how to do something, *anything*, with nearly nothing. And midnight basketball was at least something.

Coming at it from this angle—or really, putting midnight basketball in this broader social, political, and policy context—reminded me also of how the Minneapolis Department of Health and Family Support (a city department that had no staff with experience or interest in sport, recreation, or physical activity) kicked off its Stay Alive version of midnight basketball in the late 1990s. Late-night basketball wasn't the department's only option or its first choice for social intervention. It actually started out as part of the larger Violence Prevention Project undertaken by then mayor Sharon Sayles Belton in response to the exceptionally high number of homicides that hit the city, mostly in African American neighborhoods, in the summer of 1995. During its first two years, the program used its $100,000 budget to give small grants to a dozen or so community-based, violence prevention initiatives. These programs ranged from the development of a domestic violence prevention curriculum and a pilot test of "peer courts" in middle schools to a gun buyback program and a handful of different counseling and educational programs. After two years of trials and experimentation, the DHFS decided to concentrate its resources on late-night basketball. This choice was not so much because it was the cheapest (none of these programs cost that much, which was the whole point of the violence prevention initiative), nor was it because city administrators loved sport. Rather, it was because late-night basketball was the only one of the programs that evaluators (Barnes-Josiah, Ansari, and Kress 1996) concluded had any measurable success in reaching the at-risk populations identified in the project's own youth homicide studies—namely, low income, eighteen- to twenty-five-year-old men of color.

Setting midnight basketball in the context of such fiscal constraints and policy dilemmas helps us see that the high levels of public support for midnight basketball say almost as much about the state of urban social policy in late twentieth-century America as they do about youth, sports, basketball, black men, or anything else. Political leaders and policy makers like those in Minneapolis really had very few actionable ideas about where these youth and young men could be found, or what they were up to, much less how to help them or change their behaviors. And they had even fewer resources with which to work. Midnight basketball was one of the few programs that could be supported within the existing fiscal parameters that held the promise of actually interesting and attracting this difficult-to-reach, problematic population. If midnight basketball was, in the athletic metaphor of the *Chicago Tribune* editorial from December 5, 1989, a "desperation shot," it was at least a plausible, good-faith attempt to address the needs of this perpetually troubled population.

And there were a number of other aspects about midnight basketball that made it more, a lot more, than the policy equivalent of a last-second, half-court heave in a basketball game. First and perhaps most basic was its funding model and organizational structure, its fit with emerging neoliberal thinking, trends, programs, and prototypes.

Part of midnight basketball's association with neoliberalism and neoliberal social policy more specifically involved how the initiative was supported financially. In addition to the fact that midnight basketball was relatively inexpensive, it also opened up the possibility of new, nongovernment funding options through its ability to interest and enlist corporate sponsorships, foundation support, and individual private donors. Recall that Standifer's original Maryland program was funded in part by the sponsorship of a beer company. For its part, San Diego's High Five America franchise cobbled together funding from a host of sources that included NFL all-star Junior Seau's foundation as its lead donor. And even though the Chicago leagues received start-up money (which wasn't extensive to begin with) from the Department of Housing and Urban Development, the program was mainly a pilot project intended to demonstrate the viability of attracting both corporate sponsorships as well as philanthropic donors such as foundations or wealthy individuals. In other words, the ultimate plan was to demonstrate that the tab, or at least some significant portion of it, would eventually be picked up by private, nongovernmental sources.

This funding model helps explain why Jack Kemp was so willing to throw the resources and reputation of the Department of Housing and Urban Development into the initiative as well as contribute his own time and considerable personal reputation. For someone like Kemp, public-private partnerships weren't just about cost saving. What they actually represented were a new vision of government and public policy, or, to put it more precisely, a new vision of and model for the relationships among the state, markets, and civil society in providing social services and taking care of people and communities. *This* was the essence and structure of the new market-oriented welfare state in late twentieth-century America—or what has come to be called "neoliberal" social policy.

Academic labels and terms can get a bit confusing. While scholars now refer to the reform movement that Kemp and so many others represented as "neoliberalism," this is not a term Kemp himself or others in his crowd would have used. If anything, in fact, they probably would have described themselves and their policy visions as neoconservative. However, the neoliberal scholarly label is not so much a reference to political alliances (i.e., Republican or Democrat) or standard ideological orientations (i.e., progressive or conservative) as it is a more abstract, theoretical reference to political economic ideas and ideals about free markets, social contracts, and moral order that are "liberal" in a classical, Enlightenment-thinking sense. If anything, these strange semantics reveal, in my view, the overlap and confusion between social ideals and political ideologies in the United States, where republican ideologies about free-market liberalism are often described as conservative in political terms, whereas in classical political economic theory, they really represent classically liberal ideas about the power of markets, individualism, and freedom that are best, or at least classically, defined and described as liberal.

Whatever we call it, Kemp, a leading Republican inner-city advocate and policy reformer, was driven by two basic tenets when it came to dealing with urban social problems through public policy and social programming of the immediate, post-1960s period. One had to do with government and the state. Kemp and his GOP colleagues were famously and deeply suspicious of the state and its perceived inability to run social programs of any sort. Kemp's public policy statements, position papers, and speeches of the period are chock-full of descriptions of the inefficiencies of government, the red tape and excessive bureaucratization that he saw getting in the way of program delivery and social service assistance. Like that of so many other political conservatives, Kemp's criticism had an especially sharp edge when it came to policies directed toward poverty, housing, employment, and cities—for example, the programs of the so-called welfare state. Influenced by works like the populist libertarian Charles Murray's *Losing Ground* (1984), Kemp was convinced that welfare state policies and government programs from the 1960s were not only inefficient or ineffective; they actually stripped poor folks of their initiative and work ethic, their self-respect, and their sense of connection to the larger community. In other words, the government's poverty programs were deeply and fundamentally counterproductive, cultivating attitudes and behaviors that were the root of the poverty problem itself. This was the second core tenet of Kemp's thinking about government programs and state policies.

I will have more to say regarding the assumptions about inner-city culture, black men, and African American family life that are embedded in this conservative/neoliberal worldview—the culture-of-poverty critique previewed in the previous chapter—shortly. But for the moment, let me just point out that, in and of themselves, Kemp's criticisms of the shortcomings of the state as social policy provider were not particularly original or unique. What set Kemp apart from others in the Republican Party and more conservative ideological circles—and why I believe he was willing to lend his support to midnight basketball—was that he wasn't willing to leave inner-city residents and communities entirely to their own devices. Driven by his empathy for and claimed connection to African Americans—derived in large part, he always explained, from his experiences on the football field with African American teammates[5]—Kemp was passionately committed to public policies that would address the social problems of the black community and cities (see, for example, Stanfield 1996). In other words, Kemp was that rare breed: a free-market, economic conservative with an equal commitment to urban social problems—the original compassionate conservative, you might say. And his solution to the inefficiencies and shortcomings of the state, when it came to dealing with the social problems of cities and African American communities, reflected the other aspect of the neoliberal approach to social and urban policy: its embrace of the market. If the state was the problem, in short, the market was Kemp's solution.

In recent years, social theorists, political sociologists, and public policy scholars have distinguished two different faces or phases of neoliberal governance's embrace of the market. One is a basic, laissez-faire stance whose goal is to liberate agencies, organizations, and government programs from the constraints of state bureaucracies, rules, and procedures—to let them operate more like private companies, free of government regulation and oversight. Described (and criticized) most famously by cultural geographer David Harvey (2005), this is the face of neoliberal policy that took shape first, in the 1970s and 1980s. Kemp and his crowd clearly fit this bill. Across the 1990s and into the new millennium, however, policy reforms and reformers began to mobilize market logic in other, more radical ways as well.

More and more, social domains—including the state and all its various programs, policies, agencies, and initiatives—were organized and evaluated according to free-market principles and, above all else, cost-benefit analyses. In this second, more extreme extension of market logic, social policies and programs began to be transferred to private contractors and providers who were encouraged to experiment and innovate, but they were put into competition with each other for the right to provide social services in new (and presumably more cost-effective) ways (cf. Peck and Tickell 2002; W. Brown 2006; Soss, Fording, and Schram 2011).

The first, the antigovernment or laissez-faire aspect of neoliberalism, was what Jack Kemp himself was most aware of and self-consciously committed to. This commitment is perhaps best illustrated by the biggest of his initiatives as HUD secretary: enterprise zones. Kemp was convinced that the creation and facilitation of tax-free enterprise zones would produce new energy and productivity through competition, stimulating local economies and unleashing the untapped energy and potential of urban communities. The idea was that more market-oriented social programs would be closer to the ground, more responsible to the actual lives, needs, and evolving challenges of those communities and people who needed them. But the competitive, market-driven principles of evaluation and programming may have been more determinative for program operations. And, in fact, the crucial point here is that midnight basketball actually lay at the intersection of the two different facets of neoliberalism's approach to markets and policies.

As policy initiative, midnight basketball was both laissez-faire on government *and* market-driven as a mode of financing and operations, and that was what made it so attractive to someone like Kemp. With its entrepreneurial orientation and its emphasis on experimentation, midnight basketball appealed to the most libertarian impulses of neoliberalism—freeing programs and services from state regulation and offering nonstate actors the chance to compete for the opportunity to serve communities in new, innovative, and cost-effective ways. At the same time, with its use of public-private partnerships, midnight basketball embodied the shift to publicly funded and regulated programs that were nevertheless subjected to market principles of competition and performance in the social service arena. All things considered, in fact, I think it is reasonable to think that midnight basketball was at the forefront and leading edge of the reconfiguration of social policy in the neoliberal image—a near ideal-typical model, a microcosm, of neoliberal social policy in late twentieth- and early twenty-first-century America.

Athletic Idealism

Jack Kemp was not really a religious man. But he was a man of faith, and one of the things Kemp believed in was the "invisible hand" of the market. His belief in the positive, productive power of markets was unusually broad and encompassing. Unlike some Republicans (and more than a few Democrats) of the early neoliberal period, Kemp believed not only in the productive power of markets for economic growth but also in the inherent good of civil society. Indeed, Kemp's faith in a market-oriented, neoliberal vision of government and public policy was rooted in his optimism about people and American communities. It wasn't so much that Kemp thought policies constructed according to market metrics and logics would bring profits and productivity; it was that he was truly convinced regarding the capacities of free, unfettered associations of civil society to socialize and self-organize, to identify the concrete, on-the-ground needs of the community, to engage all its members, and to turn them into productive and engaged family members, citizens, and workers.[6] And if there was one thing that the secretary of Housing and Urban Development believed in as fervently as he believed in markets and civil society, it was sports and the positive social force of athletics.

A former superstar athlete and lifelong sports lover, Jack Kemp was a committed athletic idealist. Kemp never met a sports metaphor or anecdote he couldn't incorporate into his political lexicon. Indeed, campaign reporter Michael Lewis said that the stump speeches during Kemp's ill-fated 1996 presidential campaign relied so heavily on football metaphors that it was "hard to see where the football stops and the politics starts" (New Republic, October 14, 1996). These blurred lines are key to understanding Kemp's political philosophy. I think you can see athletic idealism either as one of the twin towers of Kemp's ideological commitments or as the core metaphorical system that informed his faith in markets and civil society. In learning about him, and his background in athletics, and his interest in politics, I myself lean toward thinking that his whole vision of public service, the workings of society, the role of government, and the place of politicians is rooted in his early, idealized experiences in and visions of sport.

While I don't want to get lost in political psychoanalysis, it is pretty clear that the connections between sport and political philosophy were at the root of Secretary Kemp's easy acceptance of midnight basketball. Kemp, like others, actually didn't talk a lot about midnight basketball or sport in general in pursuing the program for HUD. In fact, in all the time I've spent researching midnight basketball and Jack Kemp himself, I have never come across a passage or text in Kemp's files about midnight basketball that is worth citing (much less analyzing). For a little while, in fact, I thought maybe he wasn't as sold on midnight basketball as his public association with the concept made it appear. But eventually I came to conclude that midnight basketball was just like markets and the American spirit in Kemp's worldview: just something that made perfect sense, something that was in fact so commonsense that it didn't require any particular explanation or defense. The fact that Secretary Kemp never explicitly explained or defended the interventionist potential of one of his department's most popular pet programs doesn't mean that there wasn't a set of ideas that inspired him and informed supporters of the concept. Quite the contrary, these ideas—or really ideals and ideologies—were largely just unspoken, deeply embedded in the culture and consciousness of practitioners. And it is here, in the realm of core convictions, taken-for-granteds, and the belief in things unseen, where sport and the ideals and beliefs associated with it came into the midnight basketball analysis.

Though not particularly well formed or even self-consciously understood by advocates like Kemp, a large, unwieldy set of ideals and themes about sport were (and are) embedded in midnight basketball's otherwise mysterious popular appeal and cultural fascination. One of the most basic if usually unspoken threads of this constellation of assumptions and ideals was the belief that athletic endeavors stood as an alternative—the mantra on Standifer's letterhead—to the usual, more destructive temptations of "the street" and, moreover, constituted a special kind of safe haven for youth and young men from vulnerable, disadvantaged backgrounds. There is actually something of a tradition of this sort of analysis in scholarly writing about race and sport. Scott Brooks (2008), for example, is probably the sociologist best known for developing the idea with respect to youth basketball. Loïc Waquant (2004) gave the notion its most elaborate formulation in his well-known ethnography of boxing on the South Side of Chicago.

In describing the dialectical relationships between the boxing gym and the ghetto, Wacquant explained: "One cannot understand the relatively closed world of boxing outside of the human and ecological context in which it is anchored . . . [specifically] to the neighborhood and the grim realities of the ghetto that the gym defines itself" (2004, 17). Much of Wacquant's work focused on the community organization and social context that hosted the boxing program he studied. "By contrast to this hostile and uncertain environment," Wacquant wrote, "[boxing at] the Boys and Girls Club constitutes an island of stability and order . . . a relatively self-enclosed site . . . where one can find a respite from the pressures of the street and the ghetto, a world into which external events rarely penetrate and onto which they have little impact" (26). One of Wacquant's informants, a nineteen-year-old he called Mike who came to the gym every afternoon right after school, put it like this: "You can go there and feel good about yourself. Like I said, you feel protected, secure. You in there, aw, you're alright—it's like a second family. You know you can go there for support" (26–27). Other lines that were regularly repeated included "all the time in the gym is that much less time spent out on the street;" "it keeps me off the street;" and "I rather be here than gettin' in trouble on the streets" (27). Here, I might mention Vice President Hubert Humphrey's proposal in the late 1960s to open gyms and set up summer sports programs in inner-city neighborhoods as a hedge against the riots that had plagued major metropolitan areas in previous summers (see Hartmann 2003a, 227–31). And we certainly can't forget that basketball itself was invented by a young YMCA instructor named James Naismith who was looking for an "athletic distraction" to bring his rowdy Kansas students in line when they were stuck indoors during the long Midwestern winter months (Myerscough 1995).

The cultural appeal of midnight basketball (and all such sports-oriented crime prevention programming) went well beyond that of simple diversion and distraction. The initiative was also part of a longer, larger, and venerable American tradition of using sport for purposes of social intervention for youth, especially young men from communities of color and contexts of disadvantage. These ideals were clearly in play for the entire midnight basketball crowd. Terms like "self-esteem building," "self-discipline," and "self-respect," as well as "teamwork," "hard-work," and "community," were peppered throughout media interviews given by program officials in Chicago and Maryland as well as the official HUD and Midnight Basketball Inc. pamphlets of the period. Basketball players were also seen as role models and leaders in their communities (May 2009). Ideas about how sport provided opportunities for mobility and advancement often surfaced as well, and notions about citizenship and moral development were bandied about. When CHA chairman Vincent Lane promoted midnight basketball to the public, he put it this way: "We're going to try to move [participants] down the road to being contributing citizens" (quoted in *Chicago Reporter*, May 1990). They assumed that playing sports required and produced the qualities of self-discipline, hard work, teamwork, competitiveness, and fair play that were seen as the prerequisites for cultivating a contributing, productive member of society. Such virtues and qualities were believed to accrue organically, almost naturally or inevitably, from engaging in structured athletic competition itself. In short, sports participation was naturally socially beneficial because it both required and cultivated self-discipline and strong moral character through the virtues of effort, competition, teamwork, and fair play.

The ideology of sport as a positive, progressive socialization force took shape in the United States during the reforms of the Progressive Era. The YMCA and YWCA, Boys and Girls Clubs, and the Boy Scouts all used sports and physical activities as key to their projects of adolescent socialization and immigrant assimilation. However, this notion goes back well into nineteenth-century Anglo-Saxon culture. Initially, as historians have detailed, the idea of development and life training through sport was largely the terrain of elite and upper-middle-class European men who mobilized themselves for class purposes under the auspices of amateurism—the classic literary expression being *Tom Brown's School Days*, a nineteenth-century English story of boarding school boys' maturation through hard-nosed athletic competition.[7] While these notions took on somewhat different form for ruling elites than for ethnic minorities and the working masses, the underlying and unifying assumption was that playing sports builds character, self-esteem, and social skills that imbue otherwise undisciplined, immature young people with the principles of social order and self-control that are prerequisites for contributing, productive members of society (MacLeod 1983; Segrave 1980; see also Oriard 1991; Novak 1976).

Racial ideals and images have always been a crucial part of this conceptual package (Hartmann 2015). In proposing the midnight basketball pilot program to Kemp's office, in fact, the Chicago Housing Authority took pains to tap into ideals about natural and inherently positive connections among race, youth, and sports in American culture. And Gil Walker, the chief organizer of the Chicago league, was regularly quoted as saying that sports was an arena of access and opportunity for everyone, regardless of race, religion, class, or culture. Given that folks like Kemp and Standifer and Walker wanted to help address the problems faced by African American men and given their understanding of the importance of basketball in the black community, nothing seemed more natural and intuitive than a sport-based program.

A certain portion of midnight basketball came from sport's longstanding reputation and historical legacy as a leader in the struggle for the advancement of racial and ethnic minorities, especially African Americans. And this idealized racial history fit perfectly with an *ideology* of sport as an arena of equal opportunity and advancement for African Americans, a leader in the struggle for harmonious integration and civil rights, and a model for equity, fairness, and social change (Early 2011).

In previous research and writing on the history of race in American sport (see, especially, Hartmann 2003a, chap. 3; 2003c; 2007), I have argued that there are deep, mutually reinforcing connections among three distinct cultural elements: sport's idealized culture of competition, fair play, and merit; mainstream liberal democratic political theory; and color-blind, individualist visions of racial justice and social equality. This analysis grew out of Michael Oriard's important 1991 study of the linguistic tropes and cultural values that that have made (and continue to make) sport such a powerful and *familiar* metaphor for social life in the United States. It comes down to ideas about how social order is believed to be constituted in an individualistic, competitive culture. Basically, our idealized conceptions of sport and our conventional beliefs about democratic society share assumptions about the freely acting individual as the building block for human creativity and social order. They are also guided by the belief that individuals are to be judged (and rewarded) not on the basis of any sociological characteristics but solely on the basis of their personal merit, hard work, and actual performance, their exercise of freedom within the parameters of the equal application of the law. Sport serves as a literal model of the ideal or moral standard to which communities and social orders should aspire and by which social life itself is constituted and maintained.

Essentially, I extended Oriard's analysis to suggest that these interrelated ideals about sport culture, civil rights, and color-blind justice make sport a powerful and prominent arena for the production, reproduction, and (at least occasionally) contestation of race and visions of race in modern social life. In particular, I argued that sport's abstract, idealized sense of itself as a special realm of sociability and competitive free play within established rules of conduct parallels (and thus reinforces) not only conventional liberal democratic political ideologies, but also color-blind, individualist visions of racial justice and progress.

At the core of this vision is Martin Luther King Jr.'s fascination with St. Paul's footrace metaphor and how it could be applied to social justice—specifically the claim that a fair society, like a fair race, requires that all individuals be afforded equal opportunity. Sport, in this sense, is not only a model for social justice and racial progress; it is the concrete, institutional embodiment of the ideals of justice and progress promised in liberal democratic ideology and visions of appropriate social intervention and change. And what I came to realize in thinking back through all of this was that it was consistent with the individualist, equal opportunity ideals of the mainstream American conceptions of race relations, civil rights, and social justice that neoliberal reformers and idealists like Jack Kemp inherited from Ronald Reagan.[8]

To reiterate, these ideals and connections didn't really even need to be articulated, explained, or defended by midnight basketball supporters and admirers: they were deeply entrenched. Here I also want to suggest that this idealized vision of sport as a force for racial progress and social justice dovetailed neatly with the emerging neoliberal vision of and approach to government programs, social welfare, and public policy. The same combination of mutually reinforcing linguistic tropes and cultural commitments about the social value of sport, aspirations for racial reform, and a vision of social policy and intervention that came together in the case of midnight basketball held sway among a certain, fairly large and influential segment of mainstream, middle-class Americans. No wonder Jack Kemp—the former all-star quarterback, free-market true believer, and passionate racial reformer—saw fit to make midnight basketball one of the signature innovations of his tenure as HUD secretary (even if he didn't bother to explain it or think or talk about it much otherwise). Or that his boss (and one-time political rival) George H. W. Bush, himself a lifelong sportsman and budding compassionate conservative, was quick to jump on the midnight bandwagon as well—going so far as to make midnight basketball one of the signature programs of *his* grassroots political organization meant to mark, define, and chart the course for a new, broad-based political philosophy. All these ideas and ideals about markets and funding as well as athletics, social progress, and racial mobility came together so seamlessly, almost perfectly. It was a match made at midnight.

Underlying Assumptions about Race and Risk

Intuitive, tightly woven, and seemingly progressive as all these institutional and ideological forces may have been, a sociologist like me could not help but be aware—and increasingly concerned—that the marriage of neoliberalism, sports idealism, and individualist-meritocratic visions of racial justice that lay at the core of the midnight basketball innovation was not based in the most enlightened vision of African American men or the problems they faced. I don't mean to single out Kemp, Standifer, Bush, or any Republican for that matter. Midnight basketball had supporters across a wide range of political commitments, social backgrounds, and ideological positions—Democrats, nonpolitical community organizers, and program administrators included. Indeed, one of midnight basketball's champions in Chicago was Vincent Lane, an African American public official with designs on more influence and higher office in the Democratic Party. It is also worth recalling that Bill Clinton and his New Democrat colleagues would jump on the midnight basketball bandwagon within months of winning the 1992 elections. Thus, I see support for midnight basketball as emanating from mainstream, centrist sensibilities with broad ideological and bipartisan appeal (a cultural consensus that is almost nonexistent in today's politically polarized climate, I might add, though this is getting a bit ahead of myself).[9]

No, across ideologies, one of the biggest and most obvious shortcomings of these programs was that, in spite of occasional allusions to the contrary, midnight basketball did little to address the social conditions at the root of the problems faced by young men of color—inferior schooling, deficient housing, persistent discrimination, basic poverty and unemployment, and the like. To the extent that the earliest midnight basketball programs included *any* remedies to the structural disadvantages of the urban environment and a racialized society, these mainly involved initiatives related to jobs and job training. Standifer's flagship Maryland program, for example, offered "scholarships" for training in "truck driving, auto mechanics, and diesel mechanics," and the Chicago Housing Authority promised jobs to any participants willing to undergo four Saturday mornings of training.[10] However, these programs do not appear to have been a high priority for organizers, the job prospects were limited, and the jobs themselves were less than desirable for potential employees. I never found any evidence of actual, meaningful job placements out East, and the jobs in Chicago were entry-level, janitorial positions in the city's parks or housing departments that paid only seven dollars an hour. The Chicago opportunities were so unappealing that few participants even showed up for the minimal training. Program director Gil Walker complained publicly to the *Chicago Reporter*,[11] but my recollection is that folks around the city were not surprised. They tended to view the employment programs somewhat cynically, as more useful as recruitment devices for depleted and cash-strapped public service sector agencies than as actual employment placements intended to improve the lives of these young men. And these "opportunities" were the *only* elements of midnight basketball programming that addressed the marginal circumstances that these young men encountered on a daily basis.

This limitation was, of course, not unique to midnight basketball; it was (and is) characteristic of much neoliberal social policy (cf. Kettl 2002; Wacquant 2009). But it is useful and important to think about what motivated and justified or even just allowed such an emphasis in the first place—and it is here, in digging deeper into the ideologies behind neoliberal social policy, that we need to think critically about the racialized assumptions about street life and the culture of poverty built into these initiatives and innovations.

In a single, somewhat idiosyncratic and ostensibly color-blind program such as midnight basketball, it was (and is) impossible to isolate or specify the extent to which these policies—or lack thereof—were dictated by the racial background of the target population. American social policy is, after all, notoriously stingy and moralistic, and cutbacks were unfolding all across the social service landscape. Still, it was difficult to believe that race didn't play a part. Sociologists, political scientists, and historians have all clearly demonstrated that race and racism decisively affected social policies and politics in the late twentieth-century United States (M. K. Brown 1999; Lieberman 1998), and a plethora of studies have confirmed that neoliberal social policies were decidedly racialized in form as well as function in domains ranging from health care and housing to criminal justice, jobs programs, schools, and poverty programs (Alexander 2012; Goldberg 2008; Wacquant 2008a; Pager 2007).

For my money, one of the most grounded and far-reaching of these treatments of race and neoliberal social policy is *Disciplining the Poor* by Joe Soss, Richard Fording, and Sanford Schram (2011). Focusing on the welfare reforms that came out of the federal legislation of 1996 and using a variety of methods to analyze an impressive array of data and supporting studies, this research team has shown that what they call "poverty governance" was decisively determined by race across the whole spectrum of neoliberal social policy from policy formation to implementation and service delivery. In terms of the political discourse and legislative debates, for example, Soss, Fording, and Schram found that beliefs about black laziness and sexual irresponsibility (as reflected in racially coded terms such as "welfare queens" or the "urban underclass") were the most powerful predictors of those who wanted to scale back public aid to the poor. The authors also determined that racial assumptions and demographics not only affected the level of funding voters and policy makers supported, but also the types of policies that were created and how these programs were implemented.

At the level of policy formation, moreover, they discovered that states with higher percentages of African American aid recipients were more likely to adopt and implement the toughest policies with respect to time limits, sanctions for program violations (the inability to find a job, for example), and other infractions. In terms of actual services and program delivery, a careful analysis of caseworker activities showed that African Americans in various poverty programs were more likely to get sanctioned (to have benefits cut or withheld) than whites, and they were just as likely to get sanctioned by African American caseworkers as by whites. Moreover, at the level of treatment, *Disciplining the Poor* may be the most original and directly relevant book to the midnight basketball case at hand. Highlighting differential racial treatment allowed these scholars to show that neoliberal welfare reform and contemporary poverty policy have *overt* disciplinary dimensions that are often ignored or misunderstood by scholars and critics who focus strictly on the economic, market-based aspects. Neoliberal poverty policy is driven not only by institutional and economic considerations but also by a directive, disciplinary orientation. What we are talking about, according to Soss and his colleagues, is not just a new variant of economic liberalism but "paternalism."

Paternalism, defined by Soss, Fording, and Schram (following Lawrence Mead [1997]), is an approach to social policy charged with "bringing discipline to the lives of the poor." Its disciplinary functions seem particularly oriented and directed toward minority populations—populations who, more than others, are held responsible for their fate and thus in need of extensive personal and moral self-reform and rehabilitation. "Neoliberal-paternalist poverty governance is rooted in, and justified by, a particular image of poor people. . . . [One which] identifies the poor individual as one who is suitable for incorporation as a responsible worker-citizen but who will be unlikely to make this transition unless the state acts on its obligation to impose social order and instill self-discipline" (Soss, Fording, and Schram 2011, 81). Indeed, in the authors' view, the poverty policy transformations of the last few decades are best understood as a *double* movement that includes the embrace of both market logic and a more supervisory, disciplinary-oriented type of control and change. This recognition led Soss, Fording, and Schram to adopt the term "neoliberal paternalism" to describe contemporary poverty policy—a mode of policy governance that is "at once more muscular in its normative enforcement and more dispersed and diverse in its organization" (3).

This notion of neoliberal paternalism has helped me shape and sharpen my understanding of midnight basketball in terms of both the motivation and deep structure of this innovation, and especially with respect to how race fits into the package. When researchers and idealists talk and think about socialization and development in and through sport, they often think in proactive, seemingly agent-centered terms such as "education," "empowerment," "development," and "self-realization." However, the paternalistic context and framing reminds us of what the sport sociologist Jay Coakley has often pointed out: namely, that sport-based intervention can be (and often is) directive and controlling. There is a heavy dose of externally imposed discipline and moral compulsion built into it. Sports idealists may not be ones to call attention to intervention of any kind, obsessed as they often are with the language of freedom, volunteerism, and unfettered individual initiative, but it was clearly there in my research, revealed in how policy makers talked (what they said and didn't say) and embedded in the programming itself.

Midnight basketball, the CHA's original proposal noted, "takes an old concept—sports as a constructive character-building activity—and gives it a new twist—the organization of a structured, 'after-hours' program." In this view, young black men needed to be supervised and controlled directly. For example, the CHA believed its program would move beyond Standifer's original midnight basketball model by adding "components" that would "encourage the participants to take charge of their own lives, attain legitimate economic independence, and become constructive family members and citizens."[12] Sport was to help change all that.

And these notions of morality and rehabilitation in and through midnight basketball were quite socially specific and indeed racially charged. As idealistic as midnight basketball proponents were about sport participation "building character" and "cultivating self-discipline" among these young black men, they were equally presumptive about the source of the problems the target population faced. Consider the quote above about all the things that basketball would help young black men become. The unsaid assumption and underlying implication was that young black men were *none* of these things: they were not in control of their lives, they lacked the ability to secure jobs, and they were poor fathers, family members, and citizens. If sport was believed to instill structure, discipline, self-control, and self-esteem in young people, it was imperative that sport be brought to young African American men who were "known" to lack these virtuous personal qualities and social skills. Midnight basketball proponents assumed the behaviors and beliefs of those in poor, disadvantaged, and presumably minority communities must be directly challenged and changed, that these youth and young men were not independent, not in control of their lives, and not contributing family members and citizens. They were lacking. Indeed, once I figured out that this racialized paternalist vision saw the problems of young African American men primarily in moral terms, the Chicago project's obsession with haircuts and personal grooming, as well as its broader concerns with self-discipline, conflict resolution, and family values, suddenly made sense.

Michael Jordan and the NIKE PLAY Program

Working my way through these intersecting strands of paternalism and race, sport and neoliberalism, and the complicated history of sport as intervention,

I sometimes found it difficult to hold all the connections in my head at once, let alone articulate them clearly and consistently. One article I returned to numerous times in thinking things through was C. L. Cole's (1996) analysis of a splashy, late millennium Nike publicity campaign for youth sports and recreation whose pitchman was none other than Chicago's own Michael Jordan.

The Nike PLAY campaign was the product of a well-publicized Youth Fitness Summit held in Washington, DC, in 1993. Working in fine, neoliberal fashion with nonprofit agencies and organizations such as the Boys and Girls Clubs of America, Nike had convened the meeting in response to the decline in public facilities for recreation and sport for youth (the same developments that were the focus of Pitter and Andrews's analysis of the social problems industry in sport). The "principle" motivating the movement, according to the four-page "Revolutionary Manifesto" the company circulated around the country, was that "every child [had an] inalienable right to an active life: the joy of sport, and the pursuit of fun." "For America's youth . . . going out to play is getting tougher all the time. Budget cuts are forcing schools to scale back or eliminate sports and physical education programs. Communities can't afford the upkeep on public parks and recreation facilities. Safety issues have many parents fearful of letting children out of their sight" (quoted in Cole 1996, 379). Through PLAY—short for "*participate in the lives of America's youth*"—the company meant to create and lead a movement and network of organizations and agencies that would secure every child's "right to play."

According to Cole, the PLAY initiative was launched in direct response to a series of public relations crises Nike faced early in the 1990s.[13] Promoting this campaign in tandem with nonprofit community-based organizations allowed Nike to present itself as a representative of, or even defender of, the national community—and thus reestablish its public reputation (and probably sell a few more shoes in the process). It was, in other words, an extensive and expensive public relations ploy. But Cole's real critique (and ultimate contribution to my understanding of midnight basketball) was of the underlying assumptions about race and risk that animated the campaign and made the advertising so effective.

Despite its all-American appeal and expressed desire to serve everyone, the PLAY campaign actually depended on an unspoken but pervasive set of racial assumptions and stereotypes about African American youth. It was not so much that African American youth were overrepresented in the advertisements (although it seems they were); rather, it was *how* these youth were represented. When it came to African American youngsters, according to Cole, the PLAY campaign and its vision of the social value of sport, athletics, and physical recreation shifted—in an important and revealing way—from the rhetoric of *rights* to a language of *risks* and *needs*. In this respect, Cole's analysis parallels the reading of neoliberal dynamics in other social domains such as Nina Eliasoph's *Making Volunteers* (2011) or Kristin Luker's analysis of teenage pregnancy in *Dubious Conceptions* (1996). All children may have a right to sport, it is implied, but some need sport and its socializing influences more than others. Here the implied or imagined contrast was between how sport was perceived and presented for white, middle-class, and mostly suburban kids versus mostly minority youth from the city. "Whereas sport and physical activity are used to shore up America's bourgeois fantasy of childhood fun and play for White middle-class youth, . . . in the context of urban America," Cole concluded, "sport is not about kid's play and bodily movement but a moral and normative imperative" (1996, 386).

Cole's analysis brings out how racial imagery in the context of youth athletics was tied with different notions of risk and threat for American youth. It wasn't just that youth of color and class disadvantage were believed to need sport for their own development and growth; the rest of society—the rest of us—needed them to have it. Without sport, the implication or assumption went, children of color would fail to develop properly, and in the future, they would present challenges for the "rest of us" as they developed lives of disorder, disruption, and reliance. This is where the language of risk and risk prevention shifted, subtly but surely, from referring to education, development, and socialization to a presumed emphasis on intervention, risk reduction, violence prevention, crime control, and public safety. Certain populations were not just "at risk" for stunted development, unlikely to reach their full potential or grow into active, engaged, productive citizens, but actually likely to produce problems and disorder for society at large.

In his powerful and rightfully influential journalistic work, Jonathan Kozol (2000, 1992) has made a point of trying to reclaim the innocence and inherent meaning of the lives of inner-city children of color, insisting on their inalienable humanity and claim to all the same opportunities and supports for development and self-realization as other young people in America. This was *not* what the PLAY campaign was about. It wasn't even about sport provision for these kids. Instead, the PLAY campaign was about the resocialization and control *of* these kids through sports. And it is in this context where Mary Douglas's more governmental-symbolic critique of risk, which I alluded to above, proves more useful than standard descriptive conceptions of risk society itself. With the PLAY campaign, as with the new paternalism more generally, these kids were not "at risk"; they were "a risk." Youth and young people of color might have a right to sport for their own personal development, but more pointedly, society *needs* them to have sport. As Cole summarized: "Sport and physical activity function to regulate, discipline, and police already deviant bodies in urban areas. . . . Without sport . . . inner-city youths are at once at-risk . . . and the sites of danger" (1996, 386).

These subtle racial distinctions were most clearly revealed, according to Cole, in what the advertising campaign *didn't* say—that is, in its absences and silences. "What if there were no sports?" the first PLAY spots famously asked. "What if there were no teams? What if there were no dreams?" Interesting, powerful, haunting—these questions were left hanging. While the "what if" uneasiness underlying the campaign was presented in general, abstract terms, Cole insists that a racial subtext was made clear in the way in which African American basketball star Michael Jordan was deployed as the pitch man.

Jordan narrated the entire television ad, including the questions asking "us" to envision our selves and our society "if there were no sports." But the basketball star is only pictured in the advertisement's closing sequence. This was not, Cole explained, incidental. In her inspired, insightful reading, the image of Michael Jordan—an athlete who despite all his transcendental qualities and capacities was also an African American man, a black man—reminded viewers that without sports not only would we lose the chance to find and develop future Michael Jordans, but we would likely be left with all the more usual problems associated with black youth and young men: gangs, crime, drugs, dropouts, violence, broken families, and so on. Thus, the PLAY campaign relied not just on the rhetoric of innocence, rights, and unmet needs, but also and more pointedly on the stereotypical tropes of danger, threat, and fear in which race, particularly blackness, was central. "If we did not imagine [a black man like Jordan] in the space of sport, where would we imagine him?" Cole asked, mimicking the original Nike ad (1996, 385–86). Who would we imagine him to be? What would we imagine him to be doing?[14]

This kind of critical cultural analysis is difficult to validate or test empirically.[15] However, the important point is not whether Cole is right or wrong, but what her reading and analysis calls into focus with respect to the topic at hand—that is, its use value for making sense of midnight basketball. And in the broadest parallel, what was useful and revealing for me was the assumption that the problems of African American youth, especially African American boys and young men, are the result of the shortcomings, deficiencies, and indeed pathologies of black men, black community, and black culture. Indeed, it is here we see the doubled-edged racial logic that posits youth of color as distinctly different and uniquely "at risk"—at risk, more precisely, for not growing and developing into the citizens and productive workers society wants and expects, a risk, even more so, to societal order in general (see also Kearney and Donovan 2013).

This racialized conception of risk is made all the more pointed and poignant in view of the contrasts between midnight basketball and the PLAY campaign—specifically, the distinctive gender and generational characteristics of midnight basketball as a program. The target population for most midnight basketball programs was not teenagers, youth, or adolescents (as implied in the Nike PLAY campaign), but young men between the ages of seventeen and twenty-five, which is to say young men at or on the verge of early adulthood. The more I thought about it, the more I saw that the assumption or presupposition was that the problems young black men faced were not because of the environment they found themselves in but were believed to be the products of their own failings. Their problems were, in short, *their fault*. There was no talk of a "right" to sport for these young men. Any allusions to any kind of entitlements for the poor at the time, much less sport for its own sake, were immediately and decisively disavowed, if they came up at all. This was all because urban, African American youth and young men were deeply threatening not just to themselves but really to "the rest of us."

At one point in this project, I took a detour into research on young adults and the transition to adulthood—a strand of inquiry that has become something of a cultural and policy obsession among Americans in the last fifteen or twenty years (Swartz and Hartmann 2007). Everyone seems to be worried about young adults these days—whether they will finish school, when they will leave home, what kinds of jobs they will get, and so forth. But this discourse and worry seems less driven by fear and a need to control than an impetus to help. Indeed, what may be most notable about this research, in retrospect, is simply how absent young African American men are from the discussions of the trials and tribulations of young adulthood in the contemporary United States. It's as if they get a silent, one-sentence dismissal: it's their own fault.

Beyond Paternalism

One of the distinguishing characteristics of Nike's PLAY campaign, in Cole's description, was how it "appear[ed] to break from popular discourses on crime and seemingly shift the terms of the popular dialogue on inner-city youth in the context of dominant 'get-tough' and 'three-strikes' approach[es]" that were so prominent in the 1990s (1996, 392). This campaign appeared in a period in which both the Republican and Democratic Parties were trying to be "tough on crime," pushing for more prisons and police and stronger enforcement of laws against drugs, gangs, and violent crime (see Heclo 2001). This was at Bill Clinton and the New Democrats' insistence as much as it was driven by George H. W. Bush and the Republicans. Here it is worth recalling that even as he campaigned against Bush for the presidency, Bill Clinton made a point of showing himself and his New Democrat strategy to be tough on crime, especially crime associated with the black community.[16] The PLAY campaign directly set itself up in contrast to these trends and movements. Borrowing from other ostensibly progressive agencies and activist groups (such as Marian Wright Edelman's Children's Defense Fund), the promotion was framed as "a socially progressive program based upon a call for social and political unity around children" (Cole 1996, 384). In other words, PLAY purported a kinder, gentler alternative to address the perceived problems of at-risk inner-city communities of color.

I think Cole was right about the appeal and deeper sociocultural structure of the PLAY campaign. Indeed, where Cole's analysis is at its most important and insightful is in arguing that even though it may have looked otherwise, the Nike promotion actually depended on and played off of these tougher, more explicitly racialized policing and punishing orientations. PLAY needed them; its appeal was based on them—or, more precisely, was based on being different from them. PLAY became an attractive social movement and policy option because it posited that more insidious threats, more radical (and expensive) solutions could be avoided in a cheap, effective way: play. However, it is also essential to recognize that these points operated and were structured quite differently when it came to midnight basketball. If the whole tough-on-crime, three-strikes mentality was lurking in the background of the PLAY campaign, this emphasis and orientation was actually very much in the foreground for midnight basketball. For a certain, fairly substantial contingent of its supporters, in fact, basketball-based programming wasn't so much predicated as an alternative to a more stringent, social control—it actually was that kind of surveillance, physical containment, and complete control.

This point of comparison and contrast was crucial for me, given my initial inclination to situate midnight basketball in the historical context of liberal sports ideology as well as given the extent to which midnight basketball came to be identified with liberal, preventative approaches to social policy and sport-based intervention later in the decade (as it is still today). One of the hallmarks of contemporary theories of paternalism as social control, especially those oriented toward internal discipline and individual self-control, is the way in which this discipline and control is cultivated in, and thus carried out, by individuals themselves. In their socialization and development, in other words, individuals are taught to think and act in a particular, socially desirable fashion. So socialization is all about *self*-regulation and *self*-discipline. In Foucault's famous metaphor of the Panopticon, individuals in modern, neoliberal contexts are taught to patrol and police themselves as they internalize the norms, values, and behaviors expected of them by mainstream, middle-class society. The beauty of such a discipline-oriented paternalism is its efficiency and cost-effectiveness: the hard work of social control is carried out not so much by the system as by its subjects and their controlling of themselves.

This internalized, paternalistic disciplinary regime is the clear motivation and end goal of much sport-based intervention, and it was always present in midnight basketball. But there was also a harder-edged surveillance-and-control dimension that needs to be named and analyzed. This vision had very little faith in young black men as able to regulate and discipline themselves; in fact, it assumed they were *already, inherently* deviant and disorderly. In this view, the only thing that could be done to address the problems of young black men—which were as much the problems of society—was to supervise and control them directly, physically. Consider the assumption built into the innovation that at-risk young men needed to be kept off the streets during the late-night hours. Phrases like "get them off the streets," "keep them out of trouble," and even "make sure that they can't make trouble" permeated the discourse and talk about midnight basketball. Think also of the emphasis on the intensive involvement of law enforcement personnel: the fact that uniformed police officers were required security for all midnight basketball games, as well the fact that Standifer made such a big point of parking police paddy wagons outside the gym in the early days of the program.

The basic idea and impetus of all these measures was that as long as participants were involved in a controlled physical activity, they could not be involved in delinquency and offending. As a matter of surveillance and control, their delinquent energies and risk-oriented proclivities were physically contained and diverted toward pursuits that were contained, exciting, challenging, and physically demanding. There was nothing developmental or even rehabilitative here—nothing even really paternalistic or Foucaultian. So, while midnight basketball was a far cry from prison, it was a highly structured and intentionally controlled environment. Those in the program were off the streets and away from the general population—and everyone was believed to be safer for it. These elements of midnight basketball went well beyond an older vision of paternalism or any hope for rehabilitation, and they betrayed the assumption—indeed were *based* on the assumption—that young black men were incapable of disciplining and controlling themselves. They required constant physical supervision and control. Standifer suggested as much in an interview with the *Maryland Weekly*: "If you could fill 24 hours of a young adults['] day, you could eliminate a lot of the problems. Since we can't do that, we've chosen what we feel is the most vulnerable time frame" (quoted in Carter 1998, 30).

Like the idealistic, paternalist ideals sketched above, this use of sport as a means of direct surveillance and physical containment was not a new invention. Variations on it can be detected in the visions and activities of 1920s Progressive Era play reformers who were often quite explicit about the threats and dangers of the streets as they pushed for stricter juvenile curfew laws as well as more supervised playgrounds. One of the historical leaders of this movement, G. Stanley Hall, put particular emphasis on the social control of adolescent boys, whom he saw as particularly vulnerable, awkward, and misguided. In general, Hall believed "young people stood less in need of earnest advice than of the artful manipulation of their environment" (Kett 1977, 6)—which led to an "ideology of protection" that included not only child labor laws and educational reforms but also the implementation of juvenile curfew laws, the creation of a juvenile court system, and better organization and adult supervision of the leisure time activities of adolescents. Juvenile curfews, for example, were explicitly designed to prevent adolescents, usually fifteen years old and younger, from loitering on the streets late at night without adult supervision. Although often discussed in abstract, universalistic terms, there was little doubt that it was boys who were the primary target of these programs.[17]

Whether new or old,[18] the physical-containment-and-hard-core-control feature, perhaps more than any other single characteristic, helped account for the popularity of midnight basketball among conservatives and other law-and-order types, especially those who otherwise cared very little about sport, African American men, or the challenges of the city. Politicians and policy makers (not to mention the citizens who voted them into office) were becoming convinced that the impulse to risky behaviors and lifestyles among poor, inner-city boys and young men was so deeply rooted that it could not be prevented, just controlled and contained. If not prisons or policing, the way to deal with the problems of at-risk, inner-city youth, in this vision, was simply to get them off the streets. Rising fear of crime had become a war on crime and translated into massive public funding for more prisons and police nationwide (Mauer and The Sentencing Project 1999). This harder-edged, surveillance-and-control dimension of midnight basketball fit perfectly with what would soon be called the "new penology" (Feeley and Simon 1992; see also Garland 2002) emergent in American criminal justice circles at the time. Governance through criminalization (Simon 2007; Wacquant 2009, 2008b; Beckett and Western 2001) wasn't a particularly hopeful or constructive vision, but it fit the neoliberal moment and this vision of the social risk African American men were presumed to present.

Standifer's Genius

So what we really had with midnight basketball—at least in the first few years of its inception—were two different visions of how sport would solve the problems of inner-city young men of color. One drew on classic, liberal-paternalist ideals about sport as a force for the development, education, and socializing of otherwise poor, often minority urban youth and young men. The other saw in sport a way to physically contain and control individuals who were particularly prone to delinquency, crime, and violence. These two conceptions—what might be thought of as a *developmental* orientation (the softer, gentler approach) against what could be considered a *containment* approach (the hard-nosed vision)—had two very different perceptions of young African American men and the type and/or level of risk they posed. It is an example of what scholars have called the "left hand" and the "right hand" of neoliberal state governance (Bourdieu 1998; Soss, Fording, and Schram 2011; Wacquant 2009; see also Rios 2011).

It is easy to get enamored with the nuances and differential consequences of these contrasting visions and approaches. Running a program on a containment-and-control model that assumed participants were inherently deviant, disorderly, and prone to crime and violence, for example, led to very different programming than a set of activities oriented toward the socialization and empowerment of young adolescents into self-disciplined, self-disciplining young men. And subsequent chapters will have a lot to say about the political implications and consequences associated with each position. Important as these distinctions may be (or would become), however, this chapter is best concluded by highlighting the commonalities rather than by teasing out the contrasts. And what these two different visions of risk prevention shared were that they both fit well within the parameters of neoliberal fiscal resources and organizational templates.

In a very basic, functional way, these two seemingly divergent and otherwise competing sets of images, interests, threats, and solutions coexisted comfortably—productively—in the space of midnight basketball. Indeed, what gave midnight basketball its initial widespread public appeal and generated its bipartisan consensus was that it offered a unique and unlikely combination of traditional liberal and emerging conservative approaches to the presumed problems of "at-risk" young men of color, the risks they posed, and the kinds of solutions that were required. Conservatives could emphasize the way in which midnight basketball kept these supposedly incorrigible young men off the streets, out of public circulation, and under strict supervision. Liberals could focus on the program's traditional, liberal ideology of character building, individual worth, and racial advancement. Everyone was happy. Indeed, in one of my first publications on this project (Hartmann 2001), I argued that this uneasy combination of competing approaches to the problems of at-risk youth and young men was what constituted the real innovation and true genius of Standifer's midnight basketball concept. That is, Standifer's genius was to create a program that tapped into all these cultural images within the fiscal and organizational parameters of neoliberal public policy in a way so natural and organic that everyone not only took it for granted, but they also saw it as natural, wonderfully innovative, and appropriately opportunistic.

FOUR

A Commercial for Neoliberal Social Policy

But did it work? Was midnight basketball an effective policy innovation and social intervention? These are the questions that many people asked after midnight basketball was first introduced to the public, especially when the initial novelty of the concept wore off. Did midnight basketball—this idiosyncratic, experimental policy initiative—really make a difference? Did it have the impacts its advocates promised and its funders hoped for? Frankly, these are among the first questions that people still ask today about midnight basketball and the whole notion of sport-based risk-prevention social intervention.

The answers to these questions are complicated, and I've already been somewhat critical of the claims asserted by G. Van Standifer and his supporters in Prince George's County, Maryland. Solid evidence of effectiveness, as I've suggested, was then (as is now) difficult to come by. The early evaluations of basketball-based programs that were produced and published in the 1990s were mostly program-based case studies lacking the data, comparisons, and controls required for proper social scientific analysis and systematic conclusions. In addition, any assessment of outcomes depends on how you actually define the goals and expectations when it comes to intervention—in other words, what you mean when you ask whether the program "worked," or "was successful" or "effective" (not to mention which actual programs you are looking at). And there was little consensus or even self-conscious reflection about these different objectives among practitioners or critics. Indeed, when promoting the impact and success of their programs, operators were rarely clear whether they were talking about reducing community-level crime rates, changing individual behaviors, or providing new opportunities and resources.

I will come back to impact and effectiveness in later chapters. But at this point in the narrative, let me insist that there was at least one dimension

on which midnight basketball programs all across the board were remarkably effective and indisputably successful: public relations. In the realm of
publicity, promotion, press coverage, and media commentary, the earliest
midnight basketball programs were an unmitigated triumph.

The sheer amount of press coverage devoted to such a small, experimental program is nothing short of amazing. I can never quite get over how
extensively the HUD-supported Chicago leagues were covered in the local
media throughout their initial summer run and the amount of attention
they received in national news outlets ranging from the *New York Times* to
ABC's *Good Morning America*. The fact that nationally syndicated journalists
like George Will and Michael Wilbon both wrote columns about midnight
basketball (October 18, 1990, and April 13, 1991, respectively, in the *Washington Post*) is also quite remarkable in retrospect. What was also distinctive
about the media attention devoted to the Chicago midnight basketball initiative, as well as Standifer's Maryland model before it, was how supportive
the coverage and commentary was.

The media reporting devoted to midnight basketball was not only extensive; its tone and tenor was almost entirely positive, optimistic, and uplift-
ing. "News media perceptions," as the evaluators of the inaugural Chicago
program summarized (Kpo 1990 1), were "very favorable to the program . . .
featuring stories about the vision and good intentions of the CHA leadership, obstacles to overcome for success, and the program structure." Indeed,
the "public relations components" of the project were judged one of the biggest (if largely unanticipated) successes of the entire Chicago project. Of the
hundreds of midnight basketball stories I've collected and reviewed from
those early years of the innovation, in fact, I haven't found a single one that
could be characterized as negative, and even marginally critical comments
were few and far between.

The extensive and enthusiastic embrace of midnight basketball by media
reporters and pundits wasn't entirely incidental. Sporting celebrities, ranging from Michael Jordan and Chicago Bulls coach Doug Collins to HUD
secretary Jack Kemp, organizers, advocates, and public officials—especially
public officials—all played a capital role. For example, officials for the Minneapolis Department of Health and Family Support were huge proponents
of late-night basketball, and Mayor Sharon Sayles Belton officially justified
their Stay Alive version of midnight basketball on the grounds that it was the
only initiative successful in reaching out to young men of color and bringing
them through program doors. On this front, it is worth pointing out that in
Chicago the program was championed by newly appointed housing director Vincent Lane, a relative public newcomer with designs on completely

revamping the city's notorious public housing projects as part of his own, larger political ambitions.

Similar political and promotional agendas were at work in the San Diego program where I had my first extended, up-close-and-personal experience with basketball-based crime prevention. That operation, which received a big chunk of its funding from Chargers linebacker Junior Seau's foundation, had an advisory committee that included a prominent local doctor who had graduated from Stanford and played eight years of pro football with the Chicago Bears, a deputy district attorney who worked with the county's antigang unit, the pastor of a local community Christian church, and two state legislators, Dede Alpert and Tom Connolly. These were all folks who not only had an interest in giving back to the community but also had much larger policy visions and political aspirations. And then there is the enthusiastic embrace of midnight basketball by President George H. W. Bush in concert with his secretary of Housing and Urban Development, Jack Kemp. The president not only endorsed the midnight basketball initiative from the White House; he actually went to see the league in action and eventually made it one of three featured programs for his Points of Light Foundation.

Only the most naïve observer, I believe, would doubt that the Bush administration or any of the local leaders and political elites who celebrated their support for midnight basketball were making self-conscious, strategic decisions about devoting so much of their scarce time and attention to this small, sport-based program. But why? And with what impacts or effects? Whatever their formal explanations and justification, program administrators in Minneapolis and the mayor herself were well aware of the positive publicity of local news stories that ran every year when league play got under way at a time when the city government was under scrutiny for its difficulty in responding to a rising tide of homicides and violence in African American neighborhoods. Off the record, in fact, several program administrators admitted the program was as valuable for its public relations impact as it was for its public policy outcomes. "The mayor," one of them told me, "counted on the good press" from Stay Alive during the slow and uncertain summer months before fall elections.

Like the Minneapolis mayor, these leaders, I'm sure, all had their reasons. Politicians (and their advisors) are constantly on the lookout for opportunities to bring themselves, their campaigns, and their initiatives to broader public attention as well as to associate them with events and people that are popular with the voting public. Simply because of the number of people who follow athletes and athletic contests, competitions, and events, sports can provide just such a venue, vehicle, or stage. More than this, as Kyle Green and I have argued recently (2014), because of its ostensible apolitical character and reputation, sports supply a forum to connect with communities that bridges political and ideological divides, and being associated with popular sports or successful teams and athletes can also help build political popularity and support. Indeed, the transference of the positive feelings associated with athletes and sports can not only make a candidate more relatable or likeable, but it can also make a politician and his or her agenda more credible and legitimate. These political effects are made all the more powerful by the fact that they are typically achieved with very little self-conscious awareness on the part of the public whose favor is being curried and swayed, shaped and made.

There is an inherent intrigue and fascination with such overt, instrumental politics. However, over the course of working on this project, I have actually been less interested in partisan intentions and political strategies than with observing the symbolic effects of midnight basketball in the public sphere more generally. What I have found fascinating are the broader political messages and meanings—some of which were self-consciously developed and intentionally mobilized, others of which were less obvious or overt—that were constructed in and conveyed through the medium of midnight basketball media coverage and commentary. I am referring here to the general ideas about politics, neoliberal social policies, race, and crime control that were part and parcel of the whole package of midnight basketball reporting.

In the previous two chapters, I situated the origins of midnight basketball in the history of sport-based social interventions, the deeply racialized politics and policies of the United States, and (especially) recent, neoliberal transformations in social services, public safety, and criminal justice as a means to understand the logic and popular appeal of midnight basketball. In those chapters, I characterized midnight basketball as an expression or example of neoliberal paternalism and the new carceral state, a microcosm of American neoliberal social policy and racialized political culture. In this chapter, I invert that emphasis and analytic logic—arguing not only that midnight basketball can help us better understand broader social, cultural, and political forces, but that this small, idiosyncratic program actually played an important, active role in promoting, explaining, and justifying—in a word, legitimating—a particular, racialized vision of neoliberal social policy in the late 1990s.

Probably the most obvious political impact of midnight basketball with respect to neoliberal social policy had to do with the pivotal—if essentially symbolic, not particularly progressive, and thoroughly racialized—role that debates about it played in the legislative process that produced the federal crime bill of 1994. I studied this process in depth with my colleague Darren Wheelock and will recount that analysis in the next chapter. But in this chapter, I want to highlight and examine midnight basketball's more basic cultural or ideological functions—those stemming from and embedded in the broad, bipartisan appeal that unfolded in the initial media coverage and commentary. In particular, I want to suggest that midnight basketball was not just a microcosm of American racial ideologies or of racialized neoliberal social policy; it was an important symbol and standard-bearer for an entire orientation and approach to public policy in an era of neoliberal transformation and retrenchment. Midnight basketball was, in a nutshell, a commercial for neoliberal social policy itself.

In the rest of this chapter, I mean to develop this argument, paying particular attention along the way to the unique aspects of sporting culture that allowed it to serve such a powerful and important symbolic role in the case of midnight basketball. And here, by way of setup and preface, I should mention one additional, big-picture feature of the media coverage of midnight basketball that animates and allows this analysis: it is that many of the stories about midnight basketball that appeared in both the local and national media were not seen and reported merely as sports stories. They didn't just appear in the sports pages. Coverage was reported as general news, and commentary appeared in the editorial pages. Midnight basketball, in short, was much more than a sports story; it was a bigger, more general story charged with meaning and significance that went, as C. L. R. James might have put it, well beyond the athletic boundary.

Communication, Cultural Legitimation, and Community Building

According to the first formal, full-length assessment of a midnight basketball program I am aware of, that evaluation of the landmark Chicago league conducted by researchers at a local university (Kpo 1990), the media attention focused on midnight basketball exerted several different and distinctive effects in Chicago. One of those was that it served a basic "communication function." Media coverage, according to the evaluators' analysis, provided information to the public about both the lives of participants and the efforts of CHA leadership to improve the "quality of life" of these Chicago residents. This information was an obvious and important first step in building support for the midnight basketball initiative, helping to establish it in the community as well as to secure funding and resources for it. Another beneficial effect that the report documented was that the extensive positive publicity about the program brought buy-in and support from various midnight basketball funders, stakeholders, and even participants. In fact, the evaluators explained that media coverage provided an opportunity for individuals in the program to "make history" and served as a "source of motivation" for participation. Even more fundamentally, they found, the program's financial sponsors felt they got a great return on their investment in supporting the project (Kpo 1990, 32).

In an era of declining funding for public housing and urban programming more generally, these points about buy-in and financial support cannot be underestimated. The evaluation didn't say so explicitly, but while the CHA's $100,000 budget for midnight basketball was just a drop in the bucket of the agency's overall operating budget, it was an investment justified many times over simply on the basis of all the free, positive publicity the agency received because of it. All this attention was like a public service announcement that helped ensure the program worked well and had public support and that the bills were paid.

And what was being advertised and promoted in both the local and the national media reporting was much more than this one local, sport-based program. Media coverage and commentary about midnight basketball was also a reflection on urban social problems and public policies in a much more general, wide-ranging respect. Consider sports pundit Michael Wilbon's write-up from April 13, 1991, of the ceremony in which President George H. W. Bush named midnight basketball and G. Van Standifer as a national "Point of Light" honoree.

In his nationally syndicated *Washington Post* column, Wilbon framed the ceremony in a lighthearted, seemingly nonpolitical fashion, saying that Bush clearly enjoyed himself, talking about "dazzling nighttime shooting, courageous airborne maneuvers, and spectacular tactical wizardry." The president, as Wilbon and many others reported, clowned a bit, faking a reverse dunk at one point, and tossed around a basketball autographed by members of two local all-star teams from the league. President Bush, according to Wilbon, gushed "over and over again how glad he was to be in the gym," and Wilbon quoted him directly as saying: "I came here to see this Midnight Basketball for myself. Here, everybody wins. . . . Everyone gets a better shot at life." Importantly—and where we go from human interest reporting to (unintentional) political functioning—Wilbon suggested that Bush's energy and enthusiasm was because he saw midnight basketball as a model for his new vision and approach to government and social policy, that is, his voluntary, "thousand points of light" approach, this new, neoliberal vision of governance and social policy. To be fair, Bush himself directly suggested as much at several different moments in the press conference, and indeed, this claim was the whole point of the president's press conference and the naming of midnight basketball as an official "thousand points of light" program. However, Wilbon's rendering also brought out elements and understandings that went way beyond Bush's framing or even the official rhetoric and rationale of program officials themselves—and brought them, most importantly of all, to a much larger public audience.

Wilbon described midnight basketball as entry for these otherwise disadvantaged young men into academic seminars, vocational workshops, and family counseling. Emphasizing the importance of social networks and peer pressure, the sportswriter waxed poetic about how athletics can teach responsibility and leadership. Though he didn't mention race explicitly, Wilbon explained what the program was about (playing off of a lot of underlying assumptions about the problems and risks of inner-city, African American men, to be sure) and extolled the program as an innovative, effective new approach that was a vast improvement over other programs and approaches. I daresay that the president had fewer better, more enthusiastic (if unself-conscious) advocates of his neoliberal, "thousand points of light" approach to public policy than this one—even though the endorsement wasn't explicit or necessarily even intended as such. Midnight basketball, in Wilbon's framing, was nothing less than an advertisement for Bush's compassionate conservative agenda and a neoliberal social policy agenda more broadly.

That the message and general framing goes well beyond sport is crucial to pay attention to. Stories about midnight basketball provided a particular way of thinking about the problems of urban black men as well as the policies, programs, and potential solutions that were seen as possible within the parameters of the urban social welfare system under neoliberalism. And reporting like Wilbon's wasn't just providing neutral, objective information about these problems and policy solutions. It was also supplying readers with a particular diagnosis of the problems (young, at-risk men) and celebrating a particular agency and entire vision of how to deal with them. This is what might be called midnight basketball's "legitimating function": how the coverage and framing of midnight basketball made the emerging, new and potentially controversial neoliberal approach to social policy in the inner city—with its privatization, its combination of punitive and paternalistic objectives, and its deeply racialized character—seem appealing, rational, and uncontroversial. Here is where it becomes important to reiterate once again that stories about midnight basketball were not seen and reported merely as sports stories, and they didn't just appear in the sports pages. They were framed as bigger, more general stories about the lives of participants, the programs of housing authorities and other related government entities, and all those legislators, politicians, and policy makers charged with designing social services in inner-city neighborhoods for these residents.

What we are seeing here is a kind of collective sense-making, the formation of collective knowledge or cultural common sense where the positive, supportive coverage and commentary served the larger role of rationalizing and legitimating this entire way of looking at and addressing the social problems of inner-city youth and young men. Midnight basketball—or, more precisely, this particular way of thinking and writing and reading about the program—provided the conceptual grounds for this new, synthetic way of thinking about the perceived risks and problems of this group and for this emergent neoliberal paternalism. In and through midnight basketball, the complicated, multifaceted, and mostly structural problems of African American men could be collapsed into a single set of symptoms of the urban underclass; what's more, it was in and through midnight basketball that the public obsession with African American men could become the personification—the public face—of this concatenation of social problems. In this context, midnight basketball served as a lens through which policy makers, media pundits, and the general public could understand the deep structure and social organization of neoliberal policy as it was taking shape. In other words, midnight basketball didn't just reflect the realities of neoliberal social policy, it provided a pathway and policy model of its own, one that became a prototype and assumed an independent frame and force in the swath of neoliberal social policy.

I do not want to suggest that political elites and media pundits were self-conscious of and intentional about all of this. To the contrary, as I spent hours piecing together these ideas about the appeal and symbolic functioning of midnight basketball with respect to neoliberal social policy, it became clear that these ideas and impacts operated below the level of explicit consciousness for most midnight basketball advocates, supporters, and observers; they weren't really articulated, explained, or defended, and it didn't seem like anyone really felt they needed to be. Much as I argued for HUD secretary Jack Kemp in the previous chapter, these ideas were commonsense, taken for granted, seen and experienced as natural, intuitive, and beyond the need for conscious explication and even the realm of consciousness itself. And this, I think, is more or less the point. Although readers and reporters may not have been entirely aware of it—indeed, precisely because they were not consciously aware of it—a program like midnight basketball created under conditions of neoliberalism both an understanding of and solution to the problems of young men and the inner-city which seemed intuitively "right." Midnight basketball didn't create the consolidation of mainstream interests and ideals within the realm of institutional constraints; all the elements, both ideological and institutional, were already there. But it did provide a means and cultural place for drawing all these elements together; it galvanized and gathered these elements into a prominent but nonthreatening symbolic form.

The public popularity and symbolic utility of midnight basketball was partially the result of the semantic flexibility and useful ambiguity of the approaches to race, risk, and social intervention through sport built into the initiative that I detailed in the previous chapter. With its ambiguous, two-channel (or left-and-right-hand) ideology of development and control, containment and empowerment, support for midnight basketball appealed to both liberal and conservative constituents; it could be about welfare support and intervention, or it could signal stricter, more punitive kinds of surveillance, containment, and control. Local officials could emphasize whichever dimension of midnight basketball they believed would be received most positively and play most effectively to their crowd. A constituency that wanted a harder-edged, containment-and control orientation could emphasize the "keep 'em off the streets" (and under the watchful eye of local cops) aspects of midnight basketball; if constituents cared more about providing opportunities for self-improvement, self-discipline, and/or community building among disadvantaged youth, they could focus on the more traditional liberal virtues of sport as a site of character building, mobility, and socialization, and draw attention to the various programs, like job placement training, midnight basketball clubs often provided off the court.

But more was at work here than the ideological and metaphorical fit between the romanticized ideals of sport and racial progress and the cultural ideologies of race and social reform. There was also the unique cultural character of sport itself, the distinctive ways in which midnight basketball was understood and which were at the heart of the media coverage and commentary.

Talking about an ostensibly innovative, experimental sports program like midnight basketball also served to divert conversations that had veered into uncomfortable political terrain into a more amiable, amicable, and polite dinnertime conversation. Compared to other policy realms or social arenas, sport was an arena in which the stakes didn't seem quite so high; midnight basketball wasn't too serious or really political but ultimately "just a game." It provided a social and cultural space that people, both public leaders and the general public, could take seriously, but not *too* seriously. It provided a kind of cover not unlike what happens when friends use a line like "How 'bout them Packers?" or "Did you see the Giants game last night?" Midnight basketball didn't generate the level of scrutiny placed on other social programs. In comparison to other policy initiatives and political programs, it was almost a relief for politicians to discuss, policy makers to experiment with, and media members to cover.

I will have more to say about the sport-specific cultural dynamics and functioning of midnight basketball in the context of neoliberal social policy shortly. But before I get to that, let me develop one other point about the symbolic significance and functioning of midnight basketball in the public policy arena. It starts from the fact that the positive publicity and political legitimacy that midnight basketball brought appealed not only to a general voting public and political mainstream but also to members of the specific urban communities targeted and served by midnight basketball. Midnight basketball was, to put it bluntly, popular in the black community—a popularity reflected both in the nontraditional press as well as in the attendance that was typical at so many of the league contests in both the regular season as well as the playoffs. Recall the 80 percent approval rating in Chicago's black community, according to the *Chicago Defender*. And the positive publicity effects of midnight basketball among local community residents weren't just about abstract popular support or establishing general political legitimacy, or even about the most basic community-building functions of sport; they also had actual public safety and crime-fighting implications and possibilities.

Criminological and media scholars have suggested that the publicity effects of high-profile programs can influence community crime rates in one of two ways. On the deterrence side, public attention to a highly visible initiative like midnight basketball can show would-be lawbreakers that there's an emphasis on crime prevention in the area and underscore the extent to which law enforcement and other public officials are willing to fight against crime, thus creating a deterrent for would-be criminals. On the more proactive side, the creation of highly popular, high-profile programs such as midnight basketball can send a positive message to community members—that there's a new emphasis on community outreach and empowerment, a good-faith effort to build trust and commitment to the community broadly conceived.

The former explanation is probably the more typical in the field, and it's frequently the subject of highly publicized debate around, for example, legislation on policies involving gun laws (cf. S. D. Johnson and Bowers 2003). The second, less-developed proactive explanation has implications and consequences that are far less understood yet perhaps even more important to specify and think through in the context of basketball-based crime prevention. Here it is useful to recall the more proactive, community-oriented aspects of midnight basketball as highlighted by C. L. Cole in situating youth sports programs in the context of broader political movements and agendas. In contrast with other, more punitive urban programs and aggressive, militaristic policing expenditures (more policing, for example, or more prison funding—more aggressive and coercive approaches that do little to make a community feel safer; Weisburd and Eck 2004; Kappeler and Kraska1997; Sherman 1997), midnight basketball had a constructive, development-oriented dimension that appeared to serve and perhaps even empower young people and communities of color. It was not just reactive; it was proactive—and this was recognized and particularly well understood by members in the community. It certainly seems possible that the creation of popular, community-based programs such as midnight basketball might incline all community members (not just those in a program) to be less likely to commit crimes, not for fear of being caught, but because they feel more directly connected to and more positively served by law enforcement and social services. Midnight basketball, then, may help generate a wide and diffuse sense of community solidarity and trust that serves as a buffer against the individualistic and antisocial sentiments and behaviors that otherwise contribute to crimes against property and the community at large.

For a while, these ideas about the media coverage and social functioning of midnight basketball in the black community were essentially speculative or theoretical, and easy to lose sight of in view of my skepticism about the claims of early advocates like Standifer and Bush that midnight basketball had community-level impacts that extended well beyond the limited number of participants they directly served. However, this began to change when Brooks Depro, a colleague of mine interested in the econometric analysis of public policy initiatives, proposed to do a study of the community-level effects of midnight basketball initiatives.

Our research strategy was fairly simple and straightforward. We identified cities that were early adopters of official midnight basketball programs and then plotted changes in their average violent and property crime rates across the period from 1985 to 2001 against the rates for cities without midnight basketball (all other American cities with populations over 100,000). Our analysis (Hartmann and Depro 2006) yielded a number of surprising results. Among the most important of these was that the crime rates in cities that adopted midnight basketball appeared to decline somewhat faster than in cities without the programs *and* that these results were statistically significant (which is to say that the relationships hold even when controlling for key factors that might otherwise explain these results). In other words, we were able to confirm that cities that adopted midnight basketball programs experienced greater declines in crime rates than those that lacked midnight basketball leagues.

These results held for both violent crime rates and property crime rates, and the scope of these effects was striking. Using econometric statistical techniques, we estimated that cities that were early adopters of midnight basketball programs saw a drop in violent crime rates equal to approximately 90 offenses per 100,000 residents compared to non–midnight basketball counterparts. The results for property crime rates were even more significant and impressive. We calculated that midnight basketball cities saw a drop of approximately 390 offenses per 100,000 residents.

Given the nature of the statistical methods employed in this analysis, we did not believe that midnight basketball was directly responsible for the relatively steeper declines in crime in cities that were early adopters of midnight basketball. Effects of this magnitude cannot be attributed to the individual-level mechanisms that are the emphasis of the theoretical literature on sports-based social interventions and most assessments. Rather, we began to think about the community-level factors that could possibly account for these effects. We came up with two possible explanations. One factor that we realized would help explain these patterns had to do with the packaging or bundling of crime prevention initiatives with midnight basketball initiatives. Put differently, midnight basketball programs were usually not the only crime prevention initiatives undertaken in these communities, but rather were part of a whole package of community-based risk reduction and crime prevention programs of which midnight basketball was one high-profile component. This interpretation was supported by the fact that early adopter cities tended to have high police expenditures per capita and more social services, and seemed to be connected with the shifts toward more collaborative, partnership-type programs that came to define the midnight basketball model in the wake of the 1994 crime bill debates (see chapter 6 below).

The second factor we settled on involved the communication mechanisms and publicity effects that are the focus of this chapter. Indeed, Depro and I came to believe that the broader message about social intervention and community investment signaled by midnight basketball programs, as discussed above, had to be playing a key role. What we found regarding the particularly significant impact on property crime rates seemed consistent with this explanation, for this was all about trust in and pride about neighborhood and community. Midnight basketball was serving a powerful, symbolic role in helping generate a wide and diffuse sense of community solidarity and trust that served as a buffer against the individualistic and antisocial sentiments and behaviors that otherwise contribute to crimes against property and the community at large.

More research, of course, would need to be conducted before it is possible to definitely establish the magnitude of all the political functions and policy effects that I have suggested in this section were set in motion by midnight basketball. But something powerful and important did seem to be going on in the black community as well as mainstream society when it came to midnight basketball, something with consequences far beyond the realm of basketball and sport itself. Such good-news stories about public policies and social change were few and far between. And the most basic and important point is that the programmatic, political, and material effects I have sketched here were driven by all the free and positive publicity midnight basketball received and the symbolic and communication functions that resulted.

Sport and the Cultural Politics of Neoliberal Social Policy

Usually when Americans—scholars and regular folks alike—talk about politics they are referring to campaigns and elections, legislative debates, lobbying, party alliances and coalitions, and the making of law and public policy. With all the emphasis on electoral processes and public policy, it is easy to overlook that aspect of political life that might be called "the politics of culture" or "cultural politics." The cultural aspect of politics involves the ways in which political communities, partisan blocks, and commonsense cultural understandings are created in the first place, and how they are then consolidated, maintained, and reproduced in and through the media and popular culture as well as everyday practices, activities, and interactions. It has to do with what happens in these seemingly apolitical domains in the construction of cultural frames and social problems. It touches on how certain phenomena come to be seen as problems in need of attention or correction—what is considered core to the public interest, what is normal and typical and commonsensical, and what's not even worthy of political consideration. The cultural politics of midnight basketball is essentially what I have been talking about so far in this chapter: the symbolic, sense-making capacities and legitimating functions of a sports-based story or program like midnight basketball with respect to neoliberal social policy, racialized politics, and the role of sport therein.

Of course, I am far from the first to make these general, analytic points about culture and politics. Sociologist Joseph Gusfield ([1963] 1986) and political scientist Murray Edelman (1964) paved the way for this sort of thinking when they introduced the idea of "symbolic politics" in the middle part of the twentieth century. In more recent years, cultural studies scholars working in the tradition of Antonio Gramsci, Raymond Williams, and Stuart Hall (see, especially, Hall et al. 1978) have carved out powerful, critically oriented visions and understandings of the politics of culture, especially as they pertain to race. In fact, some of the most famous and best scholars of sport of the past decade or two have spent their time theorizing from this cultural studies perspective. Initially from a class-based, Marxist foundation but increasingly using race-critical and feminist theories, these scholars have examined how sport is central to creating and reinforcing social solidarities and collective identities (race, gender, sexuality, nationalism, etc.), and they have investigated what is seen as natural or acceptable (and thus not open to political action or contestation), which social problems are most pressing, and which policy approaches are most promising (for rich, representative collections, see Carrington and McDonald 2009; Birrell and McDonald 2000).

One obvious example would be the study of Nike's PLAY campaign by C. L. Cole that I discussed in some detail in the previous chapter. While I used that piece to help analyze and account for the popularity of midnight basketball, Cole's intention was to call attention to the crucial and often ignored role that sports programs and the public attention that surrounds them play in constituting and reproducing images and ideas about race, risk, and youth in contemporary American culture. This case and Cole's treatment of it, in other words, were about sport's capital role in the production and reproduction of racial images and stereotypes in the culture at large, or, as Cole put it, "how race is made to matter and not matter in the public imagination" (1996, 386). Most notable on this score, I think, is that the PLAY campaign featured basketball superstar Michael Jordan, one of the most famous personalities in the world at the time, a cultural icon whose shaved head was said to be more recognizable to American mall patrons than the face of the president of the United States. If Jordan didn't transcend race, he certainly transcended sport, and the attention brought by Jordan endowed the Nike advertisements with meaning and impact well beyond the world of sport itself.

A pathbreaking and perfectly on-point extension of these insights about sport, cultural construction, and political ideology can be found in Josh Newman and Michael Giardina's *Sport, Spectacle, and NASCAR Nation* (2011). In this carefully researched and meticulously argued book, Newman and Giardina document the connections between post-9/11 Republican politics and the athletic spectacle of American stock car racing. In particular, they show how the representations of race, region, religion, and nationalism that are cultivated in NASCAR races, ceremonies, and coverage dovetail with the political images, ideologies, and worldviews favored by the second President Bush and his followers in the new millennium. More than this, they demonstrate *empirically* that NASCAR culture is not only a reflection of broader social, cultural, and political formations, but actually an active, irreducible force in the making and reinforcing of these hegemonic worldviews and their associated identities. And what is perhaps most meaningful and relevant to the analysis at hand, they emphasize that what is constructed in the mutual juxtaposition of conservative ideology and race car coverage and commentary is an ideology and worldview that reproduces a whole market-based, individualistic ideology of American neoliberalism that functions to maintain existing social relationships and the privileges that go along with them.

The argument I have been trying to sketch in this chapter is derived from and intended to make a new contribution to this kind of work, these studies of the cultural politics of sport. The foundations were laid in the previous two chapters where I worked through the cultural perceptions about black men and crime that midnight basketball was based on, and the policies for intervention that were possible under the conditions of neoliberal transformation of social policy in late twentieth-century America. This kind of analysis, especially the focus on the racialization and criminalization of black men in and through an athletic arena, should be fairly familiar to most sport scholars in the cultural studies tradition. And where I have tried to push the literature and theory in a new direction is by arguing that the racialized sporting form of midnight basketball served a powerful, if subtle and often unseen role in promoting and legitimating the whole neoliberal approach to public policy and social services. My argument, in other words, is not just about the construction of ideas and identities that ultimately have political implications; it is about politics and public policy quite literally and concretely conceived. It is to argue that the cultural politics of sport may be, indeed can be, more directly, concretely, and conventionally political than we have often assumed or explored.

But what is it about sport that makes it such a powerful force for the practice and performance of these symbolic functions pertaining to politics and public policy, especially as race is implicated therein? Part of the symbolic power of sport has to do with the constellation of ideals and beliefs I referred to in the previous chapter—competition, fair play, and meritocracy—and how they parallel and overlap with many of the core elements of neoliberal political economy and reinforce the existing social status quo. The ideological elements take on far greater social significance given the extremely large number of people who participate in sport, either as players or fans, and do so frequently and intensively. That is, sport is a very big platform, with an extensive demographic reach. And the symbolic scope and social significance of sport also stem from the kind of close attention and passionate commitment that all these people bring to their engagement with sport. It is passionate, bordering at times on religious, but also not easily categorized as high culture or lower brow (cf. Riley 2010). In contrast to fans of other seemingly similar popular pursuits (such as television, film, music, media, or gaming), many of those most involved in sport hold deep, passionate beliefs about the moral value and social virtue of sport. Sport, in this popular, idealist view, is not simply entertainment, nor is it mere business or work. Rather, sport is believed to be a "good thing," a naturally and almost universally positive social force. Sport is, in short, big ideas and high ideals, the high church of modern, civic culture (Novak 1976). This is precisely why the dean of American sports journalists, Robert Lipsyte (1975), talked about sports fans as "true believers" many years ago.

The grand claims and idealized visions of sport as a special or even sacred social space figure particularly prominently with respect to racial understanding, progress, and change, especially in the American context, which I've highlighted already. African Americans have been exceptionally prominent, prolific, and successful in American athletics—especially in the most high-profile, revenue-generating sports, basketball and football—and their success has been associated with and indeed explained by the sports world's commitment to the values of competition and fair play, meritocracy, and equal opportunity for all (cf. Early 2011). Indeed, sports idealists often claim that the values and ideals of sport mirror, even model the principles of individual effort, meritocracy, and color blindness that are the foundation and essence of the liberal democratic vision of racial justice, progress, and appropriate race relations (see also Hartmann 2000; 2003c). This is not to suggest that sport is automatically and inherently a progressive racial force; I, like many sport scholars, have often been critical of a naïve embrace of such beliefs. But it is to acknowledge the enduring force of these beliefs among Americans and to insist that such deeply held ideals constitute one key aspect of the political power of all sporting phenomena.

And there is more, much more, to the political power and functioning of sport. Not everyone who participates in athletic competitions or follows sports closely is particularly aware of or interested in these high-minded, idealistic points about the positive social value and symbolic significance of sport. In spite of the grand moral claims of sports idealists, in fact, many—perhaps even most—Americans will say that sport is not an activity or pursuit of ultimate value or real social significance. They see it as a diversion or distraction, perhaps a guilty pleasure—a recreational activity or leisure pursuit to engage in and enjoy only after the real work is done, the serious stuff taken care of. "Just a game" or "mere play," they might say. In other words, as deeply passionate and fully invested as some people appear to be in sport, many others are just as quick to trivialize, deny, or dismiss sports as frivolous and unimportant—and some of those who can be most passionate in one moment can be entirely dismissive in the next. This essentially paradoxical orientation toward sport, wherein folks exhibit tremendous passion for sport but yet also minimize sport as "just a game" not to be taken too seriously, is another crucial dimension of midnight basketball's symbolic functioning and sport's unique cultural status, and it brings me to the idea of "deep play" that Clifford Geertz made famous in a classic piece of fieldwork on the Balinese cockfight.

At its core, Geertz's notion of deep play alerts us to the paradoxical status and power of sport in contemporary culture: how, on the one hand, large numbers of people play or follow sports passionately, almost religiously, in the modern world, and yet at the same time the vast majority of those sports enthusiasts minimize, trivialize, or deny that their pursuits have any larger meaning or social significance. Geertz borrowed the phrase from classical utilitarian theorist Jeremy Bentham, the originator of the Panopticon later made famous by Michel Foucault. Bentham defined deep play as "play in which the stakes are so high that it is irrational for men to engage in it at all" (quoted in Geertz 1973, 432). Geertz wasn't particularly interested in whether such play was rational, but he *was* intrigued by activities that human subjects appeared to be deeply invested in but were unwilling or unable to justify self-consciously. "Such play," according to Geertz, "is less a measure of utility . . . than it is a symbol of moral import perceived or imposed" (443), and as such could be used by the astute social analyst to reveal deeper passions and attachments, underlying beliefs, and otherwise obscure social dynamics. In Geertz's view, in other words, deep play forms are cultural objects that social analysts can use or "read" to reveal and explore beliefs, feelings, values, meanings, and commitments that are otherwise hidden, silent, protected, or obscured.

I take this notion of deep play to be a fundamental condition or character of the sporting form, a defining aspect of the social dynamics that play out in and around sport, and that shaped and determined midnight basketball's role in the cultural politics of neoliberal social policy. I am speaking here about how this deep play status allows sport to be seen as a separate and unique sociocultural domain that both matters and doesn't matter. And indeed the fact that we so often do not see these other social functions endows such "play forms" with their actual if underappreciated social significance and power. They provide a cultural cover for ideas and interactions, or activities and policies, that are otherwise impossible, improbable, or simply too controversial. And all of this is on display with midnight basketball. It is precisely *because* of sport's paradoxical, deep play structure that the symbolic significance of midnight basketball could be appropriated by so many, manipulated by some, and essentially ignored by most.

So what we have here is the combination of high-minded sports moralism, on the one hand, and deep play trivialization, on the other. Put together, these two almost conflicting cultural dimensions of sport allowed midnight basketball proponents to advance grand, ostensibly compassionate policies and claims well beyond the bounds of the athletic arena itself without really having to acknowledge or own up to what they were doing for the general public who were their intended audience.

Cover-Up and Coding: The Embeddedness of Race

The symbolic politics of a cultural form like sport—whether political, corporate, or otherwise—are not just about what you can get people to want or think; they are also about what you can lead them to ignore, assume, or forget. Any particular cultural framing, as the great Erving Goffman might have put it, necessarily limits and constrains the field of view, any conception of a public problem and its possible solutions. Joseph Gusfield's classic 1981 case study of "drinking-driving" is a case in point. Americans have adopted an understanding of the problem of drinking and driving that focuses on the moral failings of the drunk driver as an individual (drunk drivers as the culprit). Powerful though this frame may be, it does not emphasize or even acknowledge the complicit role of bars in serving drivers, beer and alcohol producers, or even a social environment that is based on cars and private drivers rather than public transportation. In similar fashion, the publicity accorded to midnight basketball programs—and their more general popularity—did more than just build support for public leaders, their vision of urban and racial problems, and their paternalist neoliberal solutions. It also pulled attention away from the deeper cutbacks and more fundamental transformations of urban policy and social programs of the period.

The late 1980s and early 1990s were, as I have mentioned several times already, an era marked by tremendous reorganization of programs and services for the poor, the powerless, and those on the margins, especially with respect to cutting back funding and programming in some domains and in others shifting responsibility away from the state to local, nonprofit organizations in metropolitan areas and communities of color (Wacquant 2008a, 2008b; Brenner and Theodore 2002; Beckett and Western 2001). I do not believe it was accidental (though, again, it wasn't entirely self-conscious or intentional either) that midnight basketball emerged as a prominent public policy innovation at just the moment that funding for both social welfare and urban development more generally was beginning to dry up.

Having midnight basketball leagues to hold up—especially with the limited funding they required and the private, nonprofit administrative structure they typically operated under—allowed leaders to avoid talking about neoliberal cutbacks and transformations and focus instead on seemingly cost-effective ways to address urban problems and "serve" impoverished and disempowered communities. The hoopla surrounding midnight basketball, in other words, didn't just manufacture consent for neoliberal reforms; it also diverted attention away from the other, more fundamental changes and shifting fiscal priorities of the era. Reading the media coverage and commentary now, you would have no way of knowing that midnight basketball was emerging right in the middle of one of the largest reorganizations of social services and welfare policy in American history (not to mention the persistent racism, segregation, and inequity that individuals in these communities lived with on a daily basis). The terrain of social amnesia and public opiates is familiar ground for critical sport scholarship and popular cultural critiques, as it has been for cultural critics at least since the Frankfurt School. Much like the famous Marxist line about religion as an opiate for the masses, this is about how sport can divert and distract attention away from other developments and activities that are arguably larger and more consequential than the dynamics of the athletic world itself.

Fiscal cutbacks and institutional transformations were not the only social phenomena obscured or distorted by midnight basketball promotion and reporting. Discussions of race, to reiterate, were curiously portrayed as well. There is no doubt that midnight basketball was a thoroughly racialized initiative. The racial demographics of neighborhoods and communities such as Glendarden, Maryland, or the housing projects of South Side, Chicago, that were "early adopters" of officially sanctioned midnight basketball leagues tended to be poorer, younger, and blacker than other American metropolitan areas (see, again, Hartmann and Depro 2006). Moreover, the images that were used to illustrate and publicize midnight basketball *always* featured young men of color, often showing them honing their skills on the court.

Once again, the April 1991 press conference in which George H. W. Bush singled out Standifer and midnight basketball as a model for his Points of Light Foundation is representative. The announcement was made in front of an all–African American audience in the center in which the Glenarden program was operated. All the photographs used to publicize the event (many of which are still used by Midnight Basketball Inc.) show Bush sharing the podium with African American men. (In my entire time researching midnight basketball, in fact, I have found only *one* photograph or other visual representation that did *not* explicitly portray an individual of color, and that was from a radical publication clearly trying to undermine the racial imagery that animated popular conceptions of the program.)

In spite of its obvious racial dimensions, however, midnight basketball was consistently and uniformly talked about and written about in the media coverage and commentary in ostensibly race-neutral, color-blind fashion. When it came to explicit talk or text, you'd almost never know that midnight basketball was a program dominated by African American men both in terms of actual participation and in terms of public perception.

For a time, I was quite troubled by this contradiction or disconnect, by the fact that even though I knew midnight basketball to be targeted to youth and young men of color, it was nonetheless overtly presented in the media in a way that made no explicit mention of race. In fact, as the research progressed past its initial phases, I was so troubled by the seemingly adamant *non*racial framing of midnight basketball in the public realm that I went to some lengths to reconsider and reestablish the racial contours and character of midnight basketball programs. But it didn't take too long to figure out that this tension or contradiction was actually a key component of the racial meaning and function of midnight basketball in the context of neoliberal politics. Even though midnight basketball was almost universally described in race-neutral, color-blind terms, it clearly functioned as a proxy or "code" for African American young men.

Racial coding—sometimes referred to as "race-baiting" or "playing the race card" outside of academic circles—refers to the way in which Americans appeal to or talk about issues that have or are believed to have racial connotations or consequences without (they hope) appearing racist or mean-spirited. These codes developed mainly out of the successes of the civil rights movement which, because it discredited biological racism on the one hand and consolidated an ideology of racial equality on the other (cf. Edsall and Edsall 1991; Schuman, Steeh, and Bobo 1985), pushed political elites to rearticulate representations of racial difference and explanations for inequality in ostensibly nonracial terms even while subtle antiblack stereotypes and perceptions remained in place (Omi and Winant 1994, esp. chap. 7). These codes tend to be deployed mostly by conservatives whose goal is to mobilize the racial fears and resentments of a largely white, Anglo-Saxon public. The 1960s-era appeals of Barry Goldwater and Richard Nixon to a "silent majority" were among the earliest such instantiations (Chambliss 1995); opposition to busing and the tax revolts of the 1970s were others. And the most (in)famous referent today is probably the 1988 Bush campaign's "Willie Horton" ad, which showed a convicted African American rapist and murderer (whose photo, not incidentally, had actually been darkened to make him appear "more black") being released on a weekend furlough from a Massachusetts prison and reoffending (Mendelberg 1997; see also Feagin and Vera 1995, 192; Kinder and Sanders 1996, chap. 9).

The way in which midnight basketball functioned in the context of neoliberal social policy was perhaps less strategic or deliberately political than standard understandings of racial coding would suggest, but I think the parallels are clear and consequential (if also disturbing). In the context of crime, the deeply entrenched images and ideas associating crime with young African American men (Pager 2007; Russell 1998; see also Entman and Rojecki 2000; Hunt 1999) had the rhetorical effect of heightening the threat of crime and raising serious questions about the types of programs and policies best suited to combating it. More specifically, support and endorsement for midnight basketball reinforced public beliefs about the supposedly pathological risk and threat posed by young black men in contemporary American cities—both what their problems were and the kinds of invasive, interventionist solutions that were required to solve those problems (or immobilize the men themselves).

Another example, from a bit later in the decade, would be the famous picture of Bill Clinton signing the bill for welfare reform, the infamous Personal Responsibility and Work Opportunity Reconciliation Act (PRWORA) in 1996, surrounded by African American women. On the one hand, as a code for race in the context of a program that was explicitly billed as a social policy innovation, publicity about and attention to midnight basketball sent a clear message that welfare problems and social policy were largely about African American communities. In addition, it also provided a cover to reinforce the least enlightened, most racist assumptions about paternalistic neoliberal social policy (in particular, that the social problems of African American communities were largely the result of their own moral failings and social shortcomings)—and the larger shifts from redistribution and social service provision to paternalism, social control, and even more containment-and-control, punitive approaches. What we see are the ways in which race is both acknowledged and disavowed, made to function in powerful ideological ways even as its very functioning is hidden and obscured from plain sight. And it is here—in these paternalist assumptions about the roots of risk and in the face of a policy regime that does little to get at their deeper structural causes—that we gain an even deeper appreciation for the racial dimensions of that political consensus I discussed in the previous chapter.

In *The Possessive Investment in Whiteness*, an essential critique of the politics and public policy of turn-of-the-millennium neoliberalism, the social historian George Lipsitz (1998) identified the consensus underlying liberal and conservative understandings of the problems of race and risk in the contemporary, neoliberal United States in explicitly racial terms. For Lipsitz, the consensus mainly involved how white Americans, both liberal and conservative, protect and preserve the privileges that go along with their skin color, without actually describing this agenda in explicit racial terms. "Liberals," according to Lipsitz, operate "under the name of respecting prevailing market practices, encouraging business investment in cities and helping the 'middle class,' conservatives under the guise of promoting state's rights, protecting private property, and shrinking the welfare state" (24).

What is more, Lipsitz identifies the shared message, implicated in midnight basketball reporting: namely, that "minority disadvantages are said to stem from innate deficiencies rather than systematic disenfranchisement and discrimination" (1998, 24; see also Scott 1997). And here we come to the deeper structure and consequence of the liberal-conservative consensus on race and the powerful, public symbolic role that midnight basketball played therein. It is a system, according to Lipsitz, that employs "indirect, inferential and covert policies that use the denial of overt racial intent to escape responsibility for racialized consequences" (216). "It disguises as *racial* problems," Lipsitz writes, "the general social problems posed by deindustrialization, economic restructuring and neoconservative attacks on the welfare state. It fuels a discourse that demonizes people of color . . . while hiding the privileges of whiteness by attributing the economic advantages enjoyed by whites to their family values, faith in fatherhood and foresight" (218). And midnight basketball accomplished these symbolic ends in a way that made its racialized underpinnings—as well as those of neoliberalism more generally (Goldberg 2008; Soss, Fording, and Schram 2011)—obvious without being blatant, easy to see yet easy to avoid talking about.

The complicated ways in which midnight basketball functioned as a racial symbol in the context of neoliberal social policy discourse are a poignant example of how race is both *made* and *made to matter* in and through sport in contemporary American culture. It is a phenomenon that appears again and again in the discourse around sport and race in the United States. This is not just about the depiction of people and communities of color; it is also about how white culture and identity are implicated—usually through invisibility and disavowal—in these constructions, with the ultimate effect of obscuring the very real outcome of maintaining and legitimating white privilege, power, and status. Connected with the sport-specific moralizing and trivializing that I explicated in the previous section, this analysis, I think, gives us a pretty solid understanding of the intersections and symbolic functioning of sport and race and midnight basketball above all in the late twentieth-century and early twenty-first-century political context. It wasn't just about race in general, or about certain conceptions of risk and the perceived pathologies of African Americans. It was about consolidating, promoting, and legitimating an entire approach to social policy and governance under conditions of neoliberalism.

Conclusion

In *Disciplining the Poor*, Soss, Fording, and Schram (2011) describe the emergence of the racialized neoliberal paternalism that they say defines contemporary poverty policy as something of an accident. Drawing on John Kingdon's (2003) influential notion of political agendas as "windows of opportunity," they suggest that the turn-of-the-millennium, bipartisan consensus around neoliberal social policy was less the result of a grand plan on the part of any particular political party or bloc than the outcome of a historical convergence of social and political forces. Included, here, would be reactions against the social policies of the 1960s, economic stagnation, the persistence and evolution of antiblack racial stereotypes in the post–civil rights era, and the return of market-based logic for social policy formation. In a political context in which partisan compromise and consensus building were becoming more and more difficult, this combination of structural forces made social services one of the few policy arenas in which something concrete could be agreed on and accomplished across party lines. This window of opportunity, according to Soss and his colleagues, allowed erstwhile political opponents to work together. The landmark overhaul of policies for the poor and underserved was, in short, less the result of some grand plan—Republican or Democrat, benevolent or otherwise—than a meeting place, a policy domain where compromise and consensus was possible, where something could be done, and where action could be taken.[1]

When I came across this interpretation (admittedly, fairly late in the process of writing this book), I realized that it had a lot in common with the argument I had formulated about midnight basketball. In the previous chapters, as you'll recall, I went to some lengths to argue that the unexpected and unlikely consensus surrounding midnight basketball had to do with how ideals and ideologies about sport and, more specifically, about sport as a mode of social intervention lined up with the visions and institutional realities of neoliberalism, race, and paternalism underlying contemporary social policy. Cheap, innovative, privately based, and carefully targeted, midnight basketball, I argued, paralleled neoliberal ideologies and realities in the United States and provided the grounds for a unique bipartisan consensus. Midnight basketball innovators couldn't take credit for these conditions and developments; they just took advantage of how they all came together. And in this chapter, I have emphasized the sport-specific characteristics that made midnight basketball such an effective tool for politicians, policy makers, and others to publicize, dramatize, and justify the shift toward neoliberal policy approaches and thinking. On this front, I have tried to suggest that these effects were achieved even in the absence of program promoters having a clear consciousness of exactly what was going on and why.

Perhaps this framing of midnight basketball's popularity and powerful effects as accidental is a bit strong, especially when it comes to the political impacts and functions I have tried to sketch in this chapter. After all, surely some of these political actors were being strategic in their discussion and deployment of midnight basketball, even if they couldn't fully articulate the cultural dimensions of sport that made it such a useful medium for communication and legitimation.

I actually experimented with arguments about the instrumental and even intentional deployment of midnight basketball symbolism for political purposes in early drafts of this chapter. Inspired by work on the uses and functions of sport in international contexts, such as Damion Thomas's (2012) pathbreaking study of African American athletes' role in the Cold War politics of the mid-twentieth century, I was hoping to highlight political figures who exhibited and employed understandings of sport as a political force that cut against the usual conventions separating sport and politics in American and Western contexts as a way to expand our scholarly conceptions of the cultural politics of sport. Similarly, informed by the role that the Olympic movement, and the International Olympic Committee more specifically, played in helping broker/facilitate the reunification of South Africa in the late 1980s and early 1990s (Mbaye 1995),[2] I thought the case of midnight basketball could contribute to a more sophisticated theory of the ways in which the supposed play space of sport provides a social context within which policy makers and political leaders can "experiment" with innovative ideas or controversial approaches, to work outside of the usual constraints of entrenched approaches to policy, the reigning partisan political coalitions, and the bright lights of media conventions more interested in conflict and contention than cooperation. However, a sympathetic but critical group of readers and reviewers pointed out—fortunately, I believe—that I didn't really have the data and material to back up such claims. They went well beyond the limits of the few, behind-the-scenes interviews I had with politicians and policy makers in my various ethnographic field sites for studying midnight basketball.

Perhaps someone can pursue these lines of inquiry into the more instrumental and intentional political dimensions of midnight basketball and sport more generally in years to come. I mean, who would really argue that presidential advisors didn't have some sense of the broader communicative and symbolic significance of celebrating a basketball-based program? But no matter how accidental or strategic, the symbolic functions of midnight basketball may prove to be, there should be little doubt of its larger significance and function in matters of contemporary neoliberal politics and public policy. Here, by way of conclusion, let me reiterate one thing that was not incidental: the powerful, paradoxical status, structure, and function of midnight basketball with respect to the racial structure, and the social significance of midnight basketball as it operated both in public policy and in the culture at large. And the key to the functional power and consequence of sport with respect to race, and in the case of midnight basketball, operated most potently because most subjects and participants were unaware of any deeper or wider social context and racial subtext. We all act out cultural structures and ideological assumptions almost habitually, without realizing that anything is going on, and it was certainly true in midnight basketball. Through sport's race-neutral, color-blind framing, our cultural assumptions about sport being either below or above politics, our willingness to believe both that "it's just a game" and "it's more than a game," midnight basketball gained a cultural power far beyond that which even the most strategic, political leaders (not to mention many literal-minded, institutionally oriented scholars) may have realized.

The political impacts and broad symbolic significance of race, culture, and neoliberal social policy as they converged in midnight basketball were not without cracks, contradictions, and fractures—and, as I will show in the next chapter, the consensus around the initiative was not to last long, at least not at the national level. But as we prepare to delve into midnight basketball's most purely political chapter, let me insist that it is precisely in this realm of the cultural, communicative, and symbolic dimensions of actual, institutional politics and political leadership that we truly realize the broader social force and political power of sport—an effect that is typically ignored by both scholars and policy makers, at least in part because as a deep play form it exerts its impacts without anyone really having to directly acknowledge and confront it.

FIVE

Breakdown and Fallout:
The Symbolic Politics of the 1994 Crime Bill

For a while, it looked like a "done deal," a "slam dunk," and an "easy win"—a "certain campaign trophy," as one reporter put it—for President William Jefferson Clinton and his Democratic colleagues in Congress (Boyer 1994, 38).[1] Operating in the centrist mode that had brought them congressional victories and the White House two years earlier, the Democratic leadership had produced a crime bill designed to appeal to all the key interest groups and political constituencies. On the one hand, the omnibus, $33 billion bill spoke to traditional Republican concerns about "law and order" and allowed moderate Democrats to appear "tough on crime" with its calls for 100,000 new police officers, more prisons, and an expansion of the death penalty. At the same time, the bill shored up left-leaning Democratic support with its long-sought ban on assault weapons and a massive collection of social programs aimed at crime prevention, risk reduction, and social intervention. In April of 1994, the bill sailed through the House of Representatives, and the Senate followed suit shortly thereafter. All that remained was for the two versions to be reconciled in conference committee over the summer recess. Because the differences were relatively minor, centering largely on the Racial Justice Act (ratified in the House but rejected in the Senate), passage appeared imminent. It would have been, could have been the cornerstone and consolidation of a new, bipartisan consensus—a neoliberal consensus—on public policy in the United States.

However, when Congress returned to Washington for a special August session to take up the compromise bill, new and powerful opposition had suddenly appeared. The intensity of this opposition was demonstrated on August 11 when the bill suffered a devastating procedural setback (by a vote of 225 to 210) in the House. The Violent Crime Control and Law Enforcement Act of 1994 (PL 103-322)—a.k.a. "the crime bill"—was ultimately ratified and signed into law by President Clinton in early September, but not until about $3 billion of spending was cut, almost all at the expense of its most prevention-oriented social policy components. In its final form, the 1994 federal crime bill—the single most important piece of criminal policy legislation of its time, still the backbone of American criminal justice policy today—ended up being less proactive (or, you might say, more punitive) than anyone could have imagined just three months earlier. It became the embodiment of what left-leaning critics would soon describe as the "iron fist and velvet tongue" of the Clinton administration's crime control policies (cf. Kramer and Michalowski 1995). Perhaps this was the new neoliberal consensus.

In any case, what explains this remarkable turn of political events? What precipitated the Republican insurgence that upset the fragile balance Democrats had so carefully crafted? As soon as I started asking such questions, I learned that the answers would be complicated and multifaceted. Led by the National Rifle Association, the gun lobby had waged war on the bill during the decisive summer weeks for its proposed ban on assault weapons. Additionally, many Republicans were outraged that the conference committee finished its work in late July but did not release copies of the 1,000-page document until the evening of August 10. GOP leaders became convinced the bill was full of unnecessary programs and provisions they'd be unable to identify or oppose because of the short timetable. These charges of political pork and procedural impropriety further exacerbated longstanding Republican concerns about the actual cost of the bill, increased federal involvement in criminal justice policy, and the folly of crime prevention in general. (More prisons and police was the mantra here.) Then there was also the aforementioned Racial Justice Act and the fact that this was all unfolding right at the start of the crucial off-year campaign season.

All these factors obviously helped shape the bill that was eventually ratified and passed into law. But what I was really interested in was the role that midnight basketball—or, to be more precise, *debates* about midnight basketball—played in determining the breakdown of the initial crime bill coalition and the eventual passage of federal crime policy. Having attuned my media antennae to midnight basketball early on, I was intrigued to see that discussions of midnight basketball had come to the fore in the context of political debates in the summer of 1994. All of a sudden, I started hearing again (and again) about midnight basketball. Even more intriguing (if disconcerting), the earlier consensus around midnight basketball appeared to have broken down—and the stakes in all of this seemed remarkably high, far beyond what one might have expected from a small sports program that had been so popular just months before.

Later, as I looked into this more closely, it seemed pretty clear to me that the debates about midnight basketball were an example of what I called in the previous chapter "racial coding"—that is, the way in which Americans can appeal to or talk about issues believed to have racial connotations or consequences without actually appearing mean-spirited, racist, or even to be talking about race at all. However, in the context of the crime bill debates, the racially coded midnight basketball program did not function, as it had earlier, to sustain neoliberalism's uneasy consensus about race, risk, and risk prevention. Rather, it appeared that midnight basketball was mobilized, strategically and intentionally, to disrupt the consensus, to upset the balance, and to try to tip the balance of power and common sense in more conservative or, I should say, Republican directions. In other words, it seemed like midnight basketball had the effect of that most (in)famous example of racial coding in recent American political history: the 1988 "Willie Horton" ad. This was the commercial that featured a convicted African American rapist and murderer who committed additional crimes while on a weekend furlough from prison, and which, in the process, made Democratic presidential nominee Michael Dukakis look "soft on crime"(Mendelberg 1997; see also Gilens 1995; Feagin and Vera 1995, 192; Kinder and Sanders 1996, chap. 9).

To test these theories (which, in fact, were the ideas that convinced me to launch a formal study of midnight basketball in the first place), I enlisted the help of a young sociologist named Darren Wheelock. Together, we began collecting public opinion polling, media coverage, political commentary, and legislative debates related to the bill. We used basic content analysis and close readings of the political discourse to document the racial character of the midnight basketball debate and suggest its impact on the legislative process. In this chapter, I recount those findings and explain how I continued to develop, deepen, and extend them over time. It is an analysis that not only deepens our understanding of the social significance of midnight basketball; it also reiterates and reproduces the broader pattern of how racial coding has functioned as a wedge issue on social policy in the post–civil rights era and helps us better appreciate the more general complications and dangers of using sports symbols for political purposes. And it all started with the breakdown of the unlikely consensus that had initially developed around midnight basketball.

The Beginning of the Breakdown

The first signs that the original consensus on midnight basketball was beginning to collapse came in April of 1994, when the previously celebrated program popped up in an NRA advertisement attacking New York senator Charles Schumer, one of the chief sponsors of the Clinton crime bill. The NRA ran full-page advertisements in *USA Today* calling Schumer, who was up for reelection, a "criminal's best friend." At the center of the ads was our favorite basketball-based initiative. However, in contrast with the depictions and opinions we have seen thus far, these ads portrayed midnight basketball as a wasteful program that was soft on crime, having more to do with social welfare than crime control, law, and order.[2] I don't know whether Republican strategists knew about the lack of evaluative research that I alluded to in previous chapters, but it certainly didn't help that midnight basketball proponents didn't have any evidence to rebut this critical characterization. In any case, Republican criticisms of the midnight basketball experiment began to find their way into the public record from this point on.

Early in the summer of 1994, conservative political talk show host Rush Limbaugh molded these scattered potshots into an all-out attack. Speaking from the platform of his nationally syndicated talk show (then at the height of its popularity), Limbaugh was not only dubious about the crime-fighting effectiveness of midnight basketball; he was *incensed* that money for such programs was available only for "qualified" communities (Limbaugh listed among these communities "those severely impacted by AIDS" and those with higher percentages of racial minorities). In his trademark mixture of irony, sarcasm, and bombast, Limbaugh castigated midnight basketball supporters for "coddling up to criminals," and with facetious if familiar hyperbole, he predicted that "the marvelous sound of bouncing basketballs will soon replace sounds of anger and destruction" (quoted in Boyer 1994, 40; see also *Time*, January 23, 1995).

Limbaugh's midsummer onslaught generated a lot of interest among conservatives on the summer state fair circuit, and Republican pollsters quickly jumped into the fray, putting out survey results suggesting that half of Americans were opposed to the program.[3] Before long, Republicans everywhere were talking about midnight basketball. In the first week of August, some fifteen Republicans legislators—including Senate leader Bob Dole (R-KS)—saw fit to criticize midnight basketball on the hallowed floors of Congress. Dozens would follow suit over the next few weeks.[4]

For many observers, participants, and program operators, the Republican attacks on midnight basketball must have come out of the blue. After all, nothing had really changed with the program in the three short years since midnight basketball was first introduced and championed by the leader of the Republication Party (a sitting president no less). Also, even though evaluators had yet to demonstrate the effectiveness of the program, no real problems had come to light in the interim either.[5] However, context, as sociologists like to say, can be everything. The context for midnight basketball in 1994 was dramatically different, the political situation in particular, than it had been just a couple of years, or even a few months, earlier. The fact that George H. W. Bush was no longer in the White House was perhaps the most obvious change. Bush's failed reelection bid discredited a whole host of his policies and initiatives—midnight basketball among them—with the Republican base. But it wasn't just that Bush lost; it was also that William Jefferson Clinton won, and the New Democrat from Arkansas turned out to be an enthusiastic midnight basketball supporter.

President Clinton's first public mention of midnight basketball came during his weekly radio address on April 16, 1994. After talking about crime problems across the country, he outlined a plan in which HUD secretary Henry Cisneros (Jack Kemp's successor) would be provided with emergency funds for "enforcement and prevention" in gang-infested public housing in cities like Chicago. As part of this package, the president assured the nation, "We'll provide more programs like midnight basketball leagues to help our young people say 'no' to gangs and guns and drugs."[6]

Clinton's endorsement alone was probably enough to upset the uneasy and unlikely political coalition Jack Kemp and George Bush had forged around midnight basketball at the national level (and that had been carved out by others in various local contexts). From the very beginning of the Clinton presidency, Republicans bristled at his ability to take programs and ideas they considered their own and shape them to his own middle-of-the-road, New Democrat program. But, having been schooled in the work of symbolic politics scholars like Joseph Gusfield ([1963] 1986) and Murray Edelman (1964), I was pretty sure the attacks on midnight basketball were not just the politics of personality and partisan bickering at work. As is so often the case with seemingly small, insignificant issues and events that receive inordinate public attention, deeper, more substantive issues—issues of neoliberal politics and policy—had to be involved.

The role of the federal government was one of the larger issues. Increased government support and bureaucratic supervision seemed to be involved in expanding funding for midnight basketball, and that perception was precisely the opposite of how many Republicans who had initially supported the initiative understood its structure and funding. They were supportive of midnight basketball (and other more proactive, preventative programs like it) because the emphasis was supposed to be on market-based principles and public-private partnerships, which had been championed by Jack Kemp. Government grants provided the seed money to get programs initiated, but then that funding and administration was to eventually be taken over at the local, community level. This was one of the key principles of the neoliberal push. However, the federal legislative provisions proposed by Democrats looked to Republicans, or at least were portrayed by them, like a move in the opposite direction. As Republican congressman Bob Inglis from South Carolina explained, the midnight basketball program may have been "valid" as a policy "experiment," but it was supposed to be "funded and operated by local governments."[7]

As such organizational and administrative concerns came to the fore, reporters and critics from all over the political spectrum began to look more closely at the structure and design of midnight basketball programs, and in doing so came to question the claim that having a couple hundred young men play basketball a few nights a week would significantly address the perceived problems of young black men. And quite soon thereafter, they actually did discover that there really wasn't any research confirming that these programs worked, certainly nothing to the extent that that standard-bearers like Standifer, Kemp, and Bush had claimed.[8]

Concerns about program design, impact, and effectiveness were particularly acute for conservatives who had been brought onto the midnight basketball bandwagon for its harder-core, "keep 'em off the streets," containment-and-control components. For those inclined to the more punitive and policing side, midnight basketball didn't—and frankly couldn't—keep participants off the streets long enough or regularly enough. They had come to realize—quite correctly, I think—that claims to crime reduction were unrealistic at best, given the operational structure of the programs. Even worse (here I am less in agreement), conservative critics began to suspect that bringing together these young men—who they saw through a deeply racialized lens as would-be criminals and thugs in the first place—putting them in the same place, could actually *exacerbate* the crime problem. Alabama representative Terry Everett was one who pushed this theme. Midnight basketball, he insisted, is "not going to halt crime—that's going to increase crime. What kind of logic keeps teenagers on the streets until well past midnight? Midnight basketball is bad and it's ugly."[9] This wasn't an entirely implausible suggestion. Not only was it questionable whether midnight was the best time for such a program, but decades of criminological research had shown that creating and facilitating peer group networks, interactions, and exchanges between already disruptive, disorderly, prone-to-violence individuals could serve to facilitate unwanted interactions and exchange. (In fact, several stories of this sort did make their way into the media later in the decade, along with at least one high-profile case of political corruption.)

Once this cloud of questions began floating around, accusations of political pork were quick to follow. For example, a congressman from southern Missouri, who granted that midnight basketball was "not without merit in theory," questioned whether the "experiment" was something "the taxpayer could afford to fund," and hypothesized that midnight basketball really just represented the president's attempt to "win favors with big city mayors and the liberals in this Congress."[10] These musings were far from the most extreme. With all this back-and-forth, all this posturing and these reversals, it didn't take a social scientist or sport specialist to realize that midnight basketball—once the poster child of a delicately balanced synthesis of liberal and conservative ideologies and approaches to social intervention and risk reduction—had gotten caught in the crossfire of a much larger controversy and political debate.

Center of a Storm

So the honeymoon was over. The midnight basketball coalition had collapsed. And the breakdown of the original, bipartisan consensus produced a metaphorical hangover that would prompt significant changes in midnight basketball philosophy and programming over the course of the rest of the decade. These changes have, for better and for worse, shaped sport-based social intervention programming into the present. But this is to get ahead of the story, as well as to see the debates over midnight basketball too narrowly. For the action and intrigue of midnight basketball in the context of the 1994 crime bill debates was not about sport-based intervention or basketball per se but about the broader symbolism and meaning basketball-based initiatives had in the legislative process. This is where the significance of midnight basketball went well beyond sport or sport-based intervention, beyond athletics and popular culture and into the realms of neoliberal politics and public policy.

To dig deeper, Wheelock and I began to examine the character and function of references to midnight basketball in both political debates and the media's coverage of those debates. The investigation took shape quickly. During congressional hearings and debates in the first three weeks of August of 1994, we found that midnight basketball was mentioned over 100 times—*one hundred*—in the *Congressional Record*, with more than 70 of these references coming during the decisive week of August 12–16. The vast majority of these references came from Republicans, every one of them was an attack of some sort, and all these attacks came in the context of debates about the federal crime bill.[11]

This obsession with midnight basketball in the context of the crime bill was reflected and reproduced in the national media as well. Over a third of the articles in our collection of mainstream national news magazines (15 of 41) contained at least one reference to midnight basketball, and seven discussed the program directly and in some detail (albeit with a less obvious partisan thrust).[12] The *New Republic*, for example, referred to midnight basketball no fewer than three times during the course of a single, one-and-one-quarter page editorial (September 5, 1994); *Time* magazine devoted a page-length insert to midnight basketball in the context of an extensive feature on the proposed crime bill (August 29, 1994). Picking up a more overtly ideological line, *Business Week* editorialized that the legislation was simply "[a] hodgepodge of untested social programs such as gang prevention and midnight basketball." While they all might sound good, according to the magazine, "there is little or no solid evidence they bring down crime" (September 5, 1994).

What was striking about all this attention is that proposed spending for midnight basketball was only a miniscule portion of the overall crime bill. This experimental sports program accounted for (at most) $50 *million* of the original $33 *billion* bill, barely a tenth of a percent of the funding, a mere fraction of a fraction. Even in terms of the dollars dedicated strictly to "prevention" ($6.9 billion), the amount to be spent on midnight basketball was negligible (Idelson 1994). That is to say, a tiny and previously uncontroversial program was suddenly and specifically a central part of the debate involving the largest and single most important criminal justice legislation of the period. This was something to take seriously, on its own terms. Wheelock and I were now convinced this was the case because the controversy surrounding midnight basketball was not really about this experimental program—it was about the crime bill itself. Midnight basketball was a symbol for other, larger issues implicated in the massive crime initiative; the 1994 debate over midnight basketball was a textbook example of "symbolic politics" at work.

The idea of targeting midnight basketball for political purposes appeared to have been spearheaded by the Republican public relations firm Craig Shirley and Associates. Its stated aim was to bring together an ad hoc coalition of conservative organizations and interests against the Democratic crime bill. The GOP consultant believed the party could do this by focusing attention on the bill's most liberal (and thus presumably vulnerable), prevention-oriented components (Carter 1998, esp. 56),[13] and it saw midnight basketball as a near-perfect symbol of the most costly and "unproven" components of the Democratic approach to crime policy.

If Limbaugh propelled midnight basketball into the public discussion, Republican consultants and strategists working behind the scenes appear to have first mapped the rhetorical strategy. The powerful Luntz Research group began by gathering polling numbers that suggested that half of Americans considered social programs like dance, art, and basketball "a complete waste of money" when it came to crime and crime prevention. Working from this finding, Luntz operatives prepared a detailed memo for the NRA advising its allies and lobbyists on how to mobilize and exploit the midnight basketball symbol.[14] Their proposed attacks played off familiar, deeply racialized stereotypes and fears about violence, crime, and social disorder as well as the accusation that a sports program was not a serious policy response.

"Americans," the memo explained, "are far more concerned that convicted criminals remain behind bars than [that] teenagers in inner cities learn to ball room dance and slam dunk from the foul line by the pale moonlight." With these racialized images and stereotypes firmly in place, the memo went on to explain that "ridicule is a powerful weapon." "Dance lessons, arts and crafts, midnight basketball and the 40,000 new social workers are all obvious targets." The Luntz group laid out various scenarios it said Republican legislators and leaders could use to exploit this situation. "Imagine the conversation between two muggers," the memo told clients to say. "One looks at his watch and says to the other: 'Hey, it's already 10:30. We'd better get in one more mugging before the game begins.'" Or, "If you want to play it straight," the memo continued, "just say: if they're under 18, they should be home studying or in bed; if they're over 18, they should be home or working the late shift." Suffice it to say, the fact that Democrats thought they could prevent crime merely by having at-risk young men play games revealed, in the Republican caricature, how laughably little Democrats knew about the hard realities of crime and criminals.

Though Wheelock and I didn't do extensive background research into exactly how coordinated this effort was, the *Congressional Record* made the road map easy to see. Almost every time midnight basketball was mentioned by Republicans in Senate and House debates, it was packaged with dance lessons and arts and crafts classes and basically treated as comical, simple-minded, or simply corrupt. In a major speech entered into the *Congressional Record* on the day after a fateful procedural vote on the bill, Senate leader Bob Dole (R-KS) argued that the American people were "not interested in spending $10–12 billion in social welfare programs like midnight basketball, dancing and self-esteem lessons." Dole relied heavily on criminologist John DiIulio, even having DiIulio's comments read into the record earlier in the proceedings, in support of the senator's claims that these programs "had very little to do with fighting crime" and were an example of classic "pork-barrel politics."[15]

Dole's invocation of DiIulio was far from incidental. The Princeton scholar was one of several academics across the country (James Q. Wilson, whose "broken windows" policing was the inspiration for Rudy Giuliani's influential remaking of law enforcement in New York City, was another) whose radical critiques of rehabilitation and prevention were being invoked and embraced by the GOP at this time in favor of more punitive approaches to criminal justice. Even politicians who were otherwise sympathetic to midnight basketball and prevention more generally found themselves uncomfortably caught up in a whole constraining set of assumptions and political alliances, forced to choose one side or the other. There is perhaps no better example than Illinois Republican Henry Hyde's ill-advised attempt to lighten the tone of debate at one point: "I have an open mind on midnight basketball. It is certainly while playing midnight basketball they are not mugging you—at least there is a referee there to blow a whistle if they do." If Hyde's awkward attempt at bipartisan humor fell flat, it was only because the racial stereotypes were now locked in and the political battle lines around midnight basketball and the crime bill had been clearly drawn.[16]

Racial Cards and Codes

Almost immediately after the amended crime bill was ratified in the fall, Democrats and others on the Left charged that the attacks on midnight basketball had been racially motivated—a classic case, in their description, of Republicans "playing the race card." Charles Schumer, for example, the Democrat from New York who was the focus of the initial midnight basketball attack ads, had offered that assessment early on: "The Republican party only succeeds when the race issue is the divide. Every time they win it is on race. . . . That's why they're going to [focus on] crime and illegal immigrants."[17] In a story entitled "The Anatomy of a Mugging," Alan Vanneman, writing in the November/December 1994 issue of *Youth Today*, a publication based in Washington, DC, claimed that the "right wing made midnight basketball the Willie Horton of the Crime Bill." Dozens more examples could be given.

As far as Wheelock and I could tell, Republicans never actually denied these charges—but they did not acknowledge them either. This presented one of the first real challenges of our study of the symbolic and racial politics surrounding the crime bill. After all, a common shortcoming of many race-card accusations and racial-coding analyses (like many conspiracy theories in general) is the inability to convincingly demonstrate the character and intent of such rhetorical symbolism.

Fortunately, in this case, empirical evidence was plentiful. We had already amassed a mountain of data and argumentation establishing the racial character and content of midnight basketball. These characteristics were confirmed in the context of crime bill debates. For example, closer, more careful inspections of the texts, as well as attention to the context within which midnight basketball references appeared, revealed that these references frequently came right before or right after names of people or neighborhoods clearly marked as African American. They were also often included alongside social problems (poverty, drugs, and welfare dependency) that scholars had demonstrated the public associated with African Americans (Entman and Rojecki 2000; Roberts 1997; J. G. Miller 1996; Lusane 1991). The August 29 *Time* magazine article quoted above contained one such instance. Midnight basketball was introduced with a quote from an individual described only as having a "blue bandanna around his head" and set in a neighborhood "five [blocks] from one of Washington [DC]'s most notorious drug markets." Similarly, when Congressman Randy "Duke" Cunningham, a Republican from San Diego (where the High Five program was located), announced that he was changing his position on the program, he used a star African American player from the Los Angeles Lakers to make his point: "Maybe Magic Johnson could play in this league but I don't want my kids to play in it."[18] In fact, when we cross-referenced midnight basketball mentions against overt racial markers elsewhere in a story, we found that they overlapped 40 percent of the time.[19]

Pictures also helped make the case. Of the dozens of pictures, cartoons, and other visual representations we collected during this period, only one contained an image of a program participant who was *not* a person of color, and this came in an editorial cartoon from an extremely progressive publication which had the clear intent of subverting the hegemony of the images usually associated with midnight basketball programs.

Probably the most compelling evidence that midnight basketball served as a proxy for race came from a little counterfactual experiment in which we looked at the media coverage of program items in the bill that contained elements similar to midnight basketball but were lacking in identifiable racial connotations. This analysis included alternative crime prevention programs such as Ounce of Prevention programs, Olympic recreation centers, after-school programs, and in-school fitness and recreation programs. Because they were organized around physical recreation of some sort, included under the broad rubric of "crime prevention," and yet lacked explicit racial connotations, provisions for these programs functioned as a kind of empirical, counterfactual test of our claim that midnight basketball was a racial symbol or code. The results of this analysis were absolutely clear and convincing:

Ounce of Prevention and after-school fitness and recreation programs were referenced most frequently (53 and 57 times, respectively), but this paled in comparison to the 374 times midnight basketball appeared in our national sample. Taking *all* recreation-oriented, prevention-type alternatives as an aggregated whole still yielded only 138 total references. And the comparative difference in the media coverage of these programs took on additional significance when we considered how expensive the provisions contained under each of these constellations of programs actually were.[20] Both Ounce of Prevention programs and Olympic training centers were budgeted at approximately $125 million in the bill, and in-school programs at $300 million. After-school programs were penciled in to receive just under $100 million per year for five years. These proposed allocations obviously stand in contrast to the $50 million to be spent on midnight basketball—yet this program was the one getting all the media attention.

So we had a start. Even though midnight basketball was pointedly *not* described as a racially targeted program, it clearly *functioned* as a proxy for "young African American men," one of those racial codes discussed in previous chapters that allow those who reference it to talk about race without actually naming that talk as such. Now we were ready to tackle the bigger, more consequential question: How did this racialized symbol, "midnight basketball," affect the political process?

Midnight Basketball Effects

Initially Wheelock and I had planned to focus on polling and public opinion since that's where most conventional racial-coding analyses are directed. However, we soon discovered that all the major polls had shown high and relatively stable levels of support for the crime bill, and that this support had remained solid throughout the year, impervious to the attacks on midnight basketball. The *Los Angeles Times*, for example, found that 53 percent of Americans polled at the end of July 1994 considered the crime bill's passage a national priority. (This had slipped slightly from a peak of 57 percent in April.) In early August, an NBC/*Wall Street Journal* poll found support for a crime bill at 57 percent; Gallup's August 15 survey found 56 percent of those polled supported the crime bill. A CBS poll conducted on August 18 found that only 28 percent of Americans *opposed* the original compromise committee version of the bill, though *support* for the compromise bill was softer (42 percent) than for the unspecified, general need for a crime bill. (A quarter of respondents said they did not know enough about the specifics of the compromise committee's version of the bill to respond.)[21] In the one poll we found that dealt specifically with the prevention-oriented components of the bill, the numbers were even stronger—almost 10 points higher (65 percent) than that for the crime bill as a whole. And this poll, conducted by Gallup on August 16 and released three days later, specifically asked respondents if they favored "providing local communities with federal tax money to provide social programs and activities for low-income children such as *Midnight Basketball*" (emphasis in original) as a proposal to reduce crime.[22] In short, then, the controversy surrounding midnight basketball had no discernable impact on public attitudes about crime, the need for federal legislation on crime, the 1994 crime bill, or even prevention programs themselves.

In light of this polling data, we realized that if midnight basketball was having an impact, it must have been operating in a less direct, more complicated fashion. Accordingly, we shifted our focus to look at framing—that is, the ways in which the racialized symbol of midnight basketball exerted its influence on elite-level discourse—how commentators, reporters, and legislators talked and thought about the crime bill and crime prevention in general. And as we dug deeper into the specifics of media coverage and political rhetoric, Wheelock and I saw that references to midnight basketball were mainly associated with increased attention to and scrutiny of the more liberal, prevention-oriented components of the bill.

After coding every article in our initial sample (all of those including a midnight basketball reference) for key issues under political debate during the decisive weeks in August (prevention, pork/political process, federal spending, gun control, prisons/police, and the Racial Justice Act),[23] we discovered midnight basketball was associated with prevention over 80 percent of the time. (Federal spending and pork/political process were the two other issues directly associated with midnight basketball, but this was only rarely the case—6.5 percent and 5.5 percent, respectively.) Republican criticisms of the crime bill via the symbol of midnight basketball not only outweighed Democratic defenses, but when the debates over the crime bill were most intense, the number of negative references to midnight basketball increased dramatically. In other words, a reference to midnight basketball more often than not functioned as an argument against the original Democratic version of the crime bill—or, to be more precise, against the prevention-oriented components of the bill. Midnight basketball references didn't just trigger general fears about crime and criminals that impinged on public opinion (as more conventional racial-coding theories would've assumed and which would have, if anything, buttressed arguments to increase criminal justice funding generally); rather, midnight basketball, functioned as a rhetorical device that made the more prevention-oriented aspects of the bill seem ill-conceived and unnecessary.

The trick was to devise tests to confirm these suspicions and figure out how these dynamics worked. To this end, we gathered a large, nationally representative sample (several thousand articles, actually) of media coverage and commentary drawn from the period when the public discourse about the crime bill was most intensive and consequential (July 31 to August 20).[24] We coded these articles and then ran a series of tests to see how crime bill articles and commentaries that mentioned midnight basketball differed from those that did not. These procedures included fairly complicated statistical analyses such as a series of cross-classification tables as well as several multifaceted logistic regression models evaluating all the "predictors" for the major crime bill arguments (that is, the key issues under political debate listed above). We also created variables to capture explicit references to race and various portrayals of crime and the social background of criminals.

Our analysis revealed that references to midnight basketball were associated with three distinctive framing patterns in the debates over federal criminal justice policy. First, when midnight basketball appeared in media coverage, the more liberal, prevention-oriented aspects of the bill received more scrutiny and criticism. Specifically, prevention went from the second-least-likely issue to be dealt with in an article on the crime bill to the single most prominent issue discussed. Simply referencing midnight basketball, in short, was functioning as an attack on prevention.

Next, we found that references to midnight basketball increased the number of times the crime issue was framed with respect to a specific population or social group (to a certain stereotype of criminals) rather than as a general social problem such as public safety. This happened for both the overall crime bill and articles in which prevention was the focal point. With respect to the construction of the prevention argument in particular, criminal images and depictions only indirectly affected by racial images and ideas were decisive in the discourse. This suggested that racially coded midnight basketball references exerted their impact concretely by transforming the overall image of crime and criminals that lurks in the background of discussions about various approaches to criminal justice policy. This is well captured by Congressman Lamar Smith's (R-TX) characterization of midnight basketball in *USA Today* as "vague social spending . . . [based] on the theory that the person who stole your car, robbed your house, and assaulted your family was no more than a would-be NBA star" (August 19, 1994). Smith was not only singling out specific social groups as the root of the crime and public safety problem; he was making it seem like criminal justice policy was about actual, already committed crimes and already convicted criminals.

Our third discovery was that midnight basketball references seemed to facilitate more direct and open references to (and discussion of) issues specific to race and African Americans. In and of itself, this function might not have been such a bad thing. Indeed, one of the chief assumptions of racial-coding critics is that it is better to have racial references and stereotypes out in the open rather than hidden behind vague inferences and obscured labels. However, when mobilized by Republicans, midnight basketball references frequently not only raised the specter of race—that is, they provided an imminent racial threat that cast doubt on any ability to prevent it—they provided a rhetorical reference point that allowed Republicans to employ racial imagery and stereotypes more freely than they otherwise might. Here, we were especially interested to discover that some 40 percent of the articles that referenced midnight basketball also contained other kinds of racial images and referents. These articles rarely talked about race directly, but racial references were there, and they were clearly associated with, if not facilitated by, talk about midnight basketball. Our conclusion was that midnight basketball was not the direct means by which racial fears were mobilized and enacted but a conduit by which explicit racial references were introduced into the political process. Once this gateway was opened, Republicans could reference race more directly without seeming like they had even brought up the issue at all.

Taken together, these findings led us to believe that midnight basketball operated on multiple levels, both overt and symbolic, in signifying the mobilized resistance against both prevention policy and the crime bill more generally. The racially coded symbol of midnight basketball functioned as a rhetorical conduit whereby racial issues and concerns could be discussed, and it determined the level of the language and discourse in and through which criminals were presented and portrayed. This use rendered "prevention" idealistic, unlikely, and unrealistic. Making prevention seem silly and misguided helped legitimate and necessitate the more punitive, prisons-and-policing emphasis favored by more conservative Republicans. What was happening, in other words, was that, in the context of the crime bill debates, images and ideas associating crime with young African American men (as conveyed through midnight basketball) heightened the perceived threat of crime and left preventative programs risible.

Caught in a Code

If we had been conducting a standard racial-coding analysis, our work would have been close to complete. Since we had established the existence of a racial code and shown the rhetorical and discursive mechanisms by which this code undermined the previous political coalition and reshaped the nature of the final legislation, writing a conclusion drawing out the more general meanings and implications would have been the only thing left to do. If only it had been that easy! What complicated our project was the fact that Republicans were not the only ones playing the symbolic politics of race with midnight basketball.

In fact, midnight basketball had begun to reemerge—a reference or two here, a quote there—in the public sphere when Democrats (that's right, Democrats) began to explore the possibility of expanding funding for the program early in the spring of the 1994 legislative session. And it was the leader of the Democratic caucus who led the charge. President Clinton made the racial images and connotations manifest in June when he spoke about midnight basketball at a housing project in Chicago. He told his predominantly African American audience that midnight basketball was a program designed to assist "people just like you." A week later, at a park in a mostly African American neighborhood in St. Louis, Clinton deflected questions about the Racial Justice Act by talking instead about "prevention programs" such as "midnight basketball." Finally, the president gave one of his most aggressive, public defenses of the crime bill—again, replete with an extended discussion of recreation and midnight basketball—in front of an all-black AME church in Atlanta, Georgia.[25]

The problem for us was not so much that Democrats "played the race card" of midnight basketball earlier and just as deliberately as Republicans (although both seem to be the case). We already knew that Democrats had at least as much of an interest and investment in the racial imagery implicitly conveyed in the symbol of midnight basketball as Republicans. And in this instance, Clinton, in a pattern that would hold for multiple policy domains and debates across the 1990s, clearly wanted to use the midnight basketball symbol to placate and appease more moderate Democrats, as well as build up his base in the African American legislative caucus, in crafting a coalition for the crime bill around prevention-oriented provisions. In other words, the president was trying to use midnight basketball to expand support for the crime bill within the framework of the larger (if uneasy) neoliberal consensus on race and social policy. The empirical problem—or really, the analytic question—was why the more liberal, Democratic mobilization of midnight basketball as a code or symbol didn't succeed. Why had the Republican story line held sway?

In her foundational study of racial coding, Tali Mendelberg (2001) offered what she called a "ray of hope" for those interested in combating racially coded political messages: racial codes, she wrote, tend to lose their appeal when their content is exposed. However, focused as Mendelberg was on conservative, Republican efforts to mobilize racial codes such as the "Willie Horton" ad, her point seemed promising for more liberal, progressive political actors because it equated racial coding with conservative ideologies and causes. Our case suggested the converse, and indeed the fallacy of this conflation—that is, in American political culture, liberals, too, can suffer the consequences if they get called out playing the politics of race. It is what we came to think of as the trap of the racial code of midnight basketball.

If formal content analysis demonstrated the decisive impact that conservative characterizations of midnight basketball had on the crime bill discourse and debate, a closer examination of the actual talk of midnight basketball in the political process helped us understand how Republican racial rhetoric and coding trumped Democratic efforts. And on this front, it was not so much the strength of the Republican onslaught against midnight basketball that was most revealing but the character, timing, and utter awkwardness of the Democratic response. The watchwords were timing and impotence.

In spite of the fact that it was their leader who had first spotlighted midnight basketball in the political process, congressional Democrats didn't even *begin* to rebut the Republican attacks on midnight basketball until August 11, a full week into the special session on the crime bill and after dozens of such charges had been levied. The first formal public defense appeared in a speech on the House floor from one of the original supporters of the initiative, Bruce Vento (D-MN), who offered a lengthy, substantive defense just before the procedural vote.[26] Vento was immediately and strongly backed by future Speaker of the House Nancy Pelosi (D-CA), whose San Francisco Bay–area district was home to one of the largest and most prominent midnight basketball leagues in the nation. Although both offered up spirited defenses of midnight basketball, they were worded in a peculiar way. No longer were Democrats touting the appeal of these programs for young, at-risk men of color. In the face of the Republican attacks, these Democrats went out of their way to defend midnight basketball in race-neutral, color-blind terms, as a general, nontargeted prevention program. In her remarks, Pelosi talked about the "midnight soccer" program targeted to Latino men and women in her district. Other Democratic representatives followed suit as they began to weigh in on the matter, abandoning the most obvious racial elements of midnight basketball and instead describing the Subtitle F provisions as "midnight sports" or "late-night basketball," eventually settling on the relatively raceless descriptor "late-night sports" by the end of the month.

The reasons for this subtle but unmistakable shift were two-fold, and they reveal the limitations of ostensibly color-blind but actually racially coded political appeals from the Left. On the one hand, Democrats were clearly trying to circumvent the racist imagery and implication of the Republican attack. Basically, they just didn't want to seem racist in their assumptions and presuppositions about the beliefs and behaviors of young black men. On the other hand, they had to be careful to avoid charges of racial favoritism and particularism that have long been anathema in American politics and which can quickly deteriorate into accusations of "reverse racism." Indeed, in a certain sense, Clinton Democrats trying to play the symbolic politics of midnight basketball were following the advice of liberal social scientists by arguing for ostensibly race-neutral, universalist policies and programs. This is what was at the time referred to as "targeting within universalism" (cf. Skocpol 1995; B. Wilson 1997). But in trying to walk this rhetorical tightrope, Democrats stripped the program of all the race-specific elements that made it so appealing in the first place. If midnight basketball was one of the few ways to reach young African American men with direct social programs, and if we "knew" those young men were struggling (whether they were at-risk or were the risk), midnight basketball held simple, inexpensive appeal. Without these basic assumptions in place, midnight basketball looked, at best, like a foolhardy, feel-good program that had no place in federal criminal justice policy.

Democrats did seem to figure this out eventually, at least to a certain extent. The day after this initial (if belated) defense, Democrats in the Senate finally acknowledged that midnight basketball was a "targeted" program and argued that was precisely what made it worthwhile as a crime prevention initiative.[27] Patricia Schroeder (D-CO), one of the program's original backers and most ardent defenders, took up this rebuttal in the House after the weekend break. But as she embraced the targeting concept, Schroeder did so in a vague fashion. She would say only that the program was targeted to "neighborhoods that need it."[28] Again, Democrats balked at employing race-specific images or connotations about the program. Defending midnight basketball explicitly in race-specific terms, when they had so long and so consistently chosen to do otherwise, would have required them to confront the racial assumptions and stereotypes about young, African American men embedded in this program—and that would quickly sound not just racialized but actually racist. And, on the other hand, a more explicit progressive argument for race targeting would have revealed the programmatic and evidentiary limitations of the midnight basketball experiment. In other words, Democrats were hemmed in, or had hemmed themselves in, on both sides.

Schroeder's tortured defense illustrated the problem. Intuitively grasping the rhetorical problems of the "neighborhoods that need it" defense, she went on to say that those were neighborhoods "where they do not have a father presence." But before she could elaborate further, she stopped herself. Schroeder was unable to continue, we came to believe, because doing so would have exposed some of the deeply racialized stereotypes and assumptions about crime and young black men that brought liberal Democrats to midnight basketball in the first place as well as the fundamental limitations and inadequacies of their prevention-oriented neoliberal social policy most broadly conceived.

A representative from South Carolina found himself in this same bind two days later. He tried to sidestep the issue by talking about targeted neighborhoods as those where "residents are stigmatized by the criminal activity occurring in their community."[29] However, this formulation rendered prevention almost incomprehensible, because it blurred the lines between those who are criminals (or would-be criminals) and those who are threatened by crime, as well as between who in these populations is "at risk" and for what—in short, who needs "prevention" and why.

Democrats, it should be noted, hit on a much more effective rhetorical strategy a few days later when they began to quote (at length) former President Bush's strong support of midnight basketball and, in particular, his "thousand points of light" recognition earlier in the decade. Three different Democratic representatives and at least one senator harkened back to Bush's early support.[30] An unexpected source also came to their aid: in a nationally syndicated opinion piece, "Why I Support the Crime Bill," published on August 18, New York mayor and Republican moderate Rudy Giuliani insisted that funding for prevention was important and appropriate. However, he also said it was necessary to "change the 'Midnight Sports Program' and make it broader and more flexible . . . so that cities can determine the types of sports program they want and not be required to have a nighttime program." Giuliani suggested, as possible alternatives, keeping schools open in the evening as well as more youth academies and other community-based innovations.

Unfortunately for Democrats, all this was too little, too late. Trapped by their own racialist assumptions as well as their limited and ambivalent commitment to prevention, Democrats and other political moderates could only talk about midnight basketball in general, race-neutral, and gender-ambiguous ways. It made the concept seem vague, vacuous, and ill conceived. Perhaps the best indication of this came on August 17 when a Democratic House member pointed out that, even in Republican versions of the crime bill, there was funding for a host of sport-and-recreation-based initiatives: sporting and recreation equipment, supervised sports programs, sports mentoring and coaching programs, Boys and Girls Clubs, and so on. "Sounds like midnight basketball to me!" he proclaimed, going on to issue a challenge: "Now is the time for Republicans to come out from under the rocks where they have been hiding . . . and accept and endorse the programs they have in fact supported."[31] Perhaps. What this representative couldn't say, however, and why Republicans would not have to answer his call, is what separated all these other sport-and-recreation-based prevention initiatives from midnight basketball: the reality of race and the unwillingness to address it fully. Midnight basketball was the only such program so thoroughly associated with young black men and the assumptions of risk, threat, and crime. Such racialized and even racist assumptions may have been built into the crime bill, and may even have been the essence of the uneasy, bipartisan consensus on neoliberal social policy and racial politics, but this was a basic truth that couldn't be trumpeted too loudly, much less mobilized too explicitly or overtly for political strategizing and positioning.

Adding Insult to Injury

One further, ironic dimension of being caught in this racial code that I really honed in on after Wheelock and I published our initial version of this research is the way in which the Democratic caucus seems to have brought this onto themselves by heightening the racial context of both crime and criminal justice earlier in the political process. I am referring here not to the symbolic politics of race but to the more overt racial politics that accompanied the proposed Racial Justice Act, the crime bill provisions put forward by the Congressional Black Caucus at the beginning of the summer in an effort to minimize racial disparities in death penalty sentencing.

On its face, the Racial Justice Act, which was composed primarily of provisions resurrected from a failed 1991 proposal (Dennis, Medoff, and Gagnier 1998), was intended to provide some pushback against some of the more racist and discriminatory elements of the crime bill (not an unreasonable proposition, given all we knew then and know now about the disproportionate negative effects of criminal justice on the black community and African American men more particularly). The debate over the Racial Justice Act unfolded primarily in June and July, just before the midnight basketball furor erupted (and, in my view, not incidentally). What was most intriguing, as I looked at the pattern more closely, was that, just shortly after this issue was decided, midnight basketball emerged as a prominent object of discussion, discourse, and debate. That is, after the *overtly racialized* Racial Justice Act dropped out of public discourse on the crime bill, the *racially coded* midnight basketball initiative came to the forefront of the debate. There was a direct, inverse relationship between references to the Racial Justice Act and midnight basketball.

In a recent study, Hana Brown (2013) found that the existence of an overt, highly published racial incident or conflict was one of the key predictors for states that passed more draconian welfare policies. Such events appear to galvanize the public and/or embolden lawmakers in some kind of subtle, less-than-conscious way. A similar kind of dynamic or relationship seems to have held sway for the relationship between the Racial Justice Act and midnight basketball on a subtler, discursive level. In the first case, the deadlock and debate over the Racial Justice Act served to bring issues of race—which had previously been notable only for their absence, for the ways in which they were built into both Democratic and Republican conceptions of crime and criminal justice, a key element of the uneasy racial consensus I described in the previous chapter—more directly into the crime bill debates. This meant that race was established as a central if contentious aspect of the debate even before midnight basketball came up for discussion. Secondly, the Racial Justice Act was eventually dropped from the bill by the Democratic leadership over the strong opposition of the more racially progressive forces within the party. This signaled that, for better or worse, explicit concerns about and attention to racial injustices were to be sidestepped in these negotiations. Ostensibly, racial disparities were not the result of procedural improprieties but rather existed because certain populations were simply more prone to crime and delinquency. The implied racial logic behind the demise of the Racial Justice Act, in other words, established a cultural context that undercut the Democratic vision of midnight basketball as an effective program in favor of the Republican one in which all such prevention programs are futile—a sort of "some people can't be helped" logic.

Not only was there a clear conservative racial logic dominating the political discourse and legislative process, but that logic was unified by the interplay of overtly and covertly racialized programs and initiatives. This pattern helps further explain both how and why Republicans were able to shift the racial meaning and transform the political impact of midnight basketball provisions. The Racial Justice Act supplied a crucial context and a substantive logic for the intense discussion and debate over the racially coded midnight basketball provisions that took place in the decisive weeks of the legislative session.

In previous chapters I suggested that both the midnight basketball experiment and neoliberal social policy more generally were driven and defined by a deeply rooted and all-too-often ignored racial consensus, one that pathologized African American men, that ignored the deeper structural conditions of poverty, inequality, and crime, and that stretched across party lines and ideological divides. I still believe this is true. However, this chapter in the story also suggests that, at other levels, the politics of race were indeed a point of cleavage with obvious political implications and policy consequences. What is also clear is that all these overt and covert racial politics would remain a thorn in the side of Clinton and the Democratic coalition for the remainder of the crime bill process and for years to come in struggles over neoliberal social policy. And Rush Limbaugh, perhaps not surprisingly, remained consistently obsessed with midnight basketball. Within a year, as the debates over Clinton's cherished welfare reform package were beginning to heat up, Limbaugh would recycle the midnight basketball episode to level a favorite accusation against the Clinton administration: reverse racism. "At a time when the black community is struggling with the notion that the route out of the ghetto is the 'N-B-A' and a Nike pair of shoes," Limbaugh proclaimed sarcastically, "here comes the administration . . . and says to parents: 'hey, we solved your problem. We're going to have your kids playing basketball from midnight to 2 a.m.'" Limbaugh went on to offer this incendiary if revealing speculation: "One wonders what the liberal mainstream media's reaction to such a proposal would have been if it had been, say, [southern Republican leader] Trent Lott's idea. I doubt the Klan itself could engineer a more bigoted government program."[32]

The Deep Play Part

All this research and analysis took Wheelock and I quite a while to work through (and even longer to get published in a journal). But even after the article appeared in print (Wheelock and Hartmann 2007), I continued to reflect on other dimensions of the political drama of the crime bill debates—its deeper cultural structure, its broader racial context, and both its general theoretical lessons and actual political impacts and implications. One line of thinking that became something of an obsession with me involved the question of how or to what extent the athletic content of the racial code shaped and determined the outcomes of this episode (as distinct from, if in relation to, the racial symbolism involved).

The sport-specific aspects of the midnight basketball symbol had (by necessity) lingered in the background of our formal racial-coding analysis. In fact, those speculative footnotes to this effect that I had included in the original drafts of our analysis had to be trimmed to meet ruthless if necessary word count limits for journal publication. Nevertheless, I remained convinced that there was more to pull out and unpack on the sport front.

The athletic aspect of midnight basketball seemed pertinent to the crime bill debates and outcome in at least two different respects, both of which illustrated and illuminated the challenges of political mobilization in and through sport's paradoxical serious-play form. One is a point I alluded to previously: how Republicans used the sports side of midnight basketball to denigrate and deride prevention programs as a whole, to make them look ill conceived and downright silly. Though not overtly, the conception and understanding of sport as "not serious," something somehow trivial or meaningless, was at the heart of the Republican attack on midnight basketball. As quoted earlier, the Luntz memo's emphasis on ridicule was perhaps the most obvious example. "Ridicule" means to poke fun at or denigrate, to reveal as silly, simpleminded, or deeply misguided. I already highlighted how the Republican caricature of midnight basketball and its consistent association with all manner of dance lessons and art classes served to suggest how little the soft-on-crime Democrats knew about the hard realities of crime and criminal justice. The key observation at this point in the analysis is that the very athletic characteristics that had made midnight basketball appear so innovative and promising as a policy innovation initially—that it was something fun, unique, engaging, and enjoyable for participants—were precisely what was used against it in these debates. The politics of the deep play form, in short, were turned on their head.

A certain set of assumptions needed to be in place for this inversion to take hold, actually, to make this charge stick. For one thing, Republicans had to jettison any aspirations of outreach, intervention, and prevention in the context of criminal justice; they had to divest themselves completely of rehabilitation as an aspect of policy. Connected with this, they grew ever more committed to the most extreme racial stereotypes about African American men and the risks they posed. If you believed that otherwise violence-prone individuals (in short, presumed criminals) could only be controlled or contained, it was foolhardy to offer fun, engaging programs that were intended to "prevent" crime through diversion and character development. What we are talking about here is the rising prominence of the superpredator criminal narrative and the end of the hope for or belief in any kind of rehabilitation. Once critics locked in on these assumptions, they could also proclaim outrage about the fact that midnight basketball programs actually claimed to manage crime by *rewarding* the presumed predators! This was the argument that prevention-oriented programs not only were ineffective crime-fighting policies but that they actually "coddled up" to criminals. In all of this, the message was that crime and violence were serious social problems that deserved better policy than fun and games for young men who might already be violent or criminalized.

It is also worth noting that in embracing the ridicule discourse, midnight basketball critics had to not only jettison the containment-and-control aspects of the program; they had to ignore or dismiss those long-standing, idealized claims about athletics being a site for the cultivation of character and self-discipline (much less an arena for the advancement of African American men and the struggle for racial equality more generally) that had been thoroughly embraced and deeply assumed by Kemp and Bush. If there had been something of an indecision or split among Republicans on the different visions of intervention embedded in midnight basketball, this moment marked the end of that uncertainty. Intervention, perhaps, even risk reduction—but crime prevention? No way. And there was certainly no room for character building, education, or development. In any case, a dismissal of traditional liberal beliefs about sport combined with exaggerated racial stereotypes about African American men reinforced and intensified the rhetorical broadside of ridicule and denigration of the idea of prevention through the symbolic significance of midnight basketball.

The second way in which the athletic aspects of midnight basketball came into play with Republican attacks against the crime bill was even more deeply structured in the culture itself: the assumptions and expectations about the appropriate relationships between sport and politics, or sport and policy, or politics and play. In the previous chapter, I mentioned that politicians and their advisors are constantly on the lookout for opportunities to associate their candidates, campaigns, and agendas with athletes, athletic competitions, and sport more generally. They do this because the transference of the positive feelings associated with athletes and sports can not only make a candidate more prominent, relatable, or likeable, but they can make a politician and his or her agenda more credible and legitimate.

What I didn't delve into at that time, however, are the cultural constraints, at least in the United States, on doing politics in and through sport. I am thinking here of cultural conventions and norms that hold sport and politics to be separate and distinct domains even when they are clearly implicated—or, as Kyle Green and I have put it, "strange, secret bedfellows" (Green and Hartmann 2014). These conventions and norms are deeply engrained in American culture. In my earlier study of the 1968 African American Olympic protests, for example, I found that the only thing advocates and critics of the movement could really agree on was that politics had no place in sports (Hartmann 1996). I used this finding, along with the language of "sacred" and "profane," to develop the idea that Americans tend to see sport as somehow sacred or special, in need of protection against the corrupting influences of "politics." Truthfully, I am never quite sure whether this is because sport is believed to be above politics—somehow special or sacrosanct—or below them. Probably it is some of both. But what is most important here are the prohibitions that lead us to believe sports and politics should not mix, the cultural taboos that want to prevent their mixing and intermingling. The result of this cultural orientation to the separation of sport and politics is not that sport is not mobilized for political purposes but that these political strategies are all driven underground—and often all the more effective because of it. This is the essence of what Ben Carrington (2010, 4) has called "the politics of the apolitical." Though this is relatively easy to spot and analyze in retrospect, actually *doing* such "apolitical politics" is a quite tricky, even dangerous proposition. This goes back to the fact that sport is at its most politically powerful when people are least aware of its political functions—when nothing important or unusual seems to be going on and when the politics are hidden or simply seen as natural and/or organic. The flipside of an ostensibly apolitical cultural arena like sport is that the political mobilization of any sporting practice, personality, or program cannot seem too contrived or strategic; it cannot be—or be seen as—deliberately manipulated or mobilized.[33]

Just as Democrats found themselves trapped in playing the racial code of midnight basketball, they were likewise said and seen to be blurring the necessary and appropriate lines between sport and politics: they were putting sport in politics (where it didn't belong) and, in doing so, cheapening the political process. Politics may be a game of sorts, a field of strategic positioning and maneuvering, in American conception and practice; however, when push comes to shove, at least in the moralistic American imagination, politics is believed, or at least desired, to be serious and rational and upright. And here the whole idea of "play"—playing the race card, playing with the political process—was set against the sanctity, or at least the gravity, of the political process. Perhaps it goes without saying that in recent years the sense that politics is "just a game" played by intellectuals, party hacks, and media elites has contributed to a pervasive dissatisfaction with politicians and the American political system in general. In any case, if the Republicans "won" the midnight basketball debate, they did so not only by exposing the Democrats' implicit racial code, but also by being able to successfully open Democrats to the charge of cheapening or corrupting the political process. Republicans could not only crow that midnight basketball was silly social policy; they could also say that their opponents were being too serious about sport and not serious enough about politics. The Democrats, their opponents charged, literally equated policy with fun and games. In sum, then, if the politics of midnight basketball were deeply structured by the symbolic politics of race, they were also shaped and determined by the tenuous, ambiguous status of serious play in the political culture.

One lesson, of course, is that this was a pretty hard package for progressive forces to mobilize for their own, political purposes. Still, I don't want to sell Republicans short, either for what they were able to accomplish politically or for the understanding of the cultural fault lines they were walking on and playing off of. In retrospect, in fact, it is not surprising that Rush Limbaugh was the figure on the Right who proved so adept in using the popular cultural stereotypes and suspicions about sport and race implicit in midnight basketball as a way to trivialize and call into question all manner of prevention programs. A limited high school football kicker but lifelong sports fan, Limbaugh got his start in radio working for the Kansas City Royals (in promotions) before moving into talk radio. He was thus well practiced in the deployment of both sports and humor for political effect, especially when it came to race.

In a little-known, but important, commentary in a collection of essays on whiteness, the American historian David Roediger (2004) has written about Limbaugh's use of silence, innuendo, implication, and satire—how, without commenting, he has been able to offer comfortable assertions and assumptions about his own position and privilege as a white male. Rush Limbaugh, of course, is a master of such rhetorical high-wire acts—of walking fine lines between cultural commentary and political punditry, innuendo and implication, politics and entertainment, talking about race and pretending to be blind to color. And this is precisely the balancing act of politics and sport he and those who followed him were able to walk with midnight basketball.

But no one is perfect, least of all Limbaugh, and one of the least proud moments of his career may best illustrate the constellation of the cultural forces of race, sport, and politics at work in the case of midnight basketball. In 2003, Limbaugh was fired from his job as an ESPN football commentator for his remarks about Philadelphia Eagles quarterback Donovan McNabb being overrated because he was African American. At one point, I took a break from my midnight basketball research to do a small-scale research paper on this incident (Hartmann 2007). The analysis focused not so much on Limbaugh's comments about race (which I believed then as I believe now spoke for themselves) but on how the mainstream media reacted to those comments. I found that, in the press, Limbaugh was not actually criticized for his racial intent, racial imagery, or racial assumptions. Rather, the pundit-turned-sportscaster was castigated by reporters and pundits (those in the world of sport and outside of it) for introducing race into an arena where it was not supposed to belong, or at least where it was not supposed to be talked about. His comments were seen as too blatant, too bold, too political, and too out of bounds. Sport, the critics held almost uniformly, was supposed to be, on the one hand, color-blind and, on the other, above (or at least separate from) the messy, uncomfortable considerations of race and politics. In criticizing McNabb, Limbaugh stepped over two different lines. He disrupted the otherwise comfortable, taken-for-granted assumptions and norms of whiteness and color blindness in sport, *and* he muddied the purity of sport's sacred play space by introducing "politics"—or, at least, the serious social concerns of race. The "mistakes" that Limbaugh made in the Donovan McNabb episode early in the new millennium, I believe, reveal the success that marked the midnight basketball mobilization in the context of the crime bill.[34]

All of which is to say, there are delicate balancing acts that politicians and pundits perform when they talk about sport and play (and sport, play, and race). No one is really innocent or neutral in this struggle over cultural forms and symbols, at least when it comes to those who attempt to mobilize sporting figures and symbols for political purposes. But what matters is public perception, and the ability to respect both the sanctity of sport and the seriousness of the political process is key. While Democrats may have been aware of some of the basic dangers and risks of playing the race card, my guess is that they—like Limbaugh when he was talking about McNabb—probably had no idea of the larger complexities and complications they were stepping into in advocating for the play of midnight basketball in the context of the crime bill.

Wrapping Up, Moving On

The final outcomes of the symbolic struggles over the meaning and significance of midnight basketball and the politics of race in the context of criminal justice policy were, once again, significant, not to be underestimated. More than $3 billion worth of programming, almost all of it prevention-oriented, was eliminated from American criminal justice policy and programming (Idelson 1994). Debates about midnight basketball—this small, experimental sports-based program—had a decisive, even staggering impact on the federal legislation that governs American criminal justice policy still today. And that criminal justice regime is among the most racially biased and punitive in the industrialized world. If there is another episode in American political history where sport has played such a powerful, it not entirely progressive role, I don't know what it is.

Yet the story of midnight basketball and neoliberal social policy was far from finished with the passage of the crime bill. For my own part, I couldn't help but wonder how things might have turned out if Democrats *hadn't* tried to fund midnight basketball in the context of crime in the first place. Late in 1993 and early in 1994, after all, there had been several different Democratic legislative initiatives working on behalf of midnight basketball. One, led by Congresswoman Patricia Schroeder (CO) and Senator Carol Moseley Braun (IL), was to include midnight basketball in an omnibus education bill—the Goals 2000: Educate America Act—designed to improve high school graduation rates nationwide. Another was initiated by National Resources Committee chair George Miller (CA) and his fellow congressman Bruce Vento (MN) as part of their proposed Urban Recreation and At-Risk Youth Act. When midnight basketball finally found a legislative home in Congress in 1994, it was as part of the Youth Development Block Grant introduced into the House version of the federal crime bill in March. (The original start-up grants for midnight basketball, those ratified in the final months of the first Bush administration, were part of an affordable housing act.)

I knew the most about the former. Moseley Braun, the first-ever African American senator in US history, was a longtime friend of Larry Hawkins and a graduate of his Office of Special Programs, the very program in which I had first worked and learned about sport-based intervention and that had served as a consultant to the Chicago-based program that first brought midnight basketball to the national stage. Indeed, during my time in Chicago, Hawkins and his group were in regular contact and communication with Moseley Braun, working on behalf of funding for youth sports and physical activity programs. I had helped write his congressional testimony on the educational value of sport, an appearance arranged by the senator's staff. That said, I had no idea how the push for youth sport programming and funding got folded into the criminal justice package of 1994.

I don't mean to be too critical here, as I wasn't involved with the decision making that went into shifting proposed support for midnight basketball and sport and recreation initiatives more generally from one domain to the other, and I know very well that special programs and initiatives inevitably must find funding and support as part of omnibus legislative packages (the one that had all the steam and momentum at that decisive point was the one involving crime). But still, I can't, even now, help but think how this all might have turned out differently if midnight basketball hadn't been included in the prevention package, singled out as one of the centerpiece, symbolic provisions of prevention. What if midnight basketball had been folded into legislation on education (as Hawkins would have wanted) or even public parks and recreation (as Minnesota's Bruce Vento would have had it)? Certainly things would have been different for the future of midnight basketball, if not for youth-based sports outreach and sport intervention more broadly conceived. And perhaps situated in a different policy domain, midnight basketball would not have been so completely racialized and thoroughly politicized.

At the same time, it kind of made sense that midnight basketball ended up in the criminal justice bill, the focal point for so much of Clinton's New Democrat politics and policy. Cutting back on social service spending, trying to deal with the problems of the inner city and African American communities, wanting to remain tough on crime, trying not to appear captive to the demands and agendas of the Left (especially of the Congressional Black Caucus) were all simultaneous initiatives for Democrats operating in the context of the politics and pressures of the period and the broader transformations of neoliberal governance and social service. In this context, it seemed almost predestined or preordained or, in more social scientific parlance, "overdetermined" that midnight basketball would end up in a legislative package of that sort. Indeed, it is for these reasons that I have, throughout this chapter, alluded to the larger political context and familiar political dynamics that unfolded across the era.

Of course, the actual outcome and broader impacts were far from what anyone on the Democratic side expected and would have hoped for. Not only was the original version of the crime bill compromised but, as congressional attention shifted from the crime bill to midterm elections back in the fall of 1994, Republicans seemed vindicated and empowered. In fact, it would not be long before the Clinton administration would suffer disastrous, if not unprecedented, off-year losses in the House and the Senate. Shortly thereafter, Newt Gingrich's controversial "Contract with America" would soon be unveiled, and neoliberal social policy would take an even more definitive and draconic turn with the passage of the Personal Responsibility and Work Opportunity Reconciliation Act of 1996 (PRWORA), the landmark welfare reform that replaced Aid to Families with Dependent Children (AFDC) with Temporary Assistance for Needy Families (TANF).

Welfare reform, both in terms of the outcomes that it has yielded and the politics that produced it, has been very widely studied and critiqued in recent years (Soss, Fording, and Schram 2011; Handler 2004; Hays 2003). Hindsight, as they say, is 20/20, and it is always dangerous to speculate too freely about the causal consequence of a single historical event. Nevertheless, it became almost impossible for me not to see how the debates and outcomes of the 1994 crime bill debate prefigured and foreshadowed a great deal of what was to come—the more punitive, carceral tone; the more disciplinary, paternalistic approach; privatization, devolution, and defunding all coming together in a gathering storm. If the 1994 crime bill debates didn't directly determine the direction and final shape of the 1996 welfare reform process, they at least presaged a great deal of what was to come, especially with respect to the (often embedded and unseen) politics of race therein (Cf. Collins and Meyer 2010). And here the memories of midnight basketball continued to haunt. Indeed, the lasting significance of the midnight basketball case was signaled a decade later, in the wake of the 2004 elections. Liberal pundits, ruminating on Republican strategies of the previous decade, repeatedly came back to midnight basketball. "Most memorably," the *New Republic* recalled, "Republicans pounced on funding for so-called 'midnight basketball'—a well-established program once promoted by George H. W. Bush—and cast it as wacky 'social spending' that coddled thugs who probably belonged in jail" (January 24, 2005).

As these developments rocked the worlds of politics and public policy, their implications were similarly seismic, if even more concrete and close to home, in the world of sport, social intervention through sport, and youth sport provision. The 1994 crime bill debates marked a decisive moment, a key turning point, for midnight basketball programs themselves, not to mention that whole class of sport-based crime prevention and social intervention programs that Pitter and Andrews called the "social problems industry" in sport. It is to that chapter of the story I turn to next.

SIX

Remodeling Sport-Based Prevention

Once the drama and political theater of the crime bill debates had played out, midnight basketball soon slipped off the media radar and out of the public eye. After the usual postmortems and political postgame commentaries (including those where Democrats self-righteously if unselfconsciously accused Republicans of playing the race card with midnight basketball), talk of midnight basketball faded into the background. Policy providers got on with the business of building prisons and revamping criminal justice programs, and legislators moved on to other policy arenas and priorities. Never again would late-night basketball—or any sports-based intervention program, for that matter—occupy the American imagination the way that it did in the early part of the last decade of the twentieth century.

The fact that most pundits, policy makers, and media members (not to mention the public at large) forgot about midnight basketball doesn't mean that basketball-based programming disappeared. It didn't, not by any stretch. By the middle of the 1990s, midnight basketball initiatives were, after all, fully functioning operations with established facilities, supportive constituencies, and (most of all) funding streams that predated congressional debate and federal legislation. And other youth and sport program operators were just beginning to figure out how to adopt and adapt elements of the midnight basketball model into their own programs and initiatives. But it was far from business as usual for midnight basketball operators and advocates. While midnight basketball (and the whole social problems industry in urban sport programming) may have survived all the political scrutiny and upheaval, folks in and around these now well-established programs felt the aftereffects of the crime bill attacks acutely. Indeed, the mid-1990s were the beginning of a new phase in the history of midnight basketball and a whole new chapter in the story of sport as social intervention and risk prevention.

Since I was in graduate school working on other research and projects at the time, I didn't have any direct, inside contact with midnight basketball program operators in the immediate wake of the crime bill controversy. However, people working in the field that I stayed in touch with told me how operators and administrators were stunned to discover the opposition midnight basketball encountered and how negatively they and their programs were perceived and portrayed in the media and public sphere. Particularly vivid in my recollection and notes are the reports that I got from Hugh "Bud" Mehan, the sociologist who was my erstwhile collaborator and mentor in Southern California. Mehan told me about an extended, emotional conversation he had with the leader of the High Five America group who ran the San Diego affiliate. Near the end of the summer, the director, Rle Nichols, put in several phone calls to Mehan, with whom, if my notes are accurate and memory correct, he didn't have more than a passing connection previously. Nichols and his staff hadn't expected nor really wanted public funding, but they had believed that they were heeding the call of the compassionate wing of the Republican Party. In Mehan's description, they were "blindsided," "demoralized," and "dumbstruck." "How," Nichols kept asking Mehan, "did this happen? How could they do this to us?" According to Mehan, Nichols and his staff were so stunned and dismayed they were almost unable to fathom or process what had happened or know how to respond. In fact, it was this confusion and frustration that led to Mehan and Nichols developing the evaluation and documentary projects that would be my first extensive, on-the-ground experience with a midnight basketball program.

Several years later, my archival research and subsequent interviews with other national and local program leaders confirmed that Nichols's reaction was not an uncommon one. Many of the informants my research assistants and I talked to also wanted to assure us that they "never received a dime" of the proposed federal money. (My own subsequent research into crime bill earmarks and expenditures confirmed that this was almost certainly the case.) But the loss of potential federal funding was perhaps the least of the problems created by the brouhaha over the crime bill. What affected midnight basketball programs even more directly and dramatically was the new skepticism and even stigma that surrounded midnight basketball and sport-based intervention more generally. This negativity was explained by Stan Hebert, director of the national midnight basketball association: "We took a real big hit when our name got caught up in the crime bill debate. People got the impression [that midnight basketball] was a government program . . . that it was a waste of money to support the program, that the people participating must be criminals" (*St. Louis Post Dispatch*, March 5, 1997).

Suffice it to say, these developments posed a huge challenge and major obstacles for midnight basketball and the entire social problems movement in sport taken as a whole. But midnight basketball organizers and operators—like so many people in the world of sport—were nothing if not resilient. They didn't give up or complain. They didn't go away, nor did they move on to something else. Rather, they turned their collective energies toward figuring out how to maintain, revitalize, and reestablish the basketball-based programs they had built up and so deeply believed in. What we are talking about is a kind of collective makeover or restart—or, in the vernacular of the construction trades, a remodeling project—driven by the contingencies and demands of the aftermath of the crime bill debates.

Like so many remodeling projects, the remaking of midnight basketball didn't happen over night, and it wasn't centrally organized or deliberately and systematically planned. (Recall that many of the programs were knock-offs, and that even the national association was really only just an informal, franchise system.) But over the course of the next three, four, maybe five years, midnight basketball organizers, working individually or loosely together in different sites all over the country, produced a tighter, more sophisticated understanding of how sport could and should be directed toward the ends of risk prevention and social intervention. This new, more developed approach was based in a more sharply formulated understanding of the problems of young men of color in urban environments and the resources available within the parameters of the emerging neoliberal social services system. It contained a less idealistic, more pragmatic vision of sport as a tool for intervention and change as well as a new emphasis on nonsport programming and programmatic connections to other, related organizations, initiatives, and resources. And perhaps most significant of all: this revised, revitalized model not only secured a future for midnight basketball; it helped chart the course for a new generation of sport-based, youth outreach and intervention initiatives in the United States and indeed all over the world. It is a generation of programs that in some respects holds closer than ever to the ideological tenets and institutional structures of neoliberal paternalism, even as sport activists and engaged scholars have tried to point out these limitations and advocate for alternative approaches.

The New Midnight Model

One of the keys to running a good, effective social program (one of the keys to doing anything well, actually) is having a clear sense of what you are trying to accomplish and what is not possible within the purview and parameters of your resources, capabilities, and goals. Such clarity of focus, as I stressed in the first chapters of this book, was not a strength of the original midnight basketball model. Although the basic programmatic features were simple and straightforward (Standifer's original program, recall, had only three explicit components or requirements: the age of the target population, the time of day of the programming, and a police presence), the earliest midnight basketball programs were marked and defined by a multifaceted, uneven, and often mixed set of images, ideas, and ideals about risk, race, and (especially) the social value of sport. While this broad, eclectic mix may have helped cultivate midnight basketball's original appeal and wide-ranging popularity, this ambiguity also created a number of problems with respect to both implementation and effectiveness in its actual service and programming (not to mention exposing it to the political controversies described in the previous chapter).

In the wake of the crime bill debacle, a clearer, more focused vision of and model for midnight basketball began to take shape. The new, remodeled edition had at least three new elements or points of emphasis. One was a sharpened focus on risk prevention and social intervention for youth and young men of color, and a concomitant de-emphasis on physical containment, public safety, and crime control. Second was the creation and implementation of a much broader, more structured range of nonsport programming, and third were more explicit and extensive connections to the programs, activities, and resources of other agencies, organizations, and initiatives working with disadvantaged communities in the inner-city. To one degree or another, I saw each of these innovations in all the various basketball-based programs that I observed and studied in San Diego and Minneapolis in the 1990s and into the new millennium; however, they were probably most well represented by and embodied in the program affiliate based in Oakland, California.

The Bay Area program, under the direction of Eric Standifer, had become a focal point for the national association in the wake of his father's unfortunate passing in 1992, as I mentioned earlier.[1] Following the crime bill fallout in the middle part of the decade, the Oakland affiliate crafted a program statement that was considerably more elaborate and developed than the one initially offered by the senior Standifer just a few years before.

> Oakland Midnight Basketball fills a void in community based programs focusing on the needs and issues affecting Oakland's "at-risk/underserved" young adults, particularly young men. . . . . Basketball is merely one of several program components, serving as the "hook" that attracts young adults to the program. Other

components include community outreach, information/referrals, case management and client advocacy, mentoring, education (including mandatory pregame workshops), and leadership development. . . . Program services are also extended to the children/families of participants, as well as the hundreds of spectators that attend OMB games and events (primarily more young adults). The program (including services provided) is free for participants.[2]

This quote (just the first paragraph of a thorough, well thought-out mission statement) captured and conveyed not only a more elaborate vision but a clearer, much more streamlined focus and rationale for the program. In other words, it reflected some real changes in philosophy, focus, and program emphasis.

Perhaps most notably and fundamentally, midnight basketball was no longer framed as a crime control program (imposed on the target population and surrounding neighborhood for the broader purposes of maintaining social order and public safety), but instead was now presented as a "community based program" whose goal was to serve the "needs and issues affecting . . . 'at-risk/underserved' young adults, particularly young men." This de-emphasis on crime control brought midnight basketball more in line with the preventionist advocates who had emerged as midnight basketball's biggest supporters and advocates at the national level during the crime bill debates, political figures such as Carol Moseley Braun, Patricia Schroeder, Charles Schumer, and President Clinton himself as well as (and perhaps most importantly) Nancy Pelosi, the Bay Area representative who would become Speaker of the House. Perhaps not surprisingly, midnight basketball programs and affiliates from the latter part of the 1990s onward also came to be far more overtly and consistently part of liberal Democratic political programs and politics. Harlem's midnight basketball program, for example, made a big deal of showing off photographs of former Democratic governor (and one-time presidential candidate) Mario Cuomo and pop star Queen Latifah appearing together for the program's opening night. (Cuomo, in fact, threw up the ceremonial tip-off.) Midnight basketball came to be championed by African American mayors in cities throughout the Midwest (in Kansas City, for example, Democratic mayor Emanuel Cleaver was described by *Sports Illustrated* on August 19, 1996, as "one of the most evangelical proponents of midnight hoops"), and Senator Paul Simon—who himself made an unsuccessful run for the presidency at one point—took up the mantel in Illinois (*Christian Century*, November 9, 1994).

This clearer, more specified rationale may have been driven to a certain extent by the exigencies of funding and post–crime bill political patronage, but it also reflected a shift away from the harder-core, more punitive and controlling elements of crime prevention toward the softer, more disciplinary and interventionist impulses of the innovation. The language of risk and risk prevention was typically retained in the Oakland program documents and practices. However, prevention in this new context came to refer not to the direct control of young people and reduction of crime and criminal activity but rather to intervention against the preconditions and factors, both individual and social, that were believed to lead to crime, deviance, and delinquency as well as to reforming and resocializing young men in the program. It also reflected a more sympathetic and sociologically nuanced understanding of the problems faced by young black men in the inner city as well as the ways in which sport could be mobilized to address these problems. In terms of the general social issues of race and risk involved, midnight basketball advocates and practitioners like those in Oakland now realized that crime and criminal justice were not the strength of their programmatic emphasis and initiative, and that, even if they had wanted it to be that way, these programs weren't large enough or comprehensive enough to contain or control young African American men in any case. Rather than trying to counter or change this, the new generation of midnight basketball advocates and administrators simply downplayed or even jettisoned the more hard-core, muscular penal elements of the initiative (for sure, in rhetoric if not in planning and practice—after all, some of it was still built in) in favor of the more proactive, "progressive" intervention-and-change aspects of the program now (or then) encapsulated under the general heading of prevention. It was this feature that brought midnight basketball more squarely in line with neoliberal paternalism as described by Soss, Fording, and Schram (2011).

Here also it is worth pointing out that while the racial specificity of the program's focus and appeal was typically still downplayed, the emphasis on gender, or more specifically on men and young men, was often accentuated. Connecting men with and serving the needs of their children and families was really a point of emphasis in Oakland. Midnight basketball was supposed to "strengthen the lives of OMB participants and their families." Indeed, a parenthetical note in the summary explained that the focus was on men because "social service programs and efforts have traditionally focused on women [and] children."

Finally, added to this new, more proactive, community-based approach was an emphasis on a whole host of nonsport, interventionist program activities and components: education and job training, for example, or resocialization such as through anger management, character building, or conflict resolution (with actual programs and structured, independent events planned). In the Oakland program and indeed the vast majority of other midnight basketball programs of the period, these were operationalized in a series of mandatory workshops that were to take place prior to games. These sessions included topics ranging from employment and educational opportunities to personal development (specified as goal setting, anger management, etc.), health, and civic responsibility. Delivered by "subject-expert facilitators," workshops were offered for "prenatal and other health care information, testing, and consultation" and "male involvement and responsibility in pregnancy and parenting"; a series of confidential surveys about "personal health history, health awareness, and health-related practices" were also conducted. Just as Soss and his colleagues described for paternalistic neoliberalism, the goal was to help these young men by teaching them to govern themselves.

A new strategy for gathering resources was also at play in the Oakland program. Connected with the belief that extensive new resources were required to deal with the multifaceted and deeply embedded problems of African American youth and young men, midnight basketball organizers came to realize that real, meaningful intervention had to be done in collaboration with a whole range of agencies, organizations, and programs. Midnight basketball, as the Oakland team described it, would "serve as a bridge between Oakland young adults and the community," "connect/re-connect young adults with the community and its resources," help "foster/develop better relations and understanding between the community and OMB participants," and "bring all aspects of community together." It was described quite accurately and appropriately as a "collaborative strategy": "Rather than duplicate [the array of organizations and services] that already exists, one of OMB's primary outreach functions is to provide linkages to community resources that can assist participants with employment training, parenting health issues, etc. . . . OMB has and maintains an extensive network of community partners and service providers that help OMB achieve its goals." In this new vision, midnight basketball was best understood not as a primary server and self-sustained, self-sufficient, totalizing solution but as a conduit or connector.

Like many in this era, the Oakland program trumpeted a long and venerable list of organizations described as "community partners." Workshops on health, for example, were conducted in collaboration with the Oakland Healthy Start programs; other events involved representatives from voter registration drives, HIV/AIDS administration, probation, family support, school districts, and the NBA's Golden State Warriors. So in this sense, midnight basketball was moving toward broader, neoliberal models not only in terms of ideology but also in terms of the institutionalization of cross-sector, networked partnerships and collaborations. Key here is the paradoxical recognition of the need for real, material resources, on the one hand, and the fact that few new resources were really available, on the other. Midnight basketball's remodelers were not trying to contest or change these limited institutional parameters; they were trying to work within them by doing a better job of pooling and coordinating the resources and programs that were already in place.

Embedded in all these new understandings and programmatic adjustments, finally, was a more focused, more pragmatic or instrumentalist vision of sport and its role in social intervention than had existed previously. It was a vision of sport as a tool for outreach and recruitment, the starting point of a much broader range and array of essentially nonsport programming, nothing more, nothing less. Although not always fully articulated in Oakland (or elsewhere), this new vision and understanding of sport was reflected in the choices program operators were making. In contrast to some other sport-based social outreach initiatives, midnight basketball operators were now less obsessed with high-profile, media-friendly events or all-star games. They were de-emphasizing training high-end athletic talent and getting scholarships or building skills for aspiring, midlevel athletes. They were also beginning to realize that midnight basketball was not about drawing big crowds or having grand-level community effects. Rather, program operators began to see the goal more in terms of using sport to provide intensive resources and to build relationships with otherwise marginalized, disaffected young men. This was not the traditional, idealized vision of sport as an arena for character building, individual development, and social mobility. Basketball, in the emerging new framework captured in the Oakland program, was now described and understood as "the 'hook' that attracts young adults to the program." This was a vision and focus that emphasized direct, individual-level interventions and effects—what athletic participation is supposed to do for youth and young adults, how it is believed to affect, challenge, and change them.

Sport-Based Intervention into the New Millennium

While the publicity and controversy brought by the crime bill presented numerous challenges for midnight basketball operations in the political arena, it actually appears to have been a boon for its visibility and influence within the world of sport-based programming oriented toward intervention, prevention, and change more generally. As I alluded to earlier, the 1990s marked an explosion in the number and variety of sport-based, intervention-oriented programs all across the United States. Programs were springing up all over the social service landscape. They ranged from small, single-sport programs located in schools or operated at community centers to citywide, multisport summertime projects run by sport experts at Olympic training centers or sports foundations, from revitalized Police Athletic Leagues to prison boot camps (Pitter and Andrews 1997; see also Cameron and MacDougall 2000; Nichols 2010). And many observers and analysts concluded that the rise of sport-based and athletically oriented intervention and programs was in no small measure due to the prominence of midnight basketball. Standifer's innovation was a catalyst, an advertisement and disseminator for that whole set of programs in the problem industry. The impact of midnight basketball's crime bill moment is suggested by the fact that eight of the nineteen programs highlighted in the 1994 National Recreation and Park Association's report "Beyond 'Fun and Games'" (Tindall 1995) listed crime prevention and public safety as a "major emphasis," and it was "risk prevention" that researchers chose as the focal point of the evaluations and assessments the organization was going to launch around the initiatives (Witt and Crompton 1996a). Similarly, when Pitter and Andrews (1997) wrote about the emerging new social problems industry in youth sport provision, the core of their focus was on the twenty-six programs in thirty different metropolitan areas that "provide sport activities as a means of reducing crime and promoting public safety" (89).

This new wave of social problems–oriented, youth sport programming was not predicated precisely on the midnight model, old or new. In the wake of the 1994 crime bill debates, there was some effort to use time effectively and keep kids "off the streets" and "out of trouble"; however, other terms and approaches were beginning to push those out, in favor of more traditional, paternalistic objectives of enrichment, education, and character building—or, in a word, "development." This new generation of programs was not only less punitive and physically controlling. It also tended to use other sports, to be oriented toward a wider range of backgrounds (girls and young women as well as boys and young men, different minority populations, and those who were economically or otherwise disadvantaged), and (perhaps most of all) to be aimed at youth and young boys and girls at earlier and earlier ages.

These shifts were actually signaled or anticipated during the crime bill debates when New York City mayor Rudy Giuliani, among others, went out of his way to lobby on behalf of the community-based prevention components of the crime bill package associated with midnight basketball. In one of his first forays onto the national political scene, Giuliani, as a Republican, tried to pitch and promote himself as a moderate, civic-minded leader dedicated to core republican values but with an interest and commitment to urban issues and solutions. In his nationally syndicated op-ed, "Why I Support the Crime Bill," published August 18, 1994, he approved of money for prisons and police but also insisted that more funding for prevention was appropriate and essential. And in advocating for additional prevention-oriented programming, he insisted on the need to "change the 'Midnight Sports Program' . . . so that cities can determine the types of sports program they want and not be required to have a nighttime program." Concluding that "the important thing is to provide young people with healthy, safe, supervised recreation," Giuliani suggested as possible models and alternatives keeping schools open in the evening as well as more youth academies outside their communities.

Giuliani was, of course, on the losing side of this debate when it came to warding off the cuts to prevention programming in the crime bill. But he was more successful in helping set the stage for the expansion of after-school programs and other related outreach efforts and program initiatives.

Although the rise of after-school intervention programs goes well beyond the bounds of our basic midnight basketball narrative, it is useful to summarize the broad parameters. It started in 1994 with the crime bill itself, which allocated $26 million to the Department of Health and Human Services for such programs, and authorized over $500 million for such programming from 1995 to 2000. And the concept of sports-oriented programs directed toward teenagers and even middle schoolers really took off in the years that followed. For example, funding for after-school programs through the US Department of Education (just one of the agencies with an after-school agenda) started at $40 million in 1998 and jumped to $846 million in 2001—when the department had 1,000 "high quality proposals" for such programs that it was unable to fund in the last grant cycle. By the end of the decade, after-school programs and related youth-oriented, community-based initiatives came to occupy the pragmatic, centrist middle for sports-oriented, social interventionist programming that Giuliani was arguing for (and that midnight basketball had once occupied).

There are several points about this new class of sport-based youth intervention programs and their relation to midnight basketball that are worth highlighting. One has to do with the rationale for such initiatives with respect to social intervention and prevention. On the one hand, after-school programs, like midnight basketball in the post–crime bill era, retained a certain emphasis on the reduction of violence and delinquency among urban

American youth; however, even more than midnight basketball, they did so
with a better, more realistic understanding of the scope and complexity of
the social problems that they were up against. As one very prominent advocate explained: "Without structured, supervised activities in the after-school
hours, youth are at greater risk of being victims of crime, or participating
in anti-social behaviors. In fact, juveniles are at the highest risk of being a
victim of violence between 2 p.m. and 6 p.m. And the peak hour for juvenile crime is from 3 p.m. to 4 p.m., the first hour that most students are
dismissed from school."[3]

Notions of "risk" and "risk prevention" continued to appear in this
context—notions that retained familiar and unsettling racial overtones—but
their meaning and policy implications shifted as well. They were beginning
to have more to do with the prevention of risky health behaviors or the fiscal liability that came with offering physical activity in supervised settings;
indeed, it wouldn't be long before risk and risk prevention in youth sports
was all about insurance liabilities and not anything resembling risk prevention in the sense of public safety or human development, which midnight
basketball was focused on. Connected with and extending from this was a
renewed emphasis on sport's importance with respect to health, fitness, and
well-being. Here it was not the paternalistic character-building or developmental aspects of sports participation that were emphasized but its physical
qualities and characteristics, and its potential ability to contribute to positive health, on the one hand, and to campaigns against obesity, drug use,
smoking, and other physically unhealthy behaviors, on the other. Indeed,
in this context the whole language of risk and risk prevention came to reference health, safety, and liability concerns—so much so that the whole emphasis on crime prevention from the midnight basketball period would be
completely absent within less than ten years, displaced entirely by concerns
about physical health and well-being (and risks therein) associated with all
manner of sport and physical activity (see Giulianotti 2009).

A third and final point has to do with the political and policy context I
alluded to previously. After-school programs were situated in the centrist,
nonpartisan cultural-political policy space that midnight basketball had
occupied in the early 1990s, prior to the radical disruption of the 1994
crime bill debate. President Clinton endorsed after-school programs in his
2000 State of the Union Address: "Let's double our investment in after-
school and summer school programs which boost achievement and keep
people off the streets and out of trouble." In support, the administration
proposed to expand the 21st Century Community Learning Center Program
by $1 billion dollars (it then had about $400 million in funding). When

he was running for governor in Texas, George W. Bush proposed spending $25 million to provide after-school programs in the state; as nominee for president, he called for a greater federal role in and support of such "youth programs." In fact, his wife, Laura Bush, made the public campaign for after-school programs one of her top priorities early in her tenure as First Lady. And as we would expect, this bipartisan support signaled that these initiatives were still contained within the fiscal and programmatic limits of neoliberalism—limited funding, tendencies toward paternalism and control, little attention to the larger structural problems of inadequate schooling, limited work opportunities, and persistent (if subtle) prejudice and discrimination.

I am not trying to suggest that this new constellation of sport-based youth intervention programming was ideal. Far from it. These initiatives were often uneven and underdeveloped in terms of the ideas that inspired and informed them. Some were more ideological and stereotyping than others, and others were little more than rationalizations for otherwise underfunded youth activities and sports leagues. Even the best of them didn't really bring new resources or support in to these communities and the problems they faced, thus limiting their larger impact, while at the same time making it easier for officials and the public to believe that there was a significant commitment to intervention and change and that meaningful change was underway. I will come back to these problems eventually. But before I do, there is another aspect of the story of midnight basketball proper that needs to be developed. It has to do with the peculiar fact that even as midnight basketball was receding in its visibility and significance stateside, the initiative was growing in popularity on the international level. Ironically, just as the idea of sport as social intervention and risk prevention was being adapted and remade in the domestic context, the midnight basketball model was taking on a whole new life in countries and cultures in other parts of the world.

Going Global[4]

One year after the 1994 crime bill debates, the first midnight basketball program outside of the United States was launched in Cologne, Germany. The German program was inspired by the idea of counteracting negative activities and "boredom" with a fun "leisure offer" that would serve as an "alternative to the nocturnal adventure" when "there are otherwise no alternative possibilities for youth" (Savic 2003). It was, according to observers, a historic move because Germany had never before offered any type of juvenile welfare service through athletics. (Organized, typically, on more of a club

model, European youth sport programs have never had the same relationship to social programs and schools as in the United States.) Within the
year, a similar initiative was established in Hamburg, and officials from other
European nations began to take notice, visiting the German programs and
laying out plans for initiatives of their own. Policy makers and program operators in England were particularly motivated. By August 2001, the National
Playing Fields Association (NPFA) in Great Britain reported that there were
twenty-five midnight basketball programs across the country, funded primarily (if not exclusively) by charitable donations (NPFA 2001). In a few short
years, there were dozens of copycat programs in countries ranging from Switzerland to Australia. A closer consideration of these programs (I will focus on
programs in four countries where the initiatives were most prominent: Germany, Switzerland, Great Britain, and Australia) reminds us of the powerful
appeal and potential impact of the general midnight basketball concept,
demonstrates the power of publicity and diffusion as well as the elasticity
of the concept, and foreshadows new directions and emphases for neoliberal, sport-based intervention and risk prevention in the new millennium.

One of the most basic similarities or parallels between international
programs and the American model had to do with sources of funding and
administrative structure and oversight. Borrowing heavily from the neoliberal American template described in chapter 3, international midnight
basketball programs were typically public-private partnerships that pieced
together resources from a hodgepodge of otherwise underfunded sources.
In Great Britain, for example, while the NPFA's patron was formally and officially the Queen of England, private organizations and corporate sponsors
provided the bulk of the funding. The pharmaceutical giant, GlaxoSmith-
Kline, for example, sponsored a November 2001 tournament, while Boots
Charitable Trust and the Mansfield Development Group, two independent
charitable organizations, were credited with supporting nineteen programs
and 492 participants in or near Mansfield, Nottinghamshire. In Germany
and Australia, it appears that there was a fairly even split of funding between
governmental agencies and private organizations. The only country where
substantial support appears to have come from governmental sources was
Switzerland—50,000 Swiss francs per year—though even this was matched by
contributions from various community groups, churches, and other private
organizations.

As in the United States, such programs were generally established in communities with high crime rates, large percentages of poor, disadvantaged
populations, and youth and young people who were often racial or ethnic
minorities (Aborginals in Australia, for example, or "new" immigrants in

Switzerland or Germany). But this was not always the case. The affiliate in Mansfield, Nottinghamshire—England's first late-night program—had high rates of crime and social unrest (sixth-worst place to live in England, only 39 percent of people felt safe) but was primarily targeted to white and poor youth. Also, many of these programs used sports other than basketball. Soccer and volleyball were popular. The Swiss program did not have formally organized teams or leagues but was more of an open-gym model that featured workshops and activities usually targeted toward younger, supposedly more malleable populations than had been targeted by midnight basketball in the United States. Here, however, it is also important to realize that this was not substantial new funding for social programs or interventions. Even in the international context, late-night sports was still, for the most part, very much like the original midnight basketball programs in the United States: social programming on the cheap, a way to reach out to certain populations or deal with certain problems that was innovative and intriguing mainly because of the limited financial commitment and institutional support there was elsewhere in the neoliberal social welfare system.

Of course, the sporting context and frame was a large part of what made these otherwise limited innovations promising and appealing. The international variations on the midnight basketball theme offered many of the usual allusions to traditional sports idealism. In his analysis of German midnight basketball programs, for example, Enes Savic (2003) stated that German officials initially started the program because of the "large participation of the youth and the statistic decrease of the criminal offenses" boasted by the American programs, but he argued that sport in general "has the function to repair and adjust negative results and a lack of insufficient socialization." He added, "Sporty activities [help] a group to learn to act and react." Elsa Davies, the first director of the NPFA, insisted that that midnight basketball "puts life into the idea of regeneration through recreation," adding that "young people are often criticized these days but Midnight Basketball seems to bring out the best in them" (NPFA 2001). Researchers from the Fachhochschule Nordwestschweiz Hochschule für Soziale Arbeit, a Swiss University, who did a report on midnight basketball in Switzerland explained in an e-mail exchange: "The young people look for an activity that is fun on one hand and on the other hand an activity that fulfills the need for affiliation and social acknowledgment." The Swiss scholars believed that basketball can offer both because "sports are naturally fun . . . [and] because basketball can already obtain the feeling of affiliation to a group, sports achievements is an important source of social acknowledgment" (cf. Sommerfeld et al. 2006).

As they got established, most of these programs began to develop and incorporate more extensive nonsport programming in variations of the sport-as-hook or sport-plus models that were beginning to become established at the time. The English model, for example, had as its motto "No Workshop, No Jumpshot." And the emphasis in nonsport programming was typically framed around goals of development and social integration. In an interview, Robert Schmuki, project manager of Midnight Basketball Switzerland told us, "Sport is just a vehicle of socialization." What was also clear was that the international programs left behind the original American emphasis on sport as a form of containment and control.

That said, if these leagues were not predicated primarily on the punitive, police-and-control model, many still required and incorporated some kind of criminal justice or law enforcement presence. But the involvement and participation of criminal justice officials was actually perhaps the most important area of contrast between the American model and the international variations.

In Germany, for example, it was not the usual police department but the juvenile justice department that was involved. In Australia as well, local police were joined by juvenile justice departments who helped determine and locate the "at-risk" youth that the program could serve. Midnight Basketball Australia's "Project Overview" states: "Those youth who are most at-risk can be targeted with the assistance of the Police Youth Liaison Officer" (Midnight Basketball Australia Ltd. 2007, 2). Both also ran and participated in the workshops and coordination of the entire program. In Britain, the local police not only supervised the programs but also played a big role in running them and setting them up by participating in the steering committee, helping to provide a "safe and structured environment" for the participants, and being present at events (BBC 1999). In Zurich, like Britain, the local city police came and supervised the program. They also made recommendations and "cooperate[d] in the participation in the meetings" (Midnight Basketball Zürich 2007). Christoph Meier, project manager of the midnight basketball program in Zurich, noted that "cooperation with the police is important for the project." He added that this police involvement helps "the young people become acquainted with the policemen in a new and good kind of way" (pers. comm., January 15, 2007). Savic (2003) spoke of the same cooperation with police in Germany, calling it "a cross-linking of different ranges [with] school, parents, youth, and police" that is necessary to the success and order of the programs. In Germany, local police thus played a multifaceted role, helping with supervision and providing input for improvement in the program while working with other administrators and participants to implement the program.

The sort of law enforcement/criminal justice involvement we found in these international programs is important as it highlights a certain emphasis on social control, but it tended to be used and understood less in the original American conception of security and safety. Instead it played a big role in helping to organize and run the programs, in a way more akin to the Police Athletic Leagues many Americans are familiar with on a community-based policing model.

There are several analytic angles about the surprising global diffusion of the midnight basketball concept to highlight. One of those is the power, resilience, and flexibility of the neoliberal restructuring of sport-based risk prevention and social intervention—the power of the broad organizational and funding structure that has emerged as well as the wide range of approaches and ideologies it could actually accommodate—an innovation that seemed fairly restrictive and focused in terms of population, vision, and goals. This emphasis seemed especially pronounced and profound for us in the context of the divergent path that the American model itself had assumed in the post–crime bill era.

In another paper, written with comparative education specialist Christina Kwauk (Hartmann and Kwauk 2011), I argue that all manner of sport-based development programming in the international context bears the same tensions and contradictions exhibited in the midnight basketball model: the tension between outreach and intervention; between sport-focused programming and non-sport-oriented social goals and objectives; and between romanticized ideals about sport as an automatically positive social force and the complicated realities of actual intervention and change. And what is missing from many such programs on the ground, in actual practice, is a more radical, transformative vision frequently associated with critical pedagogy that idealists often want to believe sport-based development can bring.

But one thing that remained compelling and consistent in the international versions of the midnight basketball model was the racial character, content, and overlay of the original American conception. I have already mentioned the social composition of international programs: while not specifically aimed at blacks, they almost always were targeted toward racial or cultural minorities and certainly to populations that were perceived as socially marginal or disadvantaged. This is obviously important and significant in itself, revealing once again the ways in which so many ideas about sport and social intervention for youth are racially informed and structured. But race came into play in international midnight basketball programs in one other, somewhat unexpected and particularly American way as well, and it brings us back to the popular and widely known cultural connections between basketball and blackness.

Basketball, it turns out, was used in many locales even where the sport wasn't necessarily a particularly popular participatory activity in that area or among that population. This was not because it was directly, immediately popular with the local youth but, rather, because of the appeal of basketball as African American culture—or, in other words, the worldwide appeal of blackness through basketball. "From the beginning of this project, it was very good to play only basketball. . . . It was very popular, the style of hip-hop and graffiti, and breakdance and basketball" (C. Meier, pers. comm., January 15, 2007). Savic reported a similar appeal in Germany, saying that the "spirit of the time can be characterized as orientation to the 'ghetto culture' of [the] black American, who is determined among other things by Streetball, Hip Hop, and XXL clothes" (2003). In view of this, the Swiss program explicitly added hip-hop music and dance into its programming. Among other contributions, this allowed "young people who would not like to play sports," to be "DJs playing music at the events" (C. Meier, pers. comm., January 15, 2007).

Talk about the construction and reproduction of racial images and ideas through sport (not to mention the ironies of midnight basketball as a social force)! This peculiar and apparently widely held fascination with basketball and blackness signals, once again, the structuring power of race itself in neo-liberal social governance, and in particular the prominence and structuring power of American blackness as a cultural form. It is just one data point to be sure—but one that puts the power of race in social policy and the global cultural imagination on full, discomforting display.

Retheorizing Sport as Prevention

If the late 1990s and early 2000s marked the appearance and proliferation of a large if rather unwieldy range of new programs utilizing youth sport for the purposes of risk prevention and social intervention in the United States and many other parts of the world, this period also witnessed a burgeoning body of research and writing on these problems-based programs. Some of this research was on specific sport-and-recreation-oriented programs like midnight basketball (Hartmann 2001), boot camps (Correira 1997), or drop-in centers (B. Wilson and White 2001), and others focused on the assessment of particular local programs (Martinek and Hellison 1997). But much of it was very broad and oriented toward specifying and theoretically unpacking the structure, operation, and utility of these sport-based social interventions, especially those related to risk prevention and crime control (Nichols 1997; Nichols and Crow 2004; Hartmann 2003; Cameron and MacDougall 2000; Coakley 2011, 2002; Danish and Nellen 1997; Witt and Crompton 1997; Spaaij 2009a, 2009b; L. Kelly 2013, 2011; Miller et al. 2007). Some of the main principles and primary insights that come out of this body of scholarship include (1) recognizing and accepting the limitations—both practical and political—of sport-based programming intended for the systematic physical containment and control of any population; (2) understanding that much of the power and potential of sport as a means for intervention is embedded in its effectiveness as a tool for outreach, recruitment, and retention of individual participants; (3) realizing the importance of nonsport programming and organizational collaborations in any sport-based program; and (4) acknowledging the imposing scope, scale, and complexity of any policy interventions of this sort.

While this chapter is not the place for a full exposition of these points, I want to highlight how the development of midnight basketball research and programming served to illustrate, illuminate, and extend these theories and this way of thinking. After all, this is a body of work that not only informs my analysis of midnight basketball in this book, but it has helped scholars, program operators, and policy makers today better understand the opportunities and limitations of sport-and-recreation-based social programming oriented toward risk prevention and social intervention (see, for discussions, Hartmann 2015, 2012b; Hartmann and Kwauk 2011).[5]

Helping to specify and clarify program objectives is one important contribution. The justifications offered by some midnight basketball supporters early on involved sport activities as a matter of physical containment, surveillance, and control. The idea, again, was that as long as participants were involved in some controlled physical activity, they would be in a controlled environment where they would not be able to engage in crime or delinquency, and they would have an outlet for their energies and any risk-oriented proclivities. For the political reasons we saw above (as well as the pragmatic fact that these programs simply weren't extensive enough to provide this level of social containment and control), midnight basketball organizers and proponents soon realized that this emphasis was neither practically feasible nor politically viable and thus shifted to a less punitive, more intervention- and prevention-oriented emphasis and approach. As the 1990s gave way to the new millennium, the emphasis in the literature moved away from crime control or even risk prevention and came to focus more on development; this theoretical shift also brought scaled-back, more realistic aspirations, expectations, and claims about the purported impacts of sport-based programming, focused almost entirely on individual-level interventions (see Coakley 2011).

Probably the most basic and most important point about the prevention-oriented youth sports programs that sport researchers and theorists have realized in reflecting back on the past twenty years of program development regards the thing that every social program must necessarily begin with: outreach and recruitment (Sandford, Armour, and Warmington 2006; Leviton and Schuh 1991). Not only are outreach and recruitment the first concern of any social policy initiative (you can't have a social program without participants); these are the areas in which all sports-based crime prevention initiatives had been able to clearly document their effectiveness and success (see Witt and Crompton 1996a).

The unique ability to recruit and retain otherwise hard-to-reach populations was true for all the various midnight basketball programs I have studied or with which I have been otherwise associated. Consider the case of a basketball-based program I worked with in Minneapolis, Minnesota, in the late 1990s called Stay Alive. I initiated research with Stay Alive with the idea of using the program as a model to assess (and hopefully document) the effectiveness of basketball-based programs. My attempts in this general project were rather unsuccessful (see the next chapter). Nevertheless, the one area that was an exception to these failures and disappointments was the Stay Alive league's ability to reach out to and recruit the otherwise hard-to-reach target population of Native American and African American men aged eighteen to twenty-five.

In 1999, the first year for which we had full data, the Stay Alive program served some 256 players. Of these, 75 percent had a residence in the city of Minneapolis proper, 60 percent were African American, and 28 percent were Native American. (The rest claimed a white, Hispanic, or "multiracial" ethnicity.) The majority (i.e., 57 percent) of participants were within the program's seventeen- to thirty-year-old target range. These numbers were a bit lower than program administrators had hoped but were explained by the presence of several teams of fifteen- and sixteen-year-olds who had entered the league in hopes of finding older, more physically mature, and experienced competition. Perhaps more important and far more positive, at least 45 percent of participants eighteen or older in the league had criminal history records with the Minneapolis Police Department.

These demographic characteristics may not sound significant, but they constituted a huge accomplishment in the context of the larger homicide prevention program of which Stay Alive was part in the city of Minneapolis. The basketball program was originally only one of a dozen pilot programs that were given small grants in the first year of the campaign. The Stay Alive program was not only continued but expanded because it was the only one of the pilot programs that actually recruited and engaged the difficult-to-reach eighteen- to twenty-five-year-old minority male population that had been identified by city researchers as the focal point of the homicide explosion. That is not to suggest that city bureaucrats were convinced Stay Alive would be an effective homicide prevention program, but that basketball was the only activity they had going that could claim to do anything remotely proactive in terms of bringing young men of color into a structured, safe environment.

Of course, recruitment is only just the beginning of any successful intervention program. Once participants are brought into a program (any program), the question quickly becomes, What does the program do with or for its participants, those that have now come in the door? This question is where the programming challenge really begins, where program design and operation are typically most varied and uneven, and where the need for better understanding and theory is most pressing and complicated.

The traditional, idealistic notion that has dominated much sport-based youth intervention over the years is that sport participation is associated—automatically, naturally—with character building, self-discipline, and socialization. The assumption here is simply that playing sports builds self-esteem and social skills that teach otherwise undisciplined and disorderly young people principles of social order and self-control. At its root, here, is the idealistic belief that simply playing sports is inherently and inevitably an effective, prosocial (and antirisk) influence. The last generation of sport scholarship has taught us to question and challenge these traditional beliefs. Contrary to most popular assumptions, sport participation, it has come to be seen, is not automatically a positive social force. Sport-based programming is better understood, like any other tool or technology, as an "empty form" (MacAloon 1995)—a practice that can be positive, but that can also be a problem if the energies involved in sport participation are not directed and channeled appropriately. Indeed, sport is best understood as a tool for development and social intervention whose influence depends on the ends toward which it is directed, how it is implemented, and the context in which it is deployed.

The notion of sport as a tool for intervention and change is not entirely a far from a new idea in the pantheon of sport programming and theory; but it is an understanding that has been revitalized and reinvigorated in recent years. My own thinking and work on these matters was shaped and informed by my continued involvement with and reflection on where I got my start in all this—that is, with Larry Hawkins, who thought of sport as a hook or a carrot, and his various sport-based initiatives and programs on the South Side of Chicago.[6] For Hawkins, this notion of sport as a hook or a tool can be a bit more complicated than first meets the eye. For one thing, it implies that sport is not automatically or inevitably a positive social or developmental force in and of itself. Stronger than this, though, it implies that sport can actually have negative impacts or outcomes if not utilized or implemented appropriately. Indeed, one of his criticisms of the inaugural Chicago league was that organizers had not devoted enough attention and programming to actively using the tool of sport involvement. It was, in other words, too much of a sports program, too beholden to the belief that sport participation alone would lead to prosocial outcomes and benefits.

An example of this notion came in a keynote address on youth sport delivered at the Institute for Athletics and Education's national conference in 1990 by a longtime supporter and board member, the well-known Chicago sociologist James Coleman. In his speech, Coleman, a former president of the American Sociological Association and author of the famous Coleman Report on education in the 1960s, described two schools that he had researched as part of his pathbreaking study of American high school culture, *Adolescent Society* (1963). In both schools, according to Coleman, the most powerful member of the teaching staff was the coach of the leading and highly successful sports team—football in the one school, wrestling in the other. Both coaches well understood their prominence and power; however, each used his position in quite different ways. Specifically, one (who happened to be the football coach) "flaunted his power" by "making jokes that were obliquely directed toward the ridicule of his players, putting pressure on teachers to keep boys eligible, and getting special privileges for his athletes" (Coleman 1991, 4). The wrestling coach, in contrast, was a creative and engaging educator who tried to "use the glory gained by his team to enhance the attractiveness and status of biology" (his classroom subject), and he "showed respect for the principal and for the other areas of activity in the school" (5). The educational outcomes of these different approaches were predictable. The life of the two schools revolved around their respective teams, but in the football school, this involvement drew energy away from schoolwork and the larger educational mission, while in the wrestling school, it fostered a deeper engagement in the school and in scholastic subject matters.

The moral of the story, for Coleman, was that the social and educational value of sport had little to do with sport itself and everything to do with the ways in which the energy and excitement of athletics was used and directed by those who participated in it. More generally, Coleman's tale of two schools made the point that the power of sport is rather like the power of any other tool, technology, or social practice: its impact and effectiveness is determined by how it is used—to what ends and in what context. So if sport was only a tool and therefore only just a starting point, what was really important was all the other, nonsport programming and activities and interventions that sport provided entrée to. The implication is that the success of a sport-based social interventionist program is largely determined by the strength of its nonsport components, what it does with young people once they are brought into the program through sport.

The most recent literature on sport and development has pushed hard on this point. Scholars have distinguished between "sport plus" and "plus sport" programs (Coalter 2009; Levermore and Beacom 2009). On the one hand, "sport plus" initiatives "give primacy to the development of sustainable sports organizations, programmes and development pathways" and then go on to address broader social issues. The "plus sport" model puts the sport/social intervention relationship the other way around, "giv[ing] primacy to social and health programmes where sport is used, especially its ability to bring together a large number of young people, to achieve some of their objectives" (Coalter 2009, 58). Clearly, this latter orientation and approach (see also Levermore 2009) is most proper and appropriate if a sport-based program is to be a significant force in the struggle against crime and delinquency. This framing also makes it easier to understand why many of the best, most effective programs include specific programming for education, mentorship, and skills training as well as what Witt and Crompton (2003) have called value-directed personal development. Time and again, case studies have revealed that the programs that are most promising and successful as crime prevention programs are those that incorporate nonsport, development-oriented elements (see, for examples, Astbury, Knight, and Nichols 2005; Witt and Crompton 1996a, 1996b).

And this is precisely why all the nonsport elements that were beginning to be the focus of midnight basketball initiatives—the connections to other agencies and organizations, the workshops and job training sessions, and the like that became the focus of the best basketball-based initiatives like the program in Oakland I discussed previously—were so crucial and important. These ideas were becoming more and more pronounced among midnight basketball practitioners and providers as the initiatives developed. Especially those who had a background in sport had been exposed to many of these elements, and some had begun to develop and incorporate such elements—both philosophical and programmatic—earlier or actually had such components that predated their formal affiliation with Midnight Basketball Inc. The High Five America program in San Diego run by Rle Nichols and his staff was one of those.

High Five offered a weekly educational component (book based for those still in school; oriented toward interview skills, job counseling, and training for school dropouts and older participants) that players were required to attend in order to be eligible to participate in league games. "Five minutes after each MBL [Midnight Basketball Leagues] game," as the organizers explained to local papers, there were classes with guest speakers on topics including drug abuse, AIDS, relationships, and conflict resolution. As Nichols put it, "Absences will not be excused. You don't show, you don't play. You are, in all likelihood, gone [from the program]" (*San Diego Union Tribune*, March 5, 1994). Eventually, in fact, the Oakland affiliate adopted this rationale and came to use a similar programming approach: "For each hour of play, participants spend a mandatory hour in workshops. The workshops cover a range of self-improvement topics such as job development, drug and alcohol use, safe sex, GED preparation and college requirements, and conflict resolution training." In addition, every "youth" joining the program had to "sign and abide by the Player Code of Conduct"—a document that included the phrase "If you miss a workshop without an excuse, you don't play." And again, what is most important here are not the specific programming elements but the big ideas, larger principles, and underlying theories of sport as a connector or conduit to other types of programs and programming that were getting implemented in the midnight basketball remodel and then beginning to circulate more broadly.

Earlier in this chapter, we saw a good deal of this approach in the program run by the Oakland Midnight Basketball affiliate. But where the Oakland affiliate was also innovative, indeed really on the cutting edge, was in combining this vision of sport-based programming with an organizational and financial model based on partnerships and collaborations with other agencies and initiatives. Here we see the parameters and pressures of the downsized, market-oriented neoliberal state pushing sport-based programming in new organizational directions. Realizing the complexity of intervention and the instrumental value (and limits) of sport as well as its own resource limitations, the Oakland affiliate put the emphasis not only on nonsport programming but even more so on connecting and partnering with other organizations, resources, and programs that would be able to help assist and serve the young men brought into its doors by basketball.

None of these insights should be taken to suggest that sport-based social intervention is easy or automatic. Not by any stretch of the imagination. In fact, one of the final points theorists have stressed is the ongoing problem of setting unrealistic hopes or expectations for all sport-based intervention-oriented initiatives. Just like any other social interventions, these programs, even at their best, are complicated, expensive, and limited in what they can accomplish. A failure to understand the realities and limitations of any such intervention can not only compromise the immediate influence and effectiveness of such efforts, but it can leave them vulnerable to public criticism and cutbacks. More than this, such programs, even when they are successful, can also serve to reinforce and exacerbate the problems faced by at-risk urban youth by deflecting public attention away from the deeper social sources of their problems.

These broader symbolic functions are, in my view, only beginning to be understood by scholars and practitioners. I talked about the political posturing that surrounded midnight basketball on the national level, as well as its consequences, already in chapters 4 and 5. But these weren't the only political episodes that involved midnight basketball. Indeed, sometimes the high-profile politics surrounding midnight basketball on more local levels was downright counterproductive with respect to larger policy and programming agendas, leading to political scrutiny and, in one instance, scandal. In St. Louis, Missouri, to be specific, an episode unfolded that would haunt for years to come—a bizarre case in which money was believed to have been embezzled from midnight basketball to pay a ransom when program director Darryl "Pee Wee" Lenard was allegedly kidnapped by a drug dealer in East St. Louis. The investigation involved the FBI and the Drug Enforcement Administration and eventually implicated the mayor himself (*St. Louis Post Dispatch*, August 24, 1997). I have not fully explored the entire scope and complexity of this incident, a chapter in itself. But let me just say that public attention and political controversy of this sort was a cautionary tale for anyone involved in sport-based intervention and change, whether theorist, practitioner, or supporter.

Conclusion

So where did all these changes and developments and transformations leave midnight basketball itself on the cusp of the twenty-first century? Obviously, things were much different for midnight basketball providers and operators in the post–crime bill era than they had been initially. With their new, more grounded model of a more connected, less utopian vision, the official national association and a host of beleaguered knockoffs and copycats definitely righted themselves, building a small cadre of programs and leagues that have sustained themselves and continue to operate even to this day. However, as the energy, excitement, public visibility, and program funding shifted in other directions, to related but differentiated sport-based initiatives, midnight basketball itself became less important, less prominent, and less visible at the national level. There should be no doubt about that. The post-1994 experience has been more about local programs than national politics. And this story, the story of actual, local programs doing their midnight basketball thing, suggests a great deal about the ongoing challenges of doing social intervention through sport—in terms of actual programming, local political conditions, and the ongoing complexities of race and risk. It is to a case study of those challenges—of putting theories into practice, and of the local conditions of race, risk, and program implementation—that I now turn.

SEVEN

Prevention in Practice:
A Field Study

WITH DARREN WHEELOCK

In 1988, the anthropologist John MacAloon delivered a keynote address at the annual Leisure Studies Association meeting in Brighton, England. It wasn't your usual academic address. Best known for his theories of spectacle and ceremony (1984) and his biography of the modern Olympic founder Pierre Coubertin (1981), MacAloon did not rehash or trumpet his previous work. Instead, he argued for the value and indeed the necessity—"the imperative," MacAloon (1992) called it—of ethnographic fieldwork in sport studies. He built his case for in-depth, on-the-ground, participant-observation studies around a critique of the research and theories of John Hargreaves, one of the real stars and stalwarts in the field. MacAloon argued against what he called the "cultural studies" approach championed by Hargreaves (1986) and his colleagues in Great Britain (see also Gruneau 1983), characterizing this work as, at its core, a top-down, deterministic approach with little concern for how structures of meaning and domination are actually understood and experienced by those on whom they impinge. As a result, MacAloon insisted, most sport scholarship misunderstood the true complexity of sport's relationship to power, didn't understand the real mechanisms at work, and missed opportunities for resistance and change. MacAloon did all of this on what was essentially Hargreaves's home turf—across the pond as they say.

It would be an understatement to say that MacAloon's wasn't the most diplomatic conference keynote address in academic history. With the benefit of hindsight, in fact, it almost goes without saying that MacAloon was more critical of the contributions of Hargreaves and his colleagues than he needed to be. To this day, their work stands as a high point of sport studies, one which continues to influence and shape the field (see Carrington 2010). Nevertheless, MacAloon's address, subsequently published in the *Sociology of Sport Journal* along with several repudiations and critiques,[1] stands as an equally important if less appreciated intervention. MacAloon's vision of the ethnographic imperative anticipated and helped clear the way for a new generation of sport scholarship and cultural approaches to the analysis of sporting forms and practices. Ethnography, in MacAloon's inspired vision, emerged as much more than a method for gathering data and information. It was actually a whole way of looking at the world—an approach to the study of social life which puts a premium on the details of people's everyday lives (what they do, the things that are meaningful and motivating to them) and is attentive to the mechanisms, processes, and practices in and through which social order is made and social life is enacted. The ethnographic approach insists, moreover, on situating these practices in the broadest possible social and theoretical frames, and tries to bring these analyses to bear on topics and questions where real action, intervention, and change are possible.

In certain grandiose respects, this entire book, this whole extended case history of midnight basketball, was inspired by MacAloon's call for more grounded, intensive involvement in the fields of sporting practice and play. It is based in the core conviction that a full understanding of the structure and significance of all sporting forms requires an intensive, multifaceted engagement with broad social and historical structures, as well as how those structures are experienced and understood by different groups of variously positioned—and often competing—social actors in their social contexts. But as this project took shape, I also came to realize that, for all the research initially conducted, I hadn't really looked closely at how midnight basketball programs actually operated on the ground, or how they were experienced and understood by those who organized them or those whom they were designed to serve. Especially in the context of the aftermath of the crime bill controversies and the consolidation of the whole neoliberal paternalist model of social service provision, what seemed to be called for was ethnography in the most basic and traditional sense of MacAloon's imperative.

With this in mind, I enlisted the help of Darren Wheelock, then a graduate student, and together we undertook an intensive, fifteen-month (two-season) field study of a crime prevention initiative in the Twin Cities called Stay Alive. It wasn't an officially sanctioned midnight basketball league, and it didn't even operate at midnight; it ran between 7:00 p.m. and 11:00 p.m.—"Minnesota midnight," as we sometimes joked. But Stay Alive was a basketball-based initiative designed on the larger, prevention-oriented model described in the previous chapter, and we were convinced it would help us better understand the challenges and complexities of sport-based risk prevention as it was practiced in actual, everyday life.

Initiated by the Minneapolis Department of Health and Family Support (DFHS) during the summer of 1998, the Stay Alive project actually consisted of two different basketball programs—the Shoot Hoops, Not Guns project of the Twin Cities Healthy Nations organization and the Ghetto Basketball Association (GBA). These grassroots, community-based programs operated a variety of sport-and-recreation-based activities on an independent basis for the better part of the year and served disadvantaged African American and Native American young men in the Minneapolis neighborhoods of Powderhorn, Phillips, and Near North. During the summer, with funding and support from the DHFS's Violence Prevention Project, they came together as partners to sponsor basketball leagues that operated between 7:00 p.m. and 11:00 p.m.

Wheelock and I got involved with Stay Alive and the GBA in the fall after the initial summer run. We had just completed a preliminary version of the analysis that I presented in chapter 5 regarding the symbolic politics surrounding midnight basketball in the 1994 federal crime bill debates, and we were looking for sites in which we could learn about how sports-based social intervention and crime prevention programs were implemented and actually operated on the local level in this new political climate and policy context. We also hoped to begin to evaluate and assess the effectiveness of such initiatives. It turned out that program administrators were, likewise, looking for researchers with university connections in order to formally evaluate and refine the program. After a series of initial meetings, we wrote a proposal to the Center for Urban and Regional Affairs (CURA) at the University of Minnesota's Public Policy School asking for assistance in funding a collaborative partnership for research, program development, and evaluation. Our proposal was approved and we were off and running.

As is so often the case with such action-oriented, community-based research, it was a complicated way to do fieldwork. Wheelock worked as an intern with the DHFS for the summer. Our original plan called for his primary duties to involve assisting in a comprehensive evaluation of the program; however, a great deal of his work, for reasons that will become clearer later, came to revolve around the basic, everyday operation and administration of the league. Thus, Wheelock spent a lot of time with program administrators and on-site with players, coaches, and referees, developing a broad, holistic view of the program in the process. I served mainly as a consultant to program administrators and project coordinators; he participated in all formal planning and evaluation meetings, attended games, and helped organize other program events. Together, we established an independent relationship with the two community-based African American league supervisors in order to assist them, as a condition of our partnership, in writing grant proposals and to help them work toward their larger, long-term aspirations of transforming GBA into a year-round, multifaceted, cultural and educational program. We also enlisted the services of two research assistants (both young African American men who were advanced undergraduate students in our department) to assist in formal observations of all program events and in conducting interviews with selected program participants.

While this level and intensity of involvement presented certain kinds of problems (especially with respect to our efforts to conduct a formal, systematic evaluation of program outcomes), it also provided tremendous access to all the parties involved. Much as Jay MacLeod described in the elegant methodological appendix to *Ain't No Makin' It* (1987), one great help was how Wheelock's own basketball knowledge and skills served to establish his credibility with numerous program participants, including the lead organizers, referees, and a number of players themselves. We accumulated detailed field notes based on his interactions with all these participants, paying special attention to their understandings of race, recreation, and social intervention. In addition, we conducted formal interviews with fifteen league players (including at least one from each team) and representatives of each of the other formal roles in the program (some twenty-five formal interviews total). And while most of our evaluation efforts fell short, they taught us a great deal about how the ideas of each person involved were implemented in positive, productive ways—and in more problematic ones.

This chapter, then, and the next are an overview of what we learned from these interactions and experiences. The present chapter focuses on the administrative organization and daily operation of the Stay Alive program. It details our initial observations and impressions of program staff and supervisors, examines how contention unfolded around questions about the social value of sport for social intervention and crime prevention, and highlights some of the unexpected tensions among program officials as well as the one, surprising point on which they all agreed. In developing this analysis, we detail the operational problems that resulted as program staff tried to implement their competing visions, and then we try to show that underlying these various conflicts and outcomes were radically different perceptions of race and risk in contemporary urban communities and the fundamentally unequal resources and power available to different actors and organizers in the program. In the following chapter, Hartmann will develop these analyses further and explain the very different ideas, interests, and perceptions of the Stay Alive program as seen through the eyes of the players themselves. Throughout, we hope you will see not only competing ideological visions and agendas, but also the fiscal and institutional limitations of neoliberal paternalism, the workings of power, and the hidden, haunting, and pervasive presence of race.

Initial Interactions and Impressions

Our first formal involvement with the Stay Alive project came in the fall of 1998, at a wrap-up meeting held at the close of the program's first summer of full-scale operation. The meeting was held at a violence prevention shelter in South Minneapolis, the primary workplace of the program's official director, Malik Rosenthal (a middle-aged African American social work professional), and his codirector, Brad Atkins (a thirty-something white male caseworker).[2] It included all the individuals who would become major players in our fieldwork over the following few years: Raphael Garcia, the Department of Health and Family Support official who administered the project for the mayor's office; Annie Klausmeyer, a program evaluator from the DHFS (an epidemiologist by training); Deon Jackson, the league's head referee (a former NFL journeyman defensive back); representatives from an all-male African American community group contracted to provide security for the league; and, of course, the three contracted, neighborhood-based site coordinators who were responsible for recruiting coaches, teams, and players and for supervising league play throughout the summer months: Frank Cauldwell, Rich Witters, and Pete Mears. We were introduced as sociologists from the "U" (the local moniker for the University of Minnesota) doing research on programs that used sport and recreation for social outreach, intervention, and violence prevention.

The meeting was convened for two purposes: to review the successes and shortcomings of the previous year's operation and to begin planning the next summer's edition. It seemed a relatively straightforward agenda, and we assumed the meeting would let us get a better sense of the program's formal structure and rationale. It would be our entry point into local understandings of the sport-race-risk nexus and for better assessing the possibility of conducting a formal evaluation of Stay Alive. Almost as soon as the meeting commenced, however, we discovered two things that would have a deep and dramatic impact on our thinking about the interactions of race, sport, and risk prevention and about sports-based crime prevention programs.

First, and most importantly, there were deep divides and disagreements among program staff. The conflicts appeared between the administrators who supervised the program for the city (Rosenthal, Atkins, and Garcia) and the more community-based, grassroots sports practitioners (Cauldwell, Witters, and, to a lesser degree, Mears) responsible for the organization and

day-to-day operation of the leagues. We saw veiled (and not-so-veiled) accusations thrown back and forth as people argued about how resources were
deployed, who got paid what, what was and was not done, who got credit
for things that went well, and who took the blame for things that didn't go
as planned.

Comparing notes on the drive home, our initial inclination was to see
these tensions as products of the usual squabbles and challenges of nonprofit, community-based partnerships among agencies and organizations
with diverse interests and agendas as well as conflicting aesthetic styles
and administrative sensibilities. On the city administration side, Garcia and
Rosenthal were your typical, fairly professional social service workers and
government bureaucrats who dressed, talked, and interacted accordingly—in
an essentially formal, professional middle-class model. In contrast, those
who handled the day-to-day operation of the program, especially Witters,
Cauldwell, and Jackson, were younger, less refined, more street cool. Not
only did they dress differently—Cauldwell usually wore the Ghetto Basketball Association T-shirts he tried to market throughout the city at sporting
venues and in the hip-hop community—but they had a much looser, flexible sense of how things should run.

As we got to know the Stay Alive program and these various parties in
the weeks and months that followed, we were satisfied that there was a good
deal of truth to our initial speculations. The fact that both the GBA and the
Shoot Hoops programs functioned as independent, self-regulated operations for all but the ten summer weeks in which they had to abide by the
rules, regulations, and requirements of the city's Stay Alive program posed
an uncomfortable working partnership that was never fully resolved (and in
which we found ourselves embroiled on more than one occasion). In working for the city during these summer months, the local grassroots operators
were forced to relinquish a certain degree of autonomy and control over
programs and participant populations they considered "their own" for the
rest of the calendar year. Power, in short, was clearly at play.

Over time, we also came to realize that these tensions ran much deeper
than style, personality conflicts, and the usual office politics of institutional
control. City supervisors and grassroots organizers were also divided by very
different understandings of the basic value and ultimate objectives of this
basketball-based initiative. More specifically, these two sets of social actors
actually had clashing conceptions of the value of sport in risk prevention
and social intervention as well as very different (if somewhat less explicit)
beliefs about the "risks" (faced or posed) and needs of the young, urban
men of color the program was intended to target and serve.

Perhaps these competing and even conflicting visions shouldn't have been surprising to us, but they were. Fresh off our initial research into the 1994 crime bill discourse and having seen the consolidation of a more refined, pragmatic vision of sport as prevention in the aftermath, we entered this field with an idealized vision. We expected to learn that the local program operators who were the subject of so much scorn and derision (or paternalism and superiority) in the national debates were fighting the good fight that politicians were avoiding. In retrospect, it's clear we expected (or hoped) that they couldn't be so petty and self-interested as to get caught up in the kinds of political struggles and conflicts that manifested themselves in the political context. In fact, we probably hoped to discover a more unified, principled, and progressive vision of sport-based intervention, one more grounded in and attentive to the real needs and concerns of the African American community and the young men themselves. Suffice it to say, these assumptions and expectations were misplaced, if not hopelessly naïve.

We will say a good deal more about these divisions and their implications as we go on, but it is important to pinpoint the one respect in which city supervisors and community-based organizers, for all their disagreements, were in complete accord. That consensus involved their attitudes toward us and the sociological critique that had drawn us to this program and the topic of late-night basketball in the first place. We are talking about our scholarly speculations that basketball-based programs like Stay Alive were based on and thus ostensibly reproductive of insidious stereotypes about young men of color in the United States. Having read all the latest literature on the sociology of sport and race, we were pretty "into" how blackness and African American stereotypes were being made and remade in the media and through these programs—and we thought they would be too. However, none of these program officials and operators—not one—was concerned with or even remotely troubled by our speculations on these issues. Even when we pointed out these ideas and possibilities explicitly (as one of us tried to do in that first meeting and as both of us attempted in individual conversations during the course of our fieldwork), they were received with "Minnesota nice"—polite silence.

It wasn't as if Stay Alive operators didn't understand our race-based critique (a word they wouldn't have used) of sport-based crime prevention programs, or even that they disagreed with it. To the contrary, when we discussed our ideas with some of these folks one-on-one, they listened attentively and even offered interesting observations and informed questions of their own. Rather, they simply didn't see these ideas as having any direct impact on or implications for them (or Stay Alive). Indeed, these ideas about race and the reproduction of racial stereotypes would *never* be a focus of discussion (much less a point of disagreement) during our entire involvement with the Stay Alive program. If Stay Alive was a program marked by deep internal differences and debates, this was the one point on which there was complete consensus—albeit consensus in the form of disinterested silence. Indeed, this receptivity—or lack thereof—was our second major discovery upon entering the field.

Part of the reason for the disinclination of Stay Alive staff to engage a radical scholarly critique of sport-based prevention programs had to do with a general skepticism about academia and intellectuals in general. It probably didn't help that we had a tendency to use terms like "critique" and to refer to "the research literature" or "experts in the field" in offering our suggestions and observations. Another factor was the deep aversion to talking directly about race that has been touched on in previous chapters. Despite being specifically targeted to young men of color (African Americans and Native Americans) and widely promoted in the ethnic media, race was not regularly or explicitly discussed, in public or in private. In an early planning meeting, in fact, a Latina consultant stressed the importance of taking a "color-blind approach" to all social work, claiming she personally "doesn't see color." And city supervisor Garcia routinely sought to deny *any* racial dimension to the participants or the program more generally. Garcia was so committed to the point, in fact, that in the year before our involvement he had insisted that a question asking for the participants' racial background be removed from the registration sheet.[3]

An even more fundamental reason for Stay Alive organizers and officials' disinterest in our racial analysis was that their program—like so many such basketball-based initiatives—was posited on the very assumptions about basketball and the problems of inner-city, minority communities our critique was directed against. Program organizers and operators may have disagreed on many things, but they all agreed that this was a population and community in real crisis. This was no mere cultural construction, no stereotype being foisted on an otherwise innocent and unsuspecting social population—it was a social reality they were intent on changing. They also saw the ideas that linked young minority men (especially those who were African American) with basketball less as negative stereotypes than as realistic representations of the cultural tastes and aesthetic preferences of this particular population. In other words, for program operators and administrators, the close cultural connections among basketball, race, and risk weren't stereotypes but realities, and as such, they were opportunities to be taken advantage of, resources to be utilized and drawn upon. Even if it did nothing else, a basketball-based program held the promise of attracting an otherwise difficult-to-reach target population.

This promise or possibility, in fact, helps explain the optimism that program administrators had about the program and their skepticism and annoyance with our cultural critiques. They didn't deny that the program drew on certain racial generalizations; obviously, these generalizations were the very foundations on which the program was built. But this rhetoric and framing was, in their view, a way to do something about the problems this community faced within the limited resources that were available. And it is in this sense—or, more precisely, in these taken-for-granted assumptions about race and risk and social intervention—that Stay Alive was entirely within the parameters of the approach to poverty governance that can properly be called neoliberal paternalism.

Competing Visions of Sport as Intervention

The fact that Stay Alive staff were uniformly *unimpressed* with our scholarly theories of the interactions of race, risk, sport, and prevention may have been the only thing they had in common. Once we got inside of the everyday operation of the program, we discovered that each of the parties involved—the administrators who funded and supervised the initiative, the organizers who ran the program on a daily basis, and even the players themselves (as I will explain in the next chapter)—had very different conceptions of the ideals and objectives of the enterprise.

The most obvious and entrenched of these differences involved competing visions of the social value of sport and pitted city supervisors Raphael Garcia, Malik Rosenthal, and, to a lesser extent, Brad Atkins against Rich Witters and Frank Cauldwell, who were responsible for the day-to-day operation of the two African American sites. Though the actual thinking and ideas behind these different visions were not always explicitly articulated (as is so often the case in the world of sport and much applied work in general), the basic conflict wasn't particularly difficult for us to identify once we got into the field and got a handle on what was going on. On the one hand, Cauldwell and Witters believed that running a good basketball program constituted an important social intervention in and of itself. When forced to articulate their ideas about the social value of sport—either by our questions or when pushed by city supervisors who had different views—Cauldwell and Witters would pay homage to familiar, time-honored, idealist lines about sport building character or providing opportunities and mobility, but their basic goal was to organize a good basketball league. For their part, Rosenthal and Garcia saw this view as a naïve, self-serving ideology perpetuated by sports lovers and former jocks. If the Stay Alive program were to continue to be funded and justified by city government, the supervisors believed, it needed to be much more than a basketball league. It needed to be focused on educational and prevention-oriented activities.

Garcia's views on sport were by far the most consistent and clearly elaborated of anyone we encountered in the field. In our very first conversation, Garcia—who was not a "sports guy" by any stretch of the imagination—expounded passionately and at length against sport-based prevention programs that offered nothing more than sports. His views were informed by his own social work experience and intuitive sense of the limits of sports idealism, but also by the research, thinking, and subsequent developments in sport-based programming and theory that followed the crime bill debates of 1994 and were discussed in the previous chapter.

Garcia and his staff had actually researched the debate and its outcomes in some depth, and they had a pretty good sense of how other basketball-based programs had responded, adapted, and evolved. Garcia had assigned staff evaluator Annie Klausmeyer to review the scholarly literature on sport-based social interventions and came away convinced that sport-only programs "didn't test out." Garcia, in other words, had done his homework. He easily discussed the belief held by many scholars that such programs were useful as "tools" for violence prevention, "carrots" to bring otherwise disinterested young men into programs. Any real program, Garcia told us early on, would have to incorporate "real programmatic elements." He didn't necessarily feel that sport was bad for communities of color (as some sport critics have suggested, arguing that sport programs can function to bring would-be criminals together, facilitating deviant networks and information channels). To his credit, he also insistently and consistently downplayed the hard-core surveillance and control elements of midnight basketball emphasized by many conservative legislators and supporters earlier in the decade. Garcia simply didn't believe that a sport program had any intrinsic social benefits in and of itself. It was just a form of play that had little or nothing to do with "real" social problems like crime, violence, and poverty. Garcia saw the possibility of broader, community influences—whether in the form of cultivating cross-cultural connections or a larger awareness of the commitment to violence prevention—but thought these could only be achieved through conscious and deliberate energy. Anything less meant not only that sport might fail to achieve its positive promises, but that it *could* (not inevitably, but possibly) serve to reproduce or reinforce problematic preexisting behaviors and social networks.

For Garcia, who worked directly for the mayor, this vision was also a matter of pragmatism. He believed, quite correctly as far as we could tell, that in the post–crime bill era sports-based programs like Stay Alive were generally perceived to be a "major thumbs down" by public policy makers, politicians, and the general public. Garcia felt such initiatives were only funded and supported to the extent that they were about *more* than sport, and even then the bar was high. If Stay Alive was seen mainly as a sports program, Garcia was convinced it would be cut entirely. At one point, as we mentioned earlier, he claimed he'd pull the plug himself: "If they [Cauldwell and Witters] want a basketball league, go ahead, just don't use 'Stay Alive' money to do it." Here, it is worth reiterating that Stay Alive was funded not through Parks and Recreation but through the Department of Health and Family Support.

We obviously had a great deal of respect and sympathy for Garcia's viewpoint; indeed, his understanding that nonsport elements were key to the success of any sport-based social intervention was one of the reasons we were drawn to Stay Alive in the first place (and, presumably, it's why he and his staff welcomed us). Sympathetic as we were, however, we also came to appreciate that the views of Cauldwell and Witters were deeper and more multifaceted than either we or Garcia had acknowledged, or a standard, idealist conception of sport would allow. At the core of their vision was a deep, intuitive sense of the importance of social solidarity and community building in and through sport for the black community. Put differently, their idea of a grassroots sports program for inner-city African American young men was part of a whole vision of recognizing and attacking antiblack stereotypes and building community in the African American neighborhoods they had grown up in. The more we learned about their background, the more this vision started to take on shape and significance and make sense to us as an alternative approach to sport as social intervention.

Both Cauldwell and Witters had grown up in the Minneapolis area and played on various touring and high school teams together (some coached by Cauldwell's dad, a college educator). Witters was a standout player who won a basketball scholarship and earned a degree from a Division I university in the Southeast. Cauldwell, though not as outstanding a player as Witters, was more political and entrepreneurial. He took college courses at several universities on the East Coast, but dropped out to concentrate on a career as a hip-hop promoter, community organizer, and self-styled entrepreneur. Both returned to Minneapolis in the early 1990s to find that no African American athletes had been invited to play in the metro area's annual Senior All-Star Game. Each saw the slight as an example of racial discrimination and injustice, and they took it on themselves to organize an alternative event for African Americans—the Inner-City All-Star Classic, which would feature outstanding African American players graduating from local high schools. Buoyed by the participation of local legend Khalid El-Amin (who eventually led the University of Connecticut to a national championship, played in the NBA, and had a long, successful career playing professionally overseas), the inaugural classic in 1994 drew a large crowd and found substantial sponsorship from local businesses. Word spread and what was once a somewhat obscure basketball game evolved into a full-fledged annual happening held at local college arenas with thousands of spectators. The game eventually became something of a fixture on the local sports scene, at least as far as the African American community was concerned. Indeed, it was something like a local, Minnesota version of the NBA's annual all-star weekend, which has come to be, at least in part, a celebration of African American history, culture, and community.

Cauldwell and Witters built the Ghetto Basketball Association on the success and vision of the classic. In addition to exposing and confronting racism and discrimination, they saw this event (and basketball more broadly) as a forum through which they could celebrate African American distinctiveness, engaging and transforming rather than simply rejecting or subverting dominant stereotypes and preconceptions. "This is *our* thing," Witters told us at one point in a discussion of the African American community. "It's where we can be ourselves and show everyone what we can do." Although they would not have put it this way (and may even cringe at the comparison), Cauldwell and Witters were not unlike queer theorists who have taken a term of derision and turned it into a site for celebration and rearticulation. This logic is precisely why Cauldwell and Witters chose the otherwise puzzling "Ghetto Basketball Association" as their organization's title. The whole *point* was to reclaim basketball in the inner-city, black community and make it a source of pride and collective identity, a symbol of excellence.

As Cauldwell and Witters got more involved with these kinds of initiatives, they developed and promoted other elements, values, and virtues of the social benefits of sport. Around the time we started working with them, for example, the classic was expanded to include some fairly minimal but symbolically significant counseling and advising sessions designed to prepare graduating seniors for the rigors, demands, and opportunities of life as collegiate student athletes. They consciously signaled the connection between athletics and academics. As the GBA took shape, the two organizers also began to espouse the belief that all individuals had a "right" to sport and "play" for their own sake; they often spoke about the lack of such basic opportunities for inner-city African American youth and young men. They even dreamed of turning their sports programs into a source of profit and productivity, the ultimate synergy of community needs and individual enterprise. We listened to their plans, looked at sketches, came up with fund-raising ideas, and even helped draft grant proposals and business plans. It was kind of fun. Indeed, in the manner that Robin Kelley (1997b, chaps. 2 and 3 especially) described for many young African American men in the inner city, Cauldwell and Witters saw sport as an economic resource, an opportunity for upward mobility through marketing their own gear and potentially founding their own community-based recreation and fitness center dedicated to basketball, hip-hop music and art, and youth programs.

These ideas were sometimes a bit haphazard, and perhaps too often a matter of convenience—it didn't take a huge leap to see them as simply self-interested (as Garcia and his staff frequently charged). The core of the concept, however, remained to celebrate (and market) African American excellence in the face of a broader culture and community that tended to see blackness in negative terms and often marginalized and excluded African Americans from mainstream institutions and events. It was a vision that gave us new purchase on the old liberal idealism about sports participation and programming being an almost automatic, inevitable progressive social force, and it helped us understand why certain African American intellectuals remained so staunchly committed to these ideals (cf. Early 2011; Wideman 2001; George 1992). Sport was not—or not *just*—about socialization or morality; nor was it about mobility for individual African American men. It was about social and symbolic significance in a culture that otherwise offered few publicly visible avenues for social solidarity, collective identification, and actual creative excellence. This was also a much different way of thinking about the irreducible, intrinsic value of sport in the black community, one that stood in fairly dramatic contrast to all the sport-as-tool, sport-as-a-means-of-intervention, sport-as-means-to-other-ends formulations and approaches that constitute and define the social problems industry of which midnight basketball is so much a part.

Suffice it to say, once we got a handle on these very different visions of the social value of sport, it became a lot easier to understand the tensions that defined the Stay Alive program. Indeed, the focus of our fieldwork came to be seeing how conflicts played out in the everyday practice of the program and what effects these dynamics had on the implementation and effectiveness of the initiative.

Design and Basic Functionality

For all its conflict and all these rather fundamental differences of vision, orientation, and experience, the Stay Alive program was far from an abject failure; in fact, in the summers in which we were most intimately involved, this Minnesota-based variation on the midnight basketball model turned out to be a fairly functional operation. Cauldwell and Witters's Ghetto Basketball Association fielded twenty teams of about ten players each (more than double the numbers from the inaugural "season"), and the new Healthy Nations branch had eight teams, all mostly composed of self-identified Native Americans. Players had usually played a lot of basketball—on high school teams, at rec centers, and in traveling leagues when they were younger—and many teams boasted at least a couple of current or former college scholarship athletes who were home for the summer. As a result, most games were serious, competitive, and entertaining. And aside from the occasional outburst, the usual disagreements with referee calls, and a technical foul or two, we saw nothing at all out of the ordinary for a league of this quality and style of play. Even the cross-site, cross-cultural play between the mostly African American GBA teams and those from the American Indian Center went smoothly and, according to our observations, offered some of the most intense, exciting games on the schedule. On any given night, there were a good number of spectators—eight of the dozen regular season games we surveyed had a high (sixty or more) to medium (twenty to sixty) number of spectators from the community. Maybe more importantly, at least with respect to community outreach goals, the league generated a lot of good will in the community and very positive media attention, in both the mainstream media (the program was featured in the *Minneapolis Star Tribune*, for example) and the African American press and airwaves (Stay Alive was a favorite of KMOJ, a local African American radio station.)

It wasn't surprising, even though we'd seen some of the cracks in the organizational foundation. Cauldwell and Witters had strong, preexisting networks in the basketball scene as well as tremendous credibility in the black community based on their work with the Inner-City All-Star Classic. And while Pete Mears, the AIC director, wasn't big in the basketball scene, he had plenty of sports ties and connections with young men in his community. The inaugural year of the program had shown this to be a pretty successful basketball league—the only program funded through the city's violence prevention initiative that had actually secured the participation of the inner-city youth and young men of color who constituted the target population. All of this, of course, was why Garcia was not only continuing but expanding city support for the program—that meant new resources, organizational stability, and expertise, including a much more focused planning and design component in the months leading up to the implementation of the second summer program.

We were most directly, if not entirely successfully, involved on the planning and design front. Garcia asked us to help piece together a plan for reengineering and racketing up the program for the coming year. Our collective efforts were guided, at least in theory, by a fifty-six-page "program planning guide" put out by the city's Department of Health and Family Support a year and a half prior (Wixon 1998). (This was Garcia and Klausmeyer's department; indeed they were both listed as members of the steering committee that produced the report). The document purported to provide a conceptual frame for thinking about violence and violence prevention as well as a "step-by-step guide" for "intervention programming and planning." This proved a more significant and revealing document for us than we initially realized.

The guide described youth violence as "an entrenched and complex problem" that required an understanding of "risk factors" and the particular "protective factors" that could be cultivated to combat the problem. Drawn mostly from the then-emerging literature on risk and resilience (it included five pages of scholarly research and references—some seventy-two citations in all—along with at least two dozen websites and policy reports), the guide presented a comprehensive list of "risk factors" explaining "youth violence and anti-social behavior." These included individual, family, community, school, and social/institutional factors that mapped, more or less, onto how the various treatments were organized—from individual and family level to community and school level all the way through law enforcement and public policy. Indeed, forty-five programs and initiatives (thirty-two pages' worth) were rated as "promising" (P), "least promising" (L), and "most promising" (M) under these headings.

There were several things about this guiding document that we couldn't help but notice. First was the limited nature of the interventions that were seen as promising. The document seemed to demonstrate a sophisticated, sociological understanding of the scope and complexity of the problem of violence in the city, both in general and as it tied to the social problems of residents. Impressively, the analysis of the crime and violence problem was rooted in a fundamentally sociological understanding of poverty, unemployment, poor schooling, and the like. The framing, like so many scholarly examinations, put a lot of emphasis on structural problems, community, and institutional risk factors such as high rates of joblessness, concentrated poverty, academic failings, persistent exposure to media violence, and the availability of drugs, alcohol, and guns. Yet the actual programs and interventions highlighted mostly fell well within the limited parameters of neoliberal funding and organizational structure. There was a blatant (if familiar) disconnect, in other words, between theory and practice. Secondly, even within the set up of "risk factors" and "protective factors," the number of protective factors (including social bonds, strong values, clear standards, and individual characteristics) paled in comparison to the risks. The document led by stating blandly that "little headway" had been made in terms of solving the problem of violence. Perhaps it goes without saying at this point in the book, but this planning guide was, for all intents and purposes, the blueprint for neoliberal paternalism as it was envisioned and would be modeled and modified in the Twin Cities area.

In addition—and perhaps even more importantly, if ironically, given the athletic foundation of the Stay Alive initiative—the guide made no mention of sport, recreation, or leisure. In other words, the department's guiding document really had no conception of or immediate place for midnight basketball or any other sport-based intervention. The closest analogue listed was "afterschool recreation programs," placed under "community level" interventions. Other programs related to social skills training, mentoring, and behavior modification programming were listed under the heading of "individual level" approaches. But there was no mention of anything that concretely resembled midnight basketball.

We should be careful here. By the time they contacted us, as noted above, Minneapolis city staff had actually done a good deal of reading on sport-based intervention—including, prominently, midnight basketball—and exhibited a fairly impressive familiarity with the research literature on the contributions and pitfalls of such approaches. But, still, the absence of sport-based initiatives in the official report presented a conundrum. City administrators and program experts had picked a violence prevention program to concentrate all their resources on, and it wasn't even on their initial radar or in their official rubric. The reasons go back to those driving factors touched on in previous chapters: with limited resources (or, more generally, under the constraints of neoliberal funding and administration), a program with a perceived ability to recruit the target population and with publicity appeal had enormous value. We all had to work within the neoliberal hand we were dealt, so midnight basketball got the (limited) nod.

In any case, as consultants and collaborators, we were all now asked to focus on the nonsport elements of the program. Garcia and his staff were concerned that, for all its previous success in attracting the target population and generating positive publicity for the mayor's office, the program had little to claim or show for itself as a violence prevention initiative. Other than getting young men off the streets for a few nights a week, maybe providing an outlet for their energies and aggression, the program really offered nothing to help with violence prevention or crime control. (Stay Alive actually had included a few job training presentations and drug counseling sessions in its first year. However, these program elements had been quite limited and essentially optional for participants.) City administrators believed—quite correctly in our view—that more extensive, nonsport programming needed to be built into the initiative and that the success (or lack thereof) had to be documented and assessed if stakeholders were to be happy and the program was to be deemed effective.

We were, at least initially, fairly optimistic about our ability to incorporate more meaningful and effective prevention components into the Stay Alive initiative. Even though Garcia's views on the social value of sport were quite different from those of Cauldwell and Witters, we did not see the visions as necessarily contradictory and, in fact, thought we could figure out how to make those views compatible in practice. So, working with all the various administrators and organizers in the off-season, we agreed on a two-pronged approach. The first component, really the core, was "life skills training." The second was a series of motivational and educational talks (to be delivered nightly) and a handful of larger, more high-profile jobs training and educational events to be held on selected Saturdays throughout the summer. These were intended to bring representatives from educational institutions, jobs training organizations, and employee recruitment firms into contact with program participants, their friends and family, and other members of the community.

Based on our knowledge of the emerging research (summarized in the previous chapter) and Hartmann's previous experience with other sport-based interventions, our advice was to incorporate the nonsport, prevention elements as much as possible into the structure, fabric, and flow of the basketball activities. Basketball, after all, was the focus of most of the energy and involvement of the participants. In terms of the life skills, for example, it was decided that the games were to begin by introducing topics right at the start of the evening, then developing and concluding the "program" during the halftime break. Similarly, when major outreach events such as job and educational fairs were to take place, we wanted to make sure that the players got the message they were required and expected to come by holding exhibition games and contests in conjunction with these activities. To integrate the sport and nonsport aspects of the program, the events were to include music, food, and other festivities in which Stay Alive teams would play unofficial exhibition games.

The Challenges of Implementation and Evaluation

Involved as we had to be in planning and design, our primary interest in partnering with the Stay Alive project was to try to document, test, and evaluate the effectiveness of a basketball-based initiative for the expressed purposes of prevention and social intervention. We initiated this fieldwork, in other words, not to do program development, but to conduct a systematic program evaluation that might even serve as a larger test case or demonstration project. These ambitions were crucial for Garcia and Klausmeyer as well. They and their bosses at city hall needed some kind of data and evidence to demonstrate the preventive effectiveness of the program if funding was to continue in future years. To these ends, we worked with Klausmeyer to devise an extensive data collection plan that involved surveys with all program participants, tracking data and records with the police department, interviews, and regular observations. As primary researchers, we developed and fielded the survey and attended all the planning and development meetings, training sessions, and special events as well as a liberal sampling of games. We worked closely with our undergraduate research assistants who attended every session of the program, conducted interviews, and prepared field reports.

It was in and through these daily—or really, nightly—observations (about which our team produced weekly reports, e-mailed regularly, and met biweekly to collectively discuss) that we were able to witness and document the success of the program as a basketball league. But to determine how and to what extent this program succeeded in intervening in the lives of young men of color was our bigger aim. Our evaluation of the prevention components of the program, then, focused on three main areas—outreach (including recruitment and retention), prevention outcomes, and implementation—and our findings reflected and reinforced our understandings of both the potentials and pitfalls of sport-based intervention.[4]

Outreach and Recruitment. The one outcome we were able to determine conclusively was that Stay Alive was successful in recruiting the notoriously hard-to-reach target population of Native American and African American men aged eighteen to twenty-five. In its second year, as alluded to in the previous chapter, the program enrolled 256 players, up from 65 in its first summer of operation. African Americans made up 68 percent and Native Americans 28 percent, and fully 75 percent listed addresses in the city of Minneapolis proper. Only 57 percent were actually between eighteen and twenty-five years old, but this was because the program enrolled several teams of seventeen-year-olds and was also popular among young men in their later twenties who had played high school or college ball with Cauldwell and Witters. Perhaps most notably, 45 percent of players eighteen years or older had "criminal history records" as defined by the Minneapolis Police Department. This group was unquestionably the otherwise hard-to-reach youth and young men of color that other programs simply couldn't attract.

We attributed the success of the Stay Alive program in terms of recruitment to two main factors. One was the appeal and popularity of basketball. Much as theories and cultural stereotypes might suggest, basketball proved a real draw for these young men. Based on our interviews and surveys, we also realized the importance of the social ties and networks formed between program coordinators and participants. This was the second reason for the recruitment success, and one that we hadn't really seen in the research literature. Witters and Cauldwell had tremendous contacts and legitimacy in the community, especially when it came to basketball. Moreover, and in contrast to other midnight basketball programs we had researched, they allowed coaches and teams to register *as teams*—meaning that they didn't hold tryouts wherein individual players were placed onto teams. Instead groups of players who knew each other registered as an entity, thereby building on their own social ties and connections.

It should be noted, however, that some retention issues emerged by the end of the summer. Several of the GBA teams saw their numbers dwindle, a few games were forfeited, and two teams from Healthy Nations dropped out completely. As we looked at the background of those teams, we quickly came to realize that this wasn't just natural attrition—it was socially structured around two main factors. For one, some teams had been less successful in terms of winning games and fell in the league standings. Those teams that were not doing well at the basketball part of the program were, unsurprisingly, mostly likely to flounder or drop out. The other factor that helped account for decreased numbers pertained to how the teams were formed. Those teams that hadn't come in as fully formed units but were an amalgam of interested yet previously unconnected individuals simply did not hang together as well, especially if they weren't seeing success on the court. Together, each of these reasons speaks to the importance of both preexisting social ties and finding a certain level of successes and competitiveness on the athletic side of any sport-based intervention initiative.

Prevention. Of course, the overriding objective of our research and evaluation was determining what happened to program participants in terms of social intervention and violence prevention. Consistent with the initial planning and organizational emphases, we wanted to look for two outcomes. One was an immediate, direct impact in terms of safety and desistance from crime, delinquency, and violence: To what extent did the program help participants become less likely to be involved in various violent and/or criminal activities? Second, we looked for the more positive, proactive outcomes such as those involving education, jobs training, or employment, and we focused specifically on the extent to which the program was able to provide access or opportunities on these fronts. What we wanted to see were the kinds of empowering, capital-building activities that were believed to promote social inclusion, provide opportunities, and (most of all) prevent crime and violence in the first place. Unfortunately, in spite of our efforts to theorize these effects, develop metrics, and collect data, our evaluative results were disappointing on both fronts. The problem wasn't so much that the data we collected suggested the program didn't work to deter crime or promote prosocial outcomes. Rather, the problem was that we weren't even able to collect enough data to offer a valid evaluation and assessment of these outcomes. This was a real disappointment for us, and a major, albeit not uncommon, failing for the program itself.

Our data collection efforts weren't a total bust. We conducted many interviews with program participants, officials, and coaches, including sit-down, question-and-answer sessions with at least one player from each of the GBA teams. Though it took much longer and was more difficult than we expected, we were also able to collect surveys from all the team captains and a majority of the players in the league. These interviews and surveys revealed an extremely high degree of satisfaction with the program. Every single individual we interviewed planned to play in the league the following year—though this typically had very little to do with its nonsport prevention programming (indeed, some might say their devotion came in spite of such programming rather than because of it).

We also did an important and revealing set of interviews with those program participants that staff had identified as "success stories"—the young men believed to have been positively affected by Stay Alive. We reached out to these exemplary or model participants to figure out what staff considered successful and to try to understand *how* the program worked when it was perceived as successful. These individuals told us how the program helped provide opportunities for educational training and changed their habits (in terms of their leisure time activities and the crowds that they typically hung out with). Interestingly, however, these stories typically had little to do with basketball or even Stay Alive—the narratives of success were mainly concerned with networking and social connections that were only tangentially related to Stay Alive and its various sports and nonsports programs.

Unfortunately, however, from a program evaluation point of view, all of this was very subjective, anecdotal, and speculative. In terms of harder, more objective data on actual social impacts and outcomes, we came up short. We didn't have any way of knowing who experienced violence or had contact with police, whether players who didn't show up for games were more or less likely to get in trouble (or take advantage of educational opportunities), or how these patterns may have been affected by participation in the program. And we certainly weren't able to track league participants after the summer's games concluded. Again, our data didn't suggest that Stay Alive didn't work; rather, we lacked the data to determine its impact one way or the other. This inability to collect the data needed for a full, systematic evaluation of the program's risk prevention effectiveness (or lack thereof) was closely connected with a set of problems Stay Alive staff had in operationalizing the agreed-on design.

Implementation. Frustrated as we were by our inability to assess its intervention and prevention impacts, it's equally important to say that, by the end of the "season," we were not convinced that the Stay Alive program could have had a significant impact anyway. This is because the nonsport ideas and program elements that were so crucial to prevention conceptualization and design (and that we had hoped to assess and demonstrate) were never really put into practice. What should have been the core of the intervention, the nonsport programming that was planned, was never fully or effectively implemented.

For example, the biggest nonbasketball component of the summer's plan was the "life skills series," which was made up of informational talks and motivational seminars. Even in the planning stages, we were not sure that these program elements would have huge effects on violence prevention. Organized by Garcia's right-hand man on the project, Malik Rosenthal, the life skills series seemed to be pitched at an individual level, conveying a message of morality and "bootstrap" ideologies of achievement and success. Our sociological inclinations led us to believe the problems these young men faced had more to do with poverty, lack of jobs and job training, institutional isolation, and racism than with personal moral shortcomings. Nevertheless, this program was really Rosenthal's baby, and he was convinced that these sessions would provide player participants with concrete information about the problems they faced and new ways to approach such challenges. He also hoped the talks would expose participants to positive role models and serve a socializing, educational function for the young men he believed lacked structure and discipline in their lives. And there wasn't really any pushback. Even Cauldwell and Witters were on board, telling us that the speakers in these sessions would help "break down media stereotypes about black men."

We, however, became leery as we watched Rosenthal shape this idea into being. The life skills series was developed and conducted by a local community activist organization known as Men of SALAAM (Sincere and Loyal African American Men). (Representatives from this organization provided security for Stay Alive, as they had the previous summer.) Rosenthal contracted with the organization to design a "curriculum" that focused on nine virtues, one for each week of the program. Each speaker would address one of the virtues (responsibility, perseverance, loyalty, etc.), and program staff—coaches, referees, site security, and so on—would stress these virtues throughout each evening's games. In many ways, they echoed politically conservative rhetoric about the true underlying problems of the inner-city and black men in particular: it's up to you to change your circumstances. It turned out, in fact, that the Men of SALAAM drew their inspiration directly from the writings of William Bennett, George H. W. Bush's former "drug czar," who actually did blame drug use and all the problems of the inner-city (and American culture more generally) on the nation's "moral failings." This orientation, a variation on old culture-of-poverty theories that operationalized the most ideological and suspect aspects of neoliberal paternalism, stood in such stark contrast to the theories and program planning materials that we had started from (as well as Garcia's own city planning guide) that it was almost unbelievable—we've never been quite sure how it ended up this way. Some combination of the easy availability and affordability of the Men of SALAAM, the paternalism that surrounded so much neoliberal policy making in the city and for African American men, and the close ties between leaders of the organization and someone in the city office seems the most likely explanation.

In a certain sense, however, these interpretations and analyses are neither here nor there. For, in the end, whatever hopes or reservations we had about the life skills program, the fact is, it was never properly put into practice. The "curriculum" was loosely conceived and poorly organized. Only one training session was held, and fewer than half of the core staff attended. Only a handful of the coaches were involved with the training, and referees, the most consistent and visible program officials on-site, were not included at all. The Shoot Hoops branch of the program (run out of the American Indian Center) opted out of the life skills series entirely. During the course of the 67 games that we (or our undergraduate research assistants) observed, some 89 life skills presentations occurred—a reasonably large number, but well short of the 134 we should have seen if the program had been conducted according to plan. Moreover, the vast majority of the life skills events we observed lasted only one minute or less—76 of 89 times consisting of little more than introductions, a group huddle, or prayer. Only three went longer than five minutes, and two of those occurred on the opening night. And recall: these program elements were supposed to be the centerpiece and signature element of Stay Alive's intervention programming. All of which is to say that the life skills portion of the Stay Alive project never really got a fair test.

Similar problems plagued the other nonbasketball aspects of the program. The education and jobs training events were ambitious and well chosen, and there were a lot of efforts to incorporate basketball showcase events and competitions into them. Cauldwell and Witters even organized a "skills showcase" of local basketball talent for community college scouts so that the best players might put their talents on display to attract scholarship offers from local colleges. (This particular program held great interest for the two grassroots organizers, bringing together their beliefs about how sport could help disadvantaged young men of color. At one point, Cauldwell even joked, "Shoot, man, I'm trying to get myself a 'ship. I still got four years of eligibility!") However, the execution of every element was problematic and haphazard. The job fair never happened, and only three local schools sent representatives to the education fair (though many made curricular and application materials available). The basketball skills and talent showcase, probably the best of the events in terms of player energy and attendance, attracted only one community college recruiter, and he only discussed the possibility of a scholarship with a player who was already in contact with other schools.

From the very beginning and on a nightly basis, the program faced constant staffing problems. We observed a full staff in place (defined as a site coordinator, timekeeper, scorekeeper, two referees, security from Men of SALAAM, and a director check-in visit) on only five of the thirty-one program days we were on-site. This situation was a recurring source of frustration and dissent among program officials. The implementation of special events was even more of a challenge. Since the program administrators and grassroots organizers had their hands full, in fact, it was often left to Wheelock to serve as the default program planner and implementation director—a role he was perhaps less trained and less prepared to perform than almost anyone else among the staff (though it did provide for an optimal ethnographic experience). Initially, Wheelock was tasked to work with Klausmeyer (the city agency's resident epidemiologist) in the evaluation and assessment of the program and to support the efforts of Cauldwell and Witters in launching their own independent year-round program. Tangentially, he would provide more general program support in assisting administrators and organizers here and there with day-to-day tasks. But, due to voids in the event components of the program, Wheelock was thrust, instead, into program development and implementation, despite having no contacts with local businesses, community college coaches, or school recruiters.

All this is to say that it was precisely those elements of the program that funders and city supervisors deemed paramount, all the nonsport elements, that were Stay Alive's weakest components. Even *our* disappointments and failures about assessment and evaluation were connected with the fundamental failures and shortcomings in implementation and delivery.[5] Much like the nonsport elements of the program, the entire data collection and evaluation plan was plagued by the inability to follow through with plans. In certain respects, the most unfortunate result was not that we didn't get to test our theories about the interventionist potential of sport; rather, it was that the program failed to put its *own* theories about sport-based prevention into practice.

EIGHT

They Got Game:
Lessons and Reflections
from the Bottom Up

Reflecting on the disappointing developments and results in the months (and ultimately) years following our first summer season with Stay Alive, my research team and I found ourselves asking two main questions: First, how did an intervention and partnership that seemed so promising, fail to live up to its own—*our* own—visions? And second, what were the larger lessons and implications of this program and experience for other basketball-based crime prevention programs—and sport-oriented social intervention more generally? Our eventual answers were derived from our review of the daily, operational demands of the program as well as our understanding of the larger neoliberal policy contexts—that is, the limits and constraints within which Stay Alive took shape and operated. But given our insider, on-the-ground research, we always started with the understandings and accounts of the various organizers themselves.

Raphael Garcia and his staff put the bulk of the blame for the failure to deliver on the nonbasketball elements of the Stay Alive project on Frank Cauldwell and Rich Witters. In addition to the fact that the city administrators saw the grassroots organizers as opportunistic, somewhat untrustworthy, and largely unprofessional and incompetent, they were also convinced that Cauldwell and Witters were just interested in basketball and didn't prioritize the elements of the program that were so crucial to the preventionist goals and programmatic requirements of a sport-based approach.

There was a certain amount of truth to the former. Cauldwell and Witters *weren't* the most careful administrators or organizers. There were often questions about daily scheduling, missed follow-up phone calls, and the like—with Wheelock, more often than not, trying to pick up the pieces, and Garcia sometimes having to step in to negotiate ongoing questions about responsibilities, documentation, and receipts. And it was no secret that Cauldwell and Witters were motivated largely by their love of basket-ball and desire to make a name for themselves in and for their community through the sport. Again, their ultimate goal was to parlay their involvement with the Stay Alive program into the creation of a larger, year-round program and community center where they would both operate youth-based sport and education programs and market their own hip-hop merchandise. (Over the course of our time working with them and as part of our agreement for doing fieldwork with them, we helped on several different funding plans and grant-writing projects to these ends.)

Nevertheless, Wheelock and I thought that laying all the blame on Cauld-well and Witters was fundamentally unfair. For one thing, they weren't trained for or experienced in social service administration. This is precisely why Garcia had brought Rosenthal and his colleague Atkins, both of whom had backgrounds and training in social service administration, on board, putting them in charge of the life skills curriculum, overall management, and administration. And ultimately the real problem in terms of adminis-tration and implementation was that Rosenthal and Atkins were not nearly as involved (or even present) as they probably should have been, given that they held primary administrative responsibility (and, as far as we could tell, received compensation for doing so). Garcia's self-chosen administrators appeared at games only sporadically and attended meetings and an event or two, but their involvement in the day-to-day workload of the program was minimal, and this was left essentially to Cauldwell and Witters, and sometimes to Wheelock and our undergraduate assistants. It wasn't neces-sarily Rosenthal's and Atkins's faults that they contributed very little (both held full-time positions in a local nonprofit domestic violence center in Minneapolis and saw their roles with Stay Alive as mostly the oversight of funds handed down by the Minneapolis Department of Health and Family Support), but it *was* the reality.

Even within these constraints, we saw that Cauldwell and Witters really did make serious, good-faith efforts in taking on the administrative and organizational responsibility to deliver a solid basketball program and the nonbasketball, violence-prevention-oriented aspects of the program. These aspiring community organizers may have been irresponsible at times, but they were hard workers and no fools. They understood the importance of the prevention programming from the point of view of city administrators and leaders—with whom they had hopes of working in the future. Good in-tentions aside, though, Cauldwell's and Witters's efforts to carry out the non-sport, prevention elements of the program plan were really stymied by two factors, both of which were somewhat beyond their immediate control. One was fairly obvious in retrospect: they had very little input into or control of the key interventionist component of the program—the life skills program. This was all on Rosenthal and his connections with the Men of SALAAM community group, and there was little Cauldwell and Witters could do if their colleagues didn't deliver. The second problem Cauldwell and Witters faced was that on a day-to-day basis they were preoccupied with the basic organization and operation of the basketball games. This one stood out as important, because it is a familiar challenge for all sport-based community organizing and social intervention.

On any given program day, the bulk of Cauldwell's and Witters's time and energy was focused on the games: getting the gyms opened and set up, making sure referees showed up, ensuring each team's roster was filled with registered participants, and trying to collect data and information for our ongoing evaluation attempts. With limited funding and staff and such a large league, this meant a lot of work. In the crush of the program's daily operation, it often proved impossible for Cauldwell and Witters to get everything done. What got pushed down the priority list was typically the nonsport programming.

To give a particularly telling example: Even before the program began, all of us involved with program design decided that participants would be required to fill out a full registration form before they could play. This was to be a hard-and-fast rule. Yet, when several teams showed up on opening night in front of the largest crowds of the season (well over one hundred fans sitting in the bleachers and standing in the aisles) without completed forms, league organizers had little choice but to let them play. While this specific incident could have been avoided with better preparation and planning, program staff found themselves in such situations regularly. When the facilities weren't ready at the beginning of a scheduled game, they had to find a way to begin games right away, or risk having frustrated players or even entire teams simply leave. If, at the last minute, a site coordinator was missing a referee and a life skills facilitator, the first call that went out was inevitably (and, we believe, necessarily) to the referee. Without a referee, players, or teams, there was not just no game; there was no program. Basketball *had* to come first.

These problems were not just a matter of low effort or even of differences in philosophy—they resulted from limited resources and time. The primary reason and rationale for the program had little to do with sport; yet it was the sport-specific part of the program that had to be the top priority and absolute necessity on a day-to-day basis. When push came to shove, the nonbasketball aspects of the program were sacrificed. Even when Rosenthal and Atkins, those program administrators most committed to the life skills and educational components of the program (and, conversely, least interested in basketball itself), were around, they made these kinds of practical choices time and again.

This isn't just an abstract, analytical point. There are real policy, programming, and implementation lessons here: this situation mirrored and highlighted the deep and fundamental tension that all sport and recreation initiatives have to face—indeed, on which they are constructed. The nonsport programmatic elements had to be tightly linked to violence prevention and risk reduction efforts in order to secure funding and community support; at the same time, the interventionist programs had to take the understandings and motivations of participants themselves seriously to avoid a "motivational mismatch" between program participants and program objectives. That is, for Stay Alive, basketball got the young men in the door. Without it, there'd be no nonsport programmatic elements, because there'd be no one to talk to.

All these efforts demand tremendous resources, knowledge, skill, and commitment. Unlike their counterparts who do not attempt to employ sport as a central programmatic feature, sport-based programs require mastery of both the cultural world of sport and the policy world of social intervention. They're more difficult, expensive, and time consuming because sport only offers a hook; the games draw people in, but the real program happens off the court. So, while looked down on in some circles, sport-based intervention, if it is to be done properly and effectively, isn't a shortcut or an easy fix: it actually requires more of operators than nonsport programming. Program providers must be experts in both sport provision and social intervention programming—and have the time, resources, staff, and facilities to make good on this. It can be more complicated and expensive than other initiatives because it imposes on its practitioners a double burden. They are caught between two different audiences and interests—and when resources are limited and push comes to shove, the nonsport aspects of the program necessarily get shortchanged (for theoretical elaboration, see Hartmann 2012b, 2003b).

The Local Politics of Neoliberal Paternalism, or The Return of Race

One of the ironies—or perhaps it is tragedies—of social policy in the neoliberal era is that it seeks to solve problems that are so complicated and deeply rooted with resources that are so, so limited. This unfortunate and almost unavoidable arrangement is the result not only of limited institutional funding and financial commitments, but also of ideologies and beliefs that the roots of these problems (and thus the appropriate policy approaches) are not systemic but individual, not structural but moral. I am referring here back to the ideas about race and risk and prevention that cohere in neoliberal paternalism as discussed in previous chapters—ideologies that put the onus for the social problems of the city on the behavioral choices and perceived moral failings of those mostly minority individuals burdened with problems of poverty, unemployment, crime, and social dislocation.

Obsessed as we all were with the proper place and appropriate use of sport in prevention and, moreover, with trying (mostly unsuccessfully) to establish and document the effectiveness of this experimental approach, these ideologies and beliefs about the roots and proper objectives of prevention did not receive much attention. Indeed for a program that was targeted specifically to African American and Native American young men, there was essentially no discussion of the risks or problems these men faced or how they might best be targeted. In retrospect, this absence was probably connected with the peculiar disinterest that Stay Alive participants, organizers, and administrators had with respect to talking about race—the race-neutral, color-blind orientations which we noticed upon entry into the field (and noted at the outset of the previous chapter). But as the project unfolded, we began to see this as a bigger, more problematic omission than we had initially appreciated. Indeed, what dawned on us especially, as later in our research and writing process we tried to reconstruct and reassess what had gone on in the field, was that the two main parties in our project were divided not only on their different visions of the value of sport but (arguably, more fundamentally) on their understandings of the problems of young inner-city men of color. In short, the two main parties or organizing players of the Stay Alive program disagreed about both the problems and needs of young, inner-city men *and* how to address these.

Ideas exemplary of neoliberal paternalism (as described in chapter 3) were built into Garcia and his supervisory staff's vision of sport programming and the needs and risks of young African American men. They believed—or, really, simply assumed—that young African American men posed a risk to themselves and to others in their neighborhoods and the Minneapolis metropolitan area as a whole. And they were focused on trying to prevent and control this risk, to prevent the violence it was believed these young men were prone to and that posed such a threat to the community at large. This wasn't (or shouldn't have been) surprising. Garcia and his staff were very much a part of this new, neoliberal system of poverty governance and paternalistic social control—its ideology and logic, its funding streams, and its underlying racial visions. Indeed, they and their colleagues were in charge of implementing programs on this model and even produced *manuals* laying all of this out.

Such thinking was almost foreign to Cauldwell and Witters. They didn't necessarily or entirely deny the social and cultural problems of young black men as imagined in neoliberal paternalism, but it wasn't really their focus or interest, nor was it reflective of their own lives and experiences and those of all the young men around them. In line with the more structural critiques often emphasized by sociologists, they saw the problems of the young men in their community as the result of features of the urban environment that were largely beyond their control: lack of good jobs, inadequate schools, and, most of all, the prejudice, discrimination, and racism of the main-stream society (with its attendant public policies and social services). That said, they really didn't think there was much that could be done to affect or change these structural realities. They weren't even what you could call "political" in this sense at all. Rather, their interest was really in calling out and confronting what might be called institutional racism by providing al-ternative resources and opportunities for young men in their community within the realm of the programs and policy options that were available to them.

The basic point here is that these were real, fundamental differences carrying with them different assumptions about policy, programming, and prevention—or, more specifically, about the needs of young African Ameri-can men and the best ways to serve these needs. Indeed, locking in on the different visions of African American men, the risks they were believed to present, and the things that needed to be done to address these risks gave us a very different purchase and perspective on Garcia and his staff's vision of sport and sport programming, calling our attention to the particular and peculiar role that sport played in the context of neoliberal paternalism.

In a certain sense, the emphasis on sport distracted attention away from other more fundamental policy and programming issues. There are two ways to see this: On the one hand, it placed an undo burden and emphasis on sport, creating expectations that were probably somewhat overblown and unrealistic. You might even say that these radically different conceptions of the social needs, risks, and requirements of young African American men undergirded and intensified the differences that surrounded the visions of sport. On the other hand, this emphasis on sport may not have been such not a bad thing—or, put somewhat more specifically, it may have served a functional purpose. Perhaps it distracted folks away from the fundamen-tal differences and debates that would have otherwise divided them and become deal-breakers. Talking about the relative value and approaches to sport, challenging as it was, may have protected against even more explosive, racial issues that would have revealed how deeply and irrevocably divided organizers were about this project, the risks it posed, and the ends toward which it was directed.

I remain uncertain about how self-conscious Cauldwell and Witters were about the very different, deeply conflicted understandings of the problems and challenges of young black men embedded in the conflicts over the Stay Alive program and the value of sport-based intervention, and even more so about the extent to which they would have understood these broader consequences or put them in an explicitly racialized context. However, I do know that ideas about race and the politics of race did seep into the Stay Alive field in other ways for Cauldwell and Witters. These involved the basic operational aspects of program administration and responsibilities that came to the fore mainly when issues of power and autonomy—or powerlessness—entered the picture. Even then, it was usually in private discussions and one-on-one conversations.

When Wheelock and I talked with them privately, Cauldwell and Witters complained (often bitterly) that they were asked to do much more than they had envisioned and were given insufficient resources and compensation to do the job. They said they were not getting paid their fair share and then were being forced to shoulder all the responsibility and blame. They probably had a point, though given our particular roles and responsibilities, we tried to steer clear of such internal administrative and fiscal debates as much as possible. But what we found ourselves attentive to in analyzing how they saw things was the context they sometimes used to make sense of the struggles when speaking to us in private. For Cauldwell and Witters, these were all about race.

Cauldwell and Witters believed the program administrators had no faith or confidence in them because of their race—or more precisely, because of how they expressed their blackness. In one revealing conversation, Cauldwell put it like this: "They see me as a black dude, a hip-hop cat and that's it. No trust—everyone is expecting me to fail. They want me to fail." At another moment he said bluntly: "[It's all about] white supremacy." Both he and Witters saw this as part of the racism and "white superiority" of those in power in society and in charge of governmental programs and policies. Ironically, the bulk of Cauldwell and Witters's ire was directed not at Garcia (whom they saw as a city bureaucrat, so they never expected him to give them much faith or respect), but at Malik Rosenthal, the African American supervisor who worked in the same community and social service sector they did. "It comes from both sides," Cauldwell told us at one point, "black and white. Even the black guys out there in their suits, they want us to fail. It's like, now that they made it, they don't want someone like me working my way in."

Some of their criticism of Rosenthal and his mainstream, bureaucratic type revolved around issues of image, identity, and style. In Cauldwell's view, Rosenthal wasn't qualified to run a basketball program like Stay Alive because he was a "nerd" who "didn't even play ball." These cultural cues served as evidence, for the grassroots organizers, that Rosenthal was out of touch with the participants in the program, unable to know what they really wanted or needed. On more than one occasion Rosenthal had been forced to ask either Cauldwell or Witters the name of a program participant. Though they never made a public show of it, they made sure that *we* knew that they saw this as a prime example of Rosenthal not being "down" with his people or their culture. But it wasn't just personal for Cauldwell and Witters. They really saw Rosenthal as a sellout to the mostly white, mainstream establishment, completely disconnected from the lives, problems, and passions of the black community he claimed to be a member of and to want to help. They suspected Rosenthal was in it for salary and status. They also believed he was actively and deliberately trying to undermine their authority and credibility with Garcia. And ultimately they were just convinced that he didn't understand the real needs and desires of inner-city African American young men.

I'm not sure it is my place to say for certain who best represented and understood the "real" or "true" needs and desires of the black community. But several points are essential and revealing. One is simply to highlight that these claims about race and the proper needs of the African American community were expressed and discussed really only indirectly, through a politics of legitimacy and cultural authenticity. Connected with this is the fact that it was only in this arena of administrative responsibility and control that these racial divisions and differences were overtly recognized or discussed in our entire engagement with the Stay Alive program. Thirdly and most importantly, we witnessed more than a few patterns and incidents that lent credibility to Cauldwell and Witters's belief that racial politics and aesthetics were key to the administrative and organizational structure of the operation. Perhaps the most significant involved their treatment relative to organizers in charge of the Native American site.

Throughout the bulk of our time in the field, we paid only minimal attention to the Native American component of the Stay Alive project, the Shoot Hoops site. This is partially because our interest in the connections between basketball and blackness had led us to focus our ethnographic observations and interviews on those two program sites that served predominantly African American populations. But it also had to do with the fact that the Shoot Hoops director, Pete Mears—"Mears" as everybody called him—wasn't interested in the Stay Alive project, its process, or its objectives (least of all our research agenda). He just wanted to offer some kind of a structured sports program for youth and young men of a certain age in his neighborhood and from his community. He was particularly disinterested in the life skills portion of the program. Mears was not unlike Caudwell and Witters in this respect, but he simply stopped attending planning meetings at some point. And he didn't return until months later when the life skills planning was complete and program officials were trying to implement it. The difference? Mears and his Native American wing of the program were actually allowed to opt out.

Initially, Mears simply did not implement any of the life skills components into his league play. He didn't so much *refuse* to do so; he just never did. Interestingly, though all of Stay Alive's city administrators knew that Shoot Hoops was going without the life skills pieces, no one did anything about it. They basically resigned themselves to it and didn't even express much concern over it. The omission of the life skills component of Mears's third of the program wasn't even considered an issue until interleague play—games between Native American and African American teams—began.

It started on an evening a few weeks into the summer program when Native American teams traveled to the African American site in South Minneapolis. While GBA players huddled together prior to the opening tip-off to hear a (typically brief) presentation on the chosen virtue for the day ("manhood," as it turned out), the players from the American Indian Center stood around, clearly unsure of what to do. This presented a problem for city supervisors: it made the African American players and their organizers, Cauldwell and Witters, painfully aware of and suspicious about the differences in their programs. Why were *they* required to have pep talks on "virtue" if the Native American teams weren't?

Confronted with this overt differential treatment at a program meeting later in the week, Garcia and Rosenthal prevailed on Mears to acknowledge the life skills component of the project, encouraging him to bring in community "elders" to make presentations of some sort before the games. Mears grudgingly hung a few posters with the nine virtues around the gym and left it at that. He never had community elders come in as was required of Cauldwell and Witters for the GBA, but then again, Garcia and his staff never brought up any concerns, either.

The difference was indicative of a larger and quite revealing pattern. Garcia and Rosenthal more or less let Mears run his league as he saw fit—even when his management completely contradicted their broader rationale, plans, and objectives; in contrast, the city administrators exerted tremendous pressure and control over Cauldwell and Witters and the GBA. It is impossible to assess the extent to which this was strictly because of racial stereotypes (as opposed to personal differences in trustworthiness and responsibility that Garcia typically emphasized), but the racial functions were hard to ignore. Comparing his African American–dominated site with that of Mears, Cauldwell told me privately at one point, "I feel like we're down on the plantation."

To be fair, there were several mitigating factors that help explain these racial differences. One involved the larger, community politics of racial equity and equality. In a metropolitan area with a large, very visible, and highly politicized Native American community, Garcia and the mayor's office needed to avoid charges of racial favoritism or preferential treatment. Moreover, though we didn't actually hear this while in the field, having a Native American program kind of shielded the whole Stay Alive initiative against accusations that the African American community was itself being unfairly targeted or stereotyped on the crime, violence, and risk front. Nevertheless, it must also be acknowledged that there was little doubt about the racial character of the administrative struggles. This gave us another angle on the racial dimensions of neoliberal paternalism—not so much with respect to the program participants as with respect to its grassroots organizers and operators.

To get to the heart of the administrative politics of race in neoliberal paternalism, let me pose this question: Why did Cauldwell and Witters put up with this anyway? Why did they continue to work with an administration that treated them this way and had a vision of programming and prevention that was so clearly and fundamentally different from their own? The answer is actually a very old and familiar story, one that came down to resources and finances, facilities and power.

The Stay Alive project was, in a certain sense, a marriage of convenience between the two main organizing parties involved. It provided funding and facilities that enabled Frank Cauldwell and Rich Witters to launch their GBA initiative, and it allowed Raphael Garcia and his staff in the Minneapolis Department of Health and Family Support to deliver popular and much-needed violence prevention programming for the mayor. Programs with multiple objectives and competing agendas are obviously far from ideal, but such arrangements were and are typical of many of the collaborations that constitute the contemporary, neoliberal social service system. And the situation was actually even somewhat more stringent and constraining for Cauldwell and Witters. Given their long-term visions and aspirations for GBA and their almost complete lack of access to funding and facilities, Stay Alive was less a marriage of convenience than a matter of necessity. Cauldwell and Witters had to "play ball" with the city officials because they didn't have a program without the city bureaucrats, their funding, and their facilities. All they had was an all-star game. (Here, it is worth mentioning that Mears's Native American league was operated out of the American Indian Center, a facility that Mears and his folks controlled independent of the recreation centers and recreational facilities the African American components were located in.) So while there may have been disagreements and conflicts about who was at fault for various program shortcomings, it was absolutely clear who had the power and authority in Stay Alive: the city supervisors, Garcia and his team.

And there is a final irony in all of this. For all of Garcia and his staff's insistence on the centrality of the interventionist aspects of the program and the visions of race and risk embedded therein, those core components of the neoliberal agenda were revealed to be the most poorly conceptualized and operated aspects of the entire initiative. Conversely, where the program was most successful was as a basketball league—both in terms of participation and play as well as in terms of visibility and popularity in the community. In other words, for all the time devoted to developing the life skills program, the conflicts between administrators and organizers, and the shifting responsibilities and duties, the final program—which is to say, Stay Alive as it was ultimately put into practice—conformed more to Cauldwell and Witters's vision of both sport and the politics of race than anyone else's. Not only was Stay Alive a strong basketball league; it was a real point of pride and symbol of success in the community. Caudlwell and Witters may have taken a lot of heat for not being able to do more on the most overt, nonsport preventionist components of the Stay Alive initiative, but ultimately it was their vision of both sport and the needs and desires of young African American men that were best served.

Oh, the ironies and complexities of race, risk, and social impact in the neoliberal context. In studying the research literature and in talking to other scholars and practitioners who have been involved with such initiatives, I have come to realize that the kind of organizational tensions, conflicts, disagreements, and shortcomings with respect to the connections between race, risk, and prevention that have been discussed in this chapter and the one before it are actually not uncommon among sport-based social interventions and violence prevention programs. And while intensive, on-site involvement with Stay Alive made my research team and I painfully aware of our inability to do much to solve these issues, it did allow us to get a first-hand, insider's view of some of the factors that help account for these shortcomings—findings that illustrate the basic, underlying tensions and challenges of almost any attempt to use sport for purposes of social intervention and change, but especially of those operating under the constraints of neoliberalism.

And before I move on, let me make two additional, big-picture points about the Stay Alive story that speak to the larger, more general issues and aims of this book taken as a whole: first, this is a story that is not just about the proper use of sport for social intervention, or just about the role of race in paternalist racial policy, but really about the relationships between these two. And, second, that there were—and are—very different visions of both sport and the needs and desires of the African American community, especially when it comes to the reasons why young black men participated in late-night basketball and what they could reasonably hope to get out of it.

But What about the Players?

With all the controversy, conflict, and intrigue that surrounded the (mostly) behind-the-scenes planning and administration of Stay Alive, my research team had to guard against losing sight of the one group involved without whom there wouldn't have been a project. I am speaking, of course, of the GBA players themselves, the young, mostly African American men who played in the league and constituted the program's target population and reason for being. Fortunately, as actual game play began each summer and our field-work shifted to the day-to-day operation of the basketball league, this was much less of a problem. This is, basically, because once the games started, the players came to occupy center stage. And in coming to see and understand the GBA and Stay Alive program from the players' point of view, my research collaborators and I came to realize yet another layer of complexity on that race-risk-sport nexus that had gotten me interested in this research project in the first place.

One of the research team's first observations and favorite points of discussion involved the disconnect between the various administrative dimensions of the Stay Alive project and the playing of the games themselves. What we quickly came to realize was that the program participants had little or no interest in or knowledge of the behind-the-scenes struggles (much less the broader political and cultural issues) that had drawn our attention to the program in the first place. In our interactions and observations and conversations, they didn't really care that much about any of the nonsport programming that was built around the games either, much less the perceptions that they were somehow an at-risk population or the claims from the mayor's office that Stay Alive and the GBA were actually social services, not sports programs. All the participants really cared about was the league and the basketball games themselves.

Throughout the entire ten-week season, we saw hard-fought games played at a surprisingly high level of play. We saw tremendous energy, excitement, and investment in the games—from warm-ups through the end of the games. And we saw young African American men playing hard, playing fair, and having fun doing so. In fact, this deep and intense level of engagement stood in obvious contrast to the kind of halfhearted, going-through-the-motions attitudes that we observed for all the various, explicitly interventionist aspects of the program. For example, attendance from the focal, nonsports events such as the job fair and the college recruitment day was, as we mentioned, not impressive. And in the life skills sessions before games, players would listen politely—ruminating, it seemed to us, more on the game ahead or trying to catch their breath during the halftime break.

These observations were not surprising, of course. Playing basketball was the main reason for these young men to be there in the first place, and as the dominant cultural script about the importance of basketball in the black community would have predicted, almost all the participants were fairly deeply invested in the game. All but one of our fifteen formal player interviewees had extensive experience playing organized and semiorganized basketball of the sort that sociologists like Scott Brooks (2009) and Reuben May (2008) have vividly described in their important ethnographies. Most had played high school ball and all had numerous years of experience playing in summer leagues (though only one-third of the program participants had aspirations to play ball at a higher level as, for example, on a college scholarship). They played seriously and, for the most part, very well. Both informal conversations and regular observations seemed to suggest that the interventionist aspects of the program were at best tolerated; it was playing the games, or simply the game itself, that mattered most to these participants.

I initially became fascinated with the idea of portraying these participants as actively refusing and resisting the program's crime prevention orientation and all the pathology, deviance, and defiance about young urban men of color it implied. This stemmed, in part, from the fact that I had spent so much time thinking and theorizing about athletic resistance in the context of my study of the 1968 African American Olympic victory stand protests as well as the then scholarly fascination with seeing political resistance and mobilization in all forms of popular culture (Hartmann 2003c). I thought—or really hoped—that here we might be seeing another level of struggle and resistance, this time between the players themselves and the whole cultural justification for the league itself. This, I speculated, might finally be the authentic young, male African American experience, the voice of the disaffected but clearly not dysfunctional young urban male of color and "resistance" in the heady, politically radical sense of the term (see Carrington 1998; Hartmann 1996; see also: Lipsitz 1998; Kelley 1997b).

Unfortunately (and as my undergraduate research assistants who were hanging out with the players in the program from day one tried to tell me from the beginning), there wasn't actually much evidence of that. GBA participants had little interest in politics, cultural or otherwise, or in any of the organizational struggles around the Stay Alive program. If anything, in the context of the concrete problems and risks these young men faced on a daily basis, their attitudes and orientations appeared more escapist. At a certain level, they were playing basketball just to have fun, stay fit, and get away from anything really serious or substantial about the broader circumstances of their lives.

In the face of this, I started to go the other analytic direction, speculating about the extent to which they were allowing themselves to be used and controlled by the Stay Alive operation. As my students and I got to know players a bit more personally through conversations, observations, and a set of formal interviews conducted by the undergraduate research assistants on the project,[1] I came to realize that this wasn't an accurate or appropriate interpretation either. GBA participants didn't see themselves as controlled or policed at all. Nor did they consider their basketball playing some kind of simple release or escape from the hardships of everyday urban life. Quite the contrary, they believed that this program was serving them and their interests quite well, thank you very much. More than a few went so far as to describe the program in the glowing terms that would accord with the theoretical language of being enabled and empowered. This became clearest when I read the transcripts that came out of the formal, structured interviews conducted during the final few weeks of the season.

Our interviews began by asking players general, open-ended questions about the program itself. The responses were very positive about almost all aspects of the league—and in no area more so than with respect to its (poorly implemented) prevention orientation and the success of the life skills components. Reflecting on these sessions, the players spoke about the need for "discipline" and "relating to others." One participant described the life skills as "cool and inspirational," a way to "learn about yourself and [a] tool for life." Another said they were "very positive." One respondent, a twenty-three-year-old with a Muslim surname who said he had been playing basketball since he was five, told us that the life skills touched on "key points in life" but that the only real answers were "in the Bible." Another interviewee felt that it "needed to be said" that Stay Alive was "not just about basketball but involved learning also." The main lesson for him and his orange squad teammates was about "unity, team unity."

To a certain extent, these responses needed to be taken with a grain of salt. Players in the Stay Alive leagues knew who was funding the league, and they also knew that our research assistants were talking to them precisely because we were supposed to be writing an evaluation that would help organizers advocate for support from the city funders for the crime prevention aspects of the program. Without being cynical or manipulative, they were simply telling us what they assumed we wanted to hear, or what they thought (probably fairly accurately) we needed to hear in order to provide an evaluation that would keep funding for the program in place. At the same time, I began to see that these positive evaluations of the prevention-focused aspects of the league were not as simple and straightforward to interpret as they seemed on first pass.

As I got further and deeper into the interview transcripts, I realized that most players had difficulty specifying exactly what it was that was positive about the basketball program or how it had affected them personally. Their answers to follow-up probes on these themes were vague and general. For example, when asked whether he had a good understanding of the program's goals and objectives, one respondent told us, "I don't exactly remember, but I feel I could relate." Pausing for a few moments, he came back to "discipline" and "organization" as the keys. When asked to specify what he had learned about these themes or skills, however, he was unable to offer any specific comments or examples and soon admitted that he didn't think the program had helped him make any positive changes in his life or life goals. And those who did acknowledge such impacts, offered answers that were fairly minimalistic: "It helped a little," an employee of a data processing company in town told us. "I mean, at least it gave me something to do." At least four of the fifteen players we did full interviews with wouldn't even say that much, admitting that they simply "couldn't relate" to the prevention parts of the program in any meaningful fashion.

And here's the thing: these responses stood in marked contrast to those offered up when respondents were asked about their more general assessment of the program and were invited to offer any suggestions they might have for improving it in the future. First of all, these overviews were uniformly positive with every single individual speaking of his plans to participate the following summer. One described it as a "great overall experience," and another said he would "absolutely participate again." More than this, when we asked about the strengths of the program or things that should be changed, we got a great deal of feedback from program participants but it was about how to improve the structure and competitiveness of the league itself, the quality of the basketball. For example, some respondents wanted more games, with at least two interviewees calling for at minimum three games per week (instead of the standard two contests). Others thought that the end of the year tournament would be better in a double elimination format. Still other suggestions included offering a higher level of competition, recruiting better referees (officials were admittedly inconsistent in their calls and often unduly influenced by complaints from coaches, fans, and players), and using earlier starting times to allow more games and easier scheduling for individuals who worked or had family obligations. One player, a nineteen-year-old with aspirations of playing college ball, wanted "more dedication from the players" to improving their games and the level of competition overall. Another individual spoke of his desire for more events and more food because that would "get the community more involved." Indeed, the desire for larger crowds, more spectators in attendance, turned out to be a recurring theme for almost every one of the players we interviewed.[2]

There were, of course, a variety of motives and interests at work here. As I mentioned above, perhaps a third of the participants had hopes of using their participation in this program and proficiency at basketball more generally as a springboard into bigger and better things along the lines of Cauldwell's and Witters's occasional flights of fancy about scholarships or professional contracts. But the majority did not. For the rest (and even for many of those who had higher aspirations), the emphasis was on recreation and fitness, socializing and having fun—nothing much different than the reasons many young men of all races and ages turn up at recreation centers and public parks to play basketball or participate in any number of other sports. Taken as a whole, these suggestions were also notable not only for their specificity but also for the thoughtfulness, force, passion, and precision in which they were offered; they were, in other words, issues that these young men were both passionate and articulate about.

This intense interest in and commitment to the basketball aspects of the program was something of a revelation for me—or, perhaps more precisely, a reminder and reevaluation of the value and function of basketball in the lives of these African American young men. I was forcefully reminded, in and through these interviews, corroborated by our observations as well, that no matter what our interest or the city's interest in crime prevention and social intervention was, Stay Alive was to these young men a basketball league first and foremost. Basketball was "the program" for these young men. One stark illustration of this came when one nineteen-year-old told us *in the life skills portion of the interview* that what he had learned in the program that would help him later in life was "to keep your hands up and play [defense] with intensity." This was his life lesson. Stay Alive, for its players, was not about crime prevention, social intervention, or anything else regardless of their own personal backgrounds and records. They simply wanted a safe, high-quality league to compete in the game that they loved to play.

These passions and commitments must be situated in the context of the decline of public parks and recreation funding and facilities nationwide at the time and since. While the Twin Cities, with their historic commitment to public parks and recreation, had seen somewhat less of this than other locales around the nation, the one issue that did hit home in Minneapolis that was unfolding elsewhere was the elimination of full-court basketball courts. Indeed, at one point as I was puzzling through these findings, a piece ran in a local weekly entitled "Bounced!" which detailed the elimination of full-court basketball in the city. The story (written by David Schimke and published in *City Pages* on June 16, 1999) explained how ten of the city's "most storied outdoor basketball facilities" had been removed by officials in Minneapolis because of a "slew of complaints by residents who live near certain city parks [and are] . . . irritated about noisy late-night games and what they see as the increasing volatility among the (mostly black) players who play them." The official rationale that was given was simple: delinquency and other illegal activities surrounding the courts. "When the contests get fierce, the court gets a reputation as *the* place to play ball. And that reputation . . . tends to attract more players than most city parks were designed to handle—either on or off the blacktop." As one officer put it, "We do watch that area, not because of who is playing, but because of what goes on around the game such as alcohol use, weapons and drug dealing."

Even in the face of these eliminations and cutbacks (which, according to a *Chicago Tribune* story from July 3, 2000, were being seen there and in many other metropolitan regions around the country), city officials I talked to insisted there were more than enough full courts available for serious players from Powderhorn to Kenwood (various Minneapolis neighborhoods). And they were probably right in a certain respect—at the time of our first work with Stay Alive, some sixty basketball courts were still open and available around the city. That said, the removal of top-flight courts had clearly left many young African American men like those in the GBA looking for competitive places to play. This might help explain the otherwise puzzling fact that the age range for the league seemed to have gone up over the two years of the program we observed. An interview with a former Minneapolis Parks and Recreation Commission supervisor on April 9, 2003, not only confirmed this policy initiative on the part of the city but related an interesting but troubling anecdote that helps explain what was going on. He shared that when senior citizens were asked why they wanted the full courts dismantled, most said that it was because they believed the courts were bringing in kids from "the outside," undesirable youths from other neighborhoods and communities around the Twin Cities. However, participation surveys revealed that most of those young people who used these facilities were actually from these very neighborhoods, usually living within blocks of these parks and playgrounds (as well as of the residences of the senior citizens themselves).

So there were no great political ideals or ideological agendas at work here for the players themselves, the young African American men targeted and served by the Stay Alive program. There were no attempts to escape the lives they were leading, no efforts to resist the government programs or the established sociopolitical regime. Stay Alive wasn't even about some unhealthy obsession with sports or unrealistic hopes for using athletics as a means out of the ghetto. Rather, what late night basketball was about was just the regular, ordinary desire of young men of color to have facilities and programs for recreation, leisure, and fitness, to make their lives as livable and enjoyable as possible under the circumstances within which they were embedded.

This brings me to a final point about social context and the broader theoretical implications of the attitudes and experiences of the league participants themselves that is signaled in the title of this chapter, "They Got Game." The title comes from the street phrase that emerged in the 1990s to describe someone who was a good basketball player. "He got game," it was said. The phrase was brought to much wider public awareness with the release of a Spike Lee film, *He Got Game*, about basketball that starred Denzel Washington and Ray Allen, the latter as high school phenom Jesus Shuttlesworth and the former as his father. (It was none other than Lee's old pal from the Nike ads of an earlier era, Michael Jordan, who delivered the line asserting that Shuttlesworth "had game.") Coming from a broken family in a poor, inner-city neighborhood, Jesus had little in life to hope for or work from—nothing other than his basketball talents and skills.

For my purposes, this title, which I used in many early presentations of the ethnographic portions of this project, is a provocative and underappreciated phrase that helps summarize and signal why it was—and is—that black athletes and members of the African American community put so much energy and attention into sports, basketball in particular. Here, it is also worth noting that the main theme of the film was that everyone (from prospective agents and college coaches to Jesus's teammates, his girlfriend, and even his own father) wants a piece of Jesus's "game." Reminiscent of Eric Lott's study of blackface minstrelsy, *Love and Theft* (2013), Jesus has the skills and talent, and they all want to profit from it. His father's final lines of advice tell Jesus that he should look out for himself or else he will be used by everyone else and end up "just another nigger like your father" (who is serving a life sentence for murder in the state penitentiary).

Extending from this, "they got game" is also a phrase that can apply to the meaning and significance of midnight basketball for the young, inner-city men who were targeted by the program as well as the communities from which they came. Folks in the African American communities targeted by midnight basketball and related sport-based social intervention programs had very limited resources aside from programs like these and their love of and ability to excel at sport. This, of course, was one of the insights and motivating points for Frank Cauldwell and Rich Witters. But what basketball (and sport more generally) meant to these folks—how it was experienced and understood, and the social functions it served—was often quite a bit different than what policy makers and program supporters intended and expected. In attending to what this "game" (or these games) meant for these young men and those in their community, I realized that there is at least one alternative to the scholarly and policy understandings of sport-based social intervention programs that we may have underappreciated, undersold, or misunderstood in focusing on the more instrumental, neoliberal political and policy context. More specifically, juxtaposing the creative ways in which young men understand and negotiate their surroundings—what Gary Alan Fine (1987) might call their "idio-cultures"—against the public discourse about sports and African American men (if not through midnight basketball then through the obsession with maintaining a "balance" between sports and education) suggests that if there is something pathological about the deeply intertwined nexus of race and sport in American culture, it may not be African American men but the American culture itself that is conflicted and problematic.

In a context in which young men like these are afforded so few opportunities and face so many stumbling blocks, it makes sense that sport provides an opportunity for fun, fitness, and competition. Who wouldn't be interested? Who wouldn't think that this was valuable in itself? Who wouldn't wonder if there weren't other kinds of opportunities for accomplishment and mobility to take advantage of? Perhaps the deeper problem with race and racialization is how difficult it seems to be for all of us to keep in mind these simple points about the kinds of activities we all want and need in our lives.

Over two decades ago in his foundational "Program for a Sociology of Sport" ([1982] 1988), the great French sociologist Pierre Bourdieu used a parable about African American athletes in prestigious American universities in the early 1970s to illustrate his depiction of the challenges of sport scholars. Despite their seeming public prominence and importance, Bourdieu explained, these student athletes found themselves in "golden ghettos" of isolation where conservatives were reluctant to talk with them because they were black, while liberals were hesitant to converse with them because they were athletes (189). In other words, Bourdieu built his project on overcoming the dualisms and dichotomies that plague sport scholarship (not to mention all sociological theory and practice): namely, that social actors deserve to be talked with and listened to, taken seriously as agents in the worlds they are made by and they continually participate in remaking. Bourdieu himself never really interrogated the African American athlete experience—and too often we as scholars and we as policy makers don't either.

The imperative to take the agency and self-understanding of young African American men seriously is, in many respects, the essence of the theoretical and methodological principles that I have tried to put into practice in this chapter. Largely as a result of prevailing cultural stereotypes and the opportunity structures they enable politically, these players and program operators have now, in the vernacular shorthand, "got game" and are thus presented with a unique vehicle for self-expression and social intervention. Perhaps it is this vision of midnight basketball that can finally have the possibility of getting beyond the racial stereotypes and images that otherwise seem so pervasive and so easy to reproduce in the context of sport-based risk prevention of any sort. To help put the aesthetic and attitude I observed among the young men who play late-night basketball in Minnesota in perspective, let me conclude this chapter by referencing a book, one of the most insightful and entertaining scholarly books you will ever read, that appeared at the same time this program was in existence, Robin Kelley's *Yo' Mama's Disfunktional!* (1997b).

In one of the first chapters of the book, Kelley wrote about the significance of pleasure and play for young people of color in contemporary urban America. The thrust of Kelley's analysis, which once appeared under the title

"Playing for Keeps: Pleasure and Profit on the Postindustrial Playground" (Kelley 1997b), is simple: that the rise of permanent unemployment, the deterioration of public institutions, and the militarization of inner-city streets and neighborhoods have created conditions where young people, especially young people of color, have little that is meaningful and rewarding to do other than engage in play forms of social practice such as graffiti, music, or sports. Rather than being just a societal opt-out or distraction, these forms of play, Kelley argues, have been channeled and transformed by some young people—Witters and Cauldwell obviously come to mind—into meaningful and indeed productive labor. "What I am suggesting," Kelley says, "is that the pursuit of leisure, pleasure, and creative expression is *labor*, and that some African American urban youth have tried to turn that labor into cold hard cash" (1997b, 45). There is nothing particularly transformative or politically radical about this, according to Kelley, but it is important and revealing nonetheless of the precarious situation of so many in these communities and the creative lengths they will go to make something of their circumstances and lives.

And for many other African American men in urban America, I would suggest, the engagement with pleasure and play is even more basic than that. In contrast to the hopes and fears of midnight basketball critics and supporters, these participants are ordinary, everyday American men in tough circumstances just looking for a few hours of recreation and physical activity a week, in an urban environment that affords them few such activities. And here is the really radical part: that what might be most desired and helpful for young men in these circumstances is not programs for risk reduction or crime prevention, not even programs for education or development, but simply facilities and programs that offer opportunities for physical fitness, recreation, and leisure. In other words, meaningful "intervention" and "change" in this context may have less to do with conventional political outreach and activism than it does with creating conditions that allow and afford the basic needs and simple pleasures of everyday human existence.

NINE

Conclusion:
In the Light of Midnight

At its most basic level, this book has been an attempt to tell the story, or perhaps solve the puzzle, of why a basketball program became such a popular and prominent solution to the problems of crime and risk and social dislocation in urban America in the early 1990s. Researching and writing this story about how this sports-based innovation first emerged and has evolved over time was something of an exercise in historical methods: locating and gathering archival documents about G. Van Standifer, the Chicago Housing Authority, and the 1994 crime bill debates; conducting oral history interviews with various leaders and actors; and gathering reports and other documentation of the project as it changed over time. Figuring out how the midnight basketball concept was adapted and operationalized in later years also called for substantial ethnographic fieldwork; and then there has been the challenge of figuring out how to collect, organize, assess, and shape this array of materials and accounts into a coherent narrative.

But this project has been much more than fact-finding, description, and storytelling. It has also been a project of sociological analysis and interpretation. That is to say, it has been about situating midnight basketball in its appropriate social and theoretical contexts and trying to grasp what is both productive and problematic about it, as well as about using midnight basketball as a lens into key dimensions of racialized neoliberal political culture and public policy and the opportunities for sport-based social intervention therein. It has also involved using this entire case study to illustrate and sketch a larger argument about sport's unique cultural characteristics and impacts in society, especially with respect to constructions of race, African American athletes, politics, and neoliberal social policy. Reviewing these larger analytic ambitions, I think, will help reiterate and frame the larger lessons of studying the rather peculiar and intriguing innovation that is midnight basketball, locking in the social and theoretical contributions of this project taken as a whole.

Midnight Basketball in Context

As an exercise in social and cultural analysis, a good deal of the work of this project involved—and indeed required—identifying the proper precursors to midnight basketball and situating this "innovation" in its appropriate social, cultural, and political contexts. More concretely, this meant that I had to explore the history of sport as social outreach and intervention. I engaged the political debates and policy transformations of the period (neoliberal paternalism, the new penology, etc.) and the ideological and cultural framings of the problems and their perceived roots and causes (especially regarding "culture of poverty" ideas). I have tried to show that midnight basketball was the product of a historic convergence of ideas about the relationships among sport; young, mostly poor, urban men of color; and social intervention given new life and form in the context of the neoliberal transformations of American social policy that coalesced in the late twentieth and early twenty-first centuries.

For a sociologist like myself interested in patterns and the more general implications of cases, this broad framing opened up whole new levels of analysis and perspective. For one thing, the existing research on these broader, more general topics provided a concrete, comparative context and set of criteria that served as a critical-theoretical touchstone for assessing the strengths and weaknesses of midnight basketball as a policy initiative. Thinking about midnight basketball as a case study of something "larger" also allowed me to reverse the analytic focus of the book in places, using midnight basketball as a lens to help deepen our appreciation of certain larger phenomena and more general social patterns. One of those was neoliberal social policy—more specifically, racialized neoliberal paternalism. I hoped, in undertaking this book, to use the intrigue of midnight basketball to cultivate understanding and awareness of racialized politics and social policies in the contemporary, neoliberal era and to contribute to these theories as well. In this context, what seemed like a single, straightforward program emerged, in fact, as a diffuse, decentralized operation involving multiple, more-or-less cooperating, coordinating agencies and actors with funding streams and rationalities all operating in the name of efficiency and cost-effectiveness and with a renewed emphasis on structure, discipline, order, and individual responsibility within broad sociopolitical groups. This organizational structure and institutional logic, such as they are, are illustrative of both neoliberal social policy and the many purposes midnight basketball served (and serves) for various stakeholders.

Studying midnight basketball as a case of larger patterns and processes also provided an opportunity to reflect on the whole idea of using sport as a means for youth development, social intervention, and change, especially in poor neighborhoods and communities of color and for so-called "at-risk" youth and young people. In fact, sport-based social intervention is the topic I am most frequently asked to talk about, and I have written on the topic a number of times in recent years (Hartmann 2003b, 2012b, 2015; see also Hartmann and Kwauk 2011). I summarized some of these insights in chapter 6 when I discussed the new theorizing about sport and intervention that grew out of the political controversies surrounding midnight basketball in the mid-1990s. Among other things, this research and fieldwork on actual basketball-based programs helped me more fully appreciate and understand that sport *can* be a powerful tool for recruitment and retention. At the same time, it also became clear that such initiatives are expensive and intensive, that development and change is far from automatic, and that it is not so much the *sport* program that produces beneficial outcomes as the nonsport programming elements that are built into, around, and onto the sport program. Much research still needs to be done in terms of assessment and evaluation of all sport-based youth intervention programs—both to confirm the effectiveness of such interventions and to refine our understandings of the mechanisms by which positive outcomes are achieved. But working through these points in the context of everything else that I have said about midnight basketball in this book provides a useful frame for helping practitioners, policy makers, and the general public better understand what sports-based crime prevention programs can reasonably be expected to accomplish (and how limited this really is), how they can be better evaluated, and, ultimately, how they can be more effectively implemented.

In the now classic paper on Balinese cockfighting, which is the source and inspiration for the ideas about "deep play" I have elaborated above, the anthropologist Clifford Geertz (1973) described cultural forms as "texts" that social analysts can read over the shoulders of their subjects. For Geertz, if social analysts and cultural critics can properly "read"—that is, situate, analyze, and contextualize—these texts, we have a powerful window onto other people's lives as well as our own, a way to interpret and communicate the ideas and meanings that constitute the lifeworlds and worldviews of human subjects in specific contexts and communities. Cultural objects and performances are stories we "tell ourselves about ourselves." This holds for social analysts as much as policy makers and regular citizens. Truth be told, this was how the analytic process worked for me at the start. I learned about neoliberal social policy and sport-based social intervention through, or because of, midnight basketball—not the other way around. And I have returned to thinking about youth recreation and sport after many years away from that line of reasoning, because patterns and trends today announce themselves in the context of sport-based youth intervention programs all across the country. The case study took me from sport to national-level culture and policy; changes in culture and policy brought me back to how sport became imbued with such promise for social intervention.

In the context of these general points about seeing midnight basketball as a case in context, this book is perhaps best understood as an iterative, extended case study—as a kind of two-channel operation. In the first phase, the goal is to situate midnight basketball (the case) in its broader social, cultural, and historical context(s) in order to provide an explanation for and better understanding of the origins, appeal, internal structure, and broader social significance of this intriguing and highly popular (if somewhat peculiar) policy innovation. In a second, back-channel operation, this framing can suggest that a fuller understanding of midnight basketball can be used to develop a deeper, more nuanced understanding of neoliberal social policy—both in terms of its own characteristics and idiosyncrasies (its racial dimensions, its ideological and organizational structures, the conflation of punishment and prevention/paternalism and penology in a single disciplinary logic) and in terms of lessons and implications for sport-based social programming and policy.

Sport as a Cultural and Political Force

Geertz's argument about the importance and impact of cultural practices like cockfights or sporting events actually went well beyond what these "texts" reflected and revealed about more general social forces and cultural patterns. As both analyst and theorist, Geertz was insistent that such cultural practices played, or at least *could* play, an important and independent role in shaping social life. In the original deep play paper, in fact, he explained the meaning and significance of the cockfight in Bali by showing how betting around the fights reproduced and reinforced the social kinship structure of local tribes and communities. Through their bets on particular animals and trainers, people in Bali demonstrated their communal ties and commitments to kin. Nothing specific or concrete *changed* in winning and losing, according to Geertz, but something definitely *happened*: social networks and ties were enacted and displayed, confirmed and reestablished. Thus, the cockfight was, in Geertz's memorable formulation, both a model *of* and a model *for* social solidarities and alliances. The Balinese may not have wanted or been able to explain their fascination with cocks and cockfighting as a reflection of their social structure (indeed, one of the most interesting aspects of the piece is that Geertz doesn't really *ask* them about it [see Crapanzano 1986]), but this practice provided a "model for" them to understand and live out their social ties and connections.

Extending this model of / model for formulation to a sports-based public policy initiative like midnight basketball is useful, I think, in letting me highlight the analysis I developed in the middle chapters of the book about midnight basketball not only as a singular policy initiative, but also as a symbolic or conceptual model of and for the larger cultural concerns and public policy approaches to the perceived risks and problems of inner-city African American men in the neoliberal era.

Midnight basketball, in these chapters, didn't just reflect the realities of neoliberal paternalism; it provided a pathway and policy model of its own, a prototype of sorts. It assumed an independent frame and force in the swath of neoliberal social policy. This applied to regular, ordinary observers as well as to policy makers and public leaders. This was my argument for a much more concrete and indeed more literally *political* understanding of the cultural politics of sport. Indeed, this modeling and sense-making through small, symbolic policy experiments was, I have come to believe, *especially* true for public leaders and political elites like Jack Kemp, who may not have been entirely self-aware about how the program was creating both an understanding of and solution to the problems of young men and the inner city. Midnight basketball seemed, to Kemp and many others, intuitively *right*. More importantly, the programs presented a synthesis of social intervention that worked for many others in the culture. Midnight basketball was an important symbol and standard-bearer for an entire orientation and approach to public policy in an era of neoliberal transformation and retrenchment. Midnight basketball gave these heretofore abstract, intuitive ideas about race and risk and social policy concrete substance and form.

Perhaps the most concrete and consequential symbolic functions midnight basketball served involved how it was used by political elites to publicize and promote their own policy reforms, program initiatives, and general, overarching approaches to government intervention. I mentioned numerous times how HUD-supported midnight basketball programs were featured in news stories nationwide, and there was really no better, more perfect example of midnight basketball being used for overt, political purposes than the first President Bush's enthusiastic embrace of it as a signature program in his official Points of Light Foundation. As I argued in the fourth chapter, "A Commercial for Neoliberal Social Policy," this publicity not only served as an advertisement for the whole Bush agenda and approach to urban and social policy, it also pulled attention away from the deeper, more fundamental cuts to and reorganization of urban policy and social programs of the period. The late 1980s and early 1990s were, as I alluded to many times in the previous pages, an era marked by tremendous transformation in policies for the poor and powerless. This also involved shifting responsibility for the public good away from the state to local, nonprofit organizations and agencies, especially in metropolitan areas and especially those serving communities of color (Wacquant 2008a, 2008b; Brenner and Theodore 2002; Beckett and Western 2001).

Having midnight basketball leagues to hold up—especially with the limited funding they required and the private, nonprofit administrative structure they typically operated under—allowed leaders to divert attention from these neoliberal transformations and focus instead on exciting and seemingly cost-effective ways to continue to do urban policy, address urban problems, or serve urban populations, albeit in quite different and clearly diminished ways. And, of course, I also emphasized that midnight basketball accomplished these symbolic ends in a way that made its racialized underpinnings—as well as those of neoliberalism more generally—obvious without being blatant, easy to see yet also not hard to avoid talking about. At local and national levels, the publicity surrounding midnight basketball served to establish the legitimacy and necessity of neoliberal approaches to crime and urban policy in an era of reformulation and reregulation. This analysis was not meant to be just about midnight basketball; it was intended to announce a much broader argument about the social significance and political power of sport in the contemporary world.

The characteristics that mark and define sport as a unique and powerful (or a uniquely powerful) social force are varied, diverse, and paradoxical. Most sport scholars start, as I suggested in the introduction, with the basic material facts involving the large number of people who participate in sport in one way or another. They consider the depth and sheer intensity of the energy, resources, and emotion so many people invest in sport participation. In this project, I've tried to add at least three additional dimensions to our theories of the cultural significance and political consequence of sport: sport's high-minded idealism and moralism, especially with respect to racial progress, mobility, and change; the paradoxical trivialization of sport that Clifford Geertz's concept of deep play calls into focus; and the deeply embedded norms and convictions that hold sport and politics separate in contemporary American and Western culture, what Ben Carrington (2010) dubbed "the politics of the apolitical."

I take these moralist, ludic, and political/apolitical factors—which sometimes operate on their own, but often work in combination(s)—as keys to many of the questions and puzzles and ironies that shape this narrative. The high-minded moralism that surrounds much sport, especially with respect to young people of color, helps explain, for example, what made midnight basketball so amazingly and unexpectedly popular as an approach to social intervention, even in a culture that is typically disdainful of state sport policy. At the same time, its paradoxical play status helps account for how midnight basketball was able to tap into high ideals about sport even as its social and political significance was disavowed by many of its most ardent operators, supporters, and funders. The ludic aspects of sport in American culture, especially in combination with prevailing ideals about the need to keep sport and politics separate and distinct, are also key to understanding how midnight basketball was mobilized in different ways and to different political effects in various social, cultural, and legislative settings. Indeed, in some ways sport's social and political effects were most pronounced in the places where they were least seen such as national media coverage of the original program or the organization infighting that I described in chapter 7. I have argued it is precisely *because* of sport's paradoxical, deep play structure that the symbolic significance of midnight basketball could be appropriated by so many, easily manipulated by some, and plausibly denied by others. And the powerful norms about sport and politics are also why, on occasion, this political mobilization could easily backfire.

Such ironies appear again and again in this narrative, in both national political discourse and grassroots program operations, and they help us understand (I hope) not only midnight basketball but also the cultural structure and social significance of sport itself. In fact, I am convinced that these moralistic, ludic, and apolitical factors are fundamental conditions or dimensions of the sporting form, defining aspects of the social and political dynamics that play out in and around sport.

While this study of midnight basketball has depended on and has been intended to further develop our theories of the cultural form and sociopolitical functions of sport in the contemporary world, I want to be sure that my attention to the unique cultural status of sport hasn't overshadowed or obscured another distinctive aspect and objective of the project as a whole: its racial analytic aspects and ambitions. The powerful, paradoxical status, structure, significance, and functions of sport are not, in my view, incidental to the racial structure and social significance of midnight basketball (and perhaps even sport more generally). No, much more than this, I think the unique cultural status of sport actually parallels and even *heightens* the racial dimensions of the midnight basketball project.

The most basic and concrete point to highlight in this respect is how, and the very large extent to which, sport functions as a race-making force in contemporary American culture. This is a fundamental, guiding assumption of this project. A part of sport's role in constructing racial images and ideals goes back to ideas about sport as providing unique opportunities for mobility and advancement for racial minorities, as an idealized space for modeling appropriate race relations in contemporary culture. But here I also want to call attention to the unparalleled importance of sport as a site for the cultivation and consumption of African American icons, heroes, and success stories. Sport is a genuinely unparalleled arena in terms of its role in creating images—both positive and negative—of African American men in American culture, as well as in terms of its importance for black community, culture, and identity. No single sporting practice exemplifies this function more than midnight basketball and the programs and spaces it has created (or that have been created in its name) throughout this country.

This is not to idealize or romanticize the role of basketball or any other sport in the construction of race in American culture. As sport scholars are quick to remind us all, the history of race and sport in the United States is marked by persistent racial stereotyping and discriminatory practices; by conflict, backlash, and counterresistance; and by subtler, more "enlightened" versions of contemporary stereotyping and racism. And sports-oriented racial images and representations are as likely (perhaps even more so) to contribute to the construction of subtle but powerful racial stereotypes, images of difference based on physical superiority, mental inferiority, and moral ambiguity or depravity. Surely there has been much of that in this narrative, and I probably don't need to recount my various analyses of all the racial subtext built into the whole notion of sport as a tool for outreach and intervention—especially with respect to risk and risk prevention in the post–civil rights, neoliberal context. Recall here that even in the most local and perhaps ideal setting of this project, the Minnesota-based program my students and I spent several years working with, the politics of authority, resource distribution, and even style reared their heads in forms that were clearly driven by ideologies and assumptions based on race and racism.

Such are the paradoxes and contradictions of sport's racial construction, of sport as a race-making space. The multifaceted and contested dynamics of race that play out in and through sport are on a very large stage. They have meaning and significance well beyond the confines and boundaries of the

204 / Chapter Nine

sporting world itself. This is what I have called "sport as a contested racial ter-rain" (Hartmann 2000). The racial dynamics of the sports world are a drama for all to see, a model, a metaphor, or a vehicle by which people in "the rest of the society" understand—for better or worse, more accurately or less so—perceived problems of the black community and potential solutions for them. What happens in the world of sport reflects and informs—indeed, educates—many Americans in their understandings of race in general and African Americans in particular.

Midnight Basketball's "Longue Durée"

Midnight basketball is now at least thirty years old, and I've been reading, re-searching, and thinking about the innovation, its evolution, and its broader social and theoretical significance for at least half of that time. These are not insignificant amounts of time for a policy innovation or a research project. In-deed, I have sometimes felt a kindred spirit with the historians of the French *Annales* school. These scholars called their approach to the study of history the "longue durée" to capture their emphasis on long-term historical struc-tures and slowly evolving processes. Frustrating as it can be for scholars and policy makers interested in the latest thing and more immediate changes, this extended, big-picture orientation has provided a certain, very useful analytical distance and historical perspective. It has allowed me to see mid-night basketball—and the dynamics of race, sport, and social intervention more generally—from many different angles.

This "long view" has also proved indispensable in those years (such as the first decade of the new millennium) when scholarly interest in sport-based crime prevention began to wane and/or midnight basketball dropped out of the public view almost altogether. Actually, to a certain degree, this is still the case today. To be sure, there is still a Midnight Basketball Inc., late-night sports-based programs can still be found in many communities, and a plethora of youth intervention programs still have sport or some competi-tive physical activity as a significant component of their programming. But on the whole, policy makers, funders, and the general public, especially those most interested in sports and athletics, have moved on to other in-novations and programs, at least on the sport and recreation front. In fact, if you do a Google search on "sports and risk" or "prevention and sport," what you find is that these terms, either in scholarly or more public circles, have come now to focus on issues of health, safety, liability, and injury.

It is not entirely clear to me whether the decline of research and writ-ing on sport-based social intervention and crime prevention has resulted from a lack of interest in these approaches, or whether it instead represents a retreat back into more idealistic and, from my perspective, naïve beliefs about sport's capacity to be an automatically positive, prosocial force in the lives of young people. To a certain extent, I suspect the latter. After all, the idea of "development" in and through sport is more popular than ever (Coakley 2011); many of these programs and ideas now focused on more global or international levels are little more than traditional sport romanticism (Hartmann and Kwauk 2011; see also Coalter 2010; Darnell 2007; Giulianotti 2004; Kidd 2008; Levermore and Beacom 2013). While disconcerting in some ways, these transformations and shifts are, for someone like me, all food for thought, material for analysis and critique. And in the most recent years, one thing that has not only kept me going but kept this research project and its ideas relevant is that this crazy, idiosyncratic concept of midnight basketball still resonates with lots of folks and pops up in a surprising array of contexts.

Some of these references and recollections are positive, productive, and forward-looking; others are far more problematic. On the latter front, for example, in June of 2014 a story came out of Memphis that five teens were shot in the aftermath of a midnight basketball tournament held as part of an event designed to keep "teens and guns off the streets."[1] Though all the teens were reported to be alive and in recovery, this incident and the reports of it, gave rise to a whole, predictable set of concerns about the purported dangers of offering sport and recreation programs in inner-city neighborhoods and communities. On the other end of the political spectrum was a story by Dave Zirin for the *Nation's Police and Law Enforcement* blog on September 10, 2013, about how the NYPD was accused of using sport-based programs as a means to monitor and control Arab American, Muslim, and South Asian organizations, players, and their families which led to e-mails and phone calls about the misuses and abuses of sport-based programs by public officials and criminal justice professionals.

I don't know that midnight basketball will ever again be as central to public policy for cities and crime as it was at the end of the previous century, or even to youth sport policy more generally. But it does still resonate; it casts a long shadow. Stories and incidents like these call midnight basketball to mind for many folks and get them thinking, once again, about the potential benefits and pitfalls of sport-based social intervention and change, about initiating, improving, or evaluating sport-based social intervention programs of all shapes and sizes. Just as it was paradigmatic for a whole generation of sports providers back in the 1990s, midnight basketball remains a touchstone and a model for many politicians and policy makers with respect to sport-based intervention as well as criminal justice policy more generally, and, I believe, we have lessons to learn from it. Hopefully this project can help those of us who care about youth sports, social intervention, public policy, and politics to be more informed and constructive when we encounter these dynamics and debates in coming years. But I'm not always sure.

Perhaps the most intriguing yet also disconcerting example of midnight basketball's continued resonance and long, complicated shadow came in September of 2014 on the twentieth anniversary of the Clinton crime bill (just as I was beginning to dive into the penultimate round of reviews and revisions on this manuscript). This milestone yielded a whole series of stories and recollections (some of which I was interviewed for) about midnight basketball, its role in federal legislative policy, and the innovation itself. Many of these were framed in terms of a reconsideration of federal criminal justice policy and the explosion of incarceration more generally, especially given its disproportionate impacts on African American men. For many, the policy that got put into place had since been revealed as too punitive, too controlling, with not enough attention to intervention and prevention. As the title of one National Public Radio story put it, "20 Years Later, Part of Major Crime Bill Viewed as Terrible Mistake" (September 15, 2014). Without any apparent recollection of the tortured racial politics that surrounded midnight basketball back in 1994, it was invoked as a more constructive and cost-effective alternative to traditional punitive, prison-and-police models.

Here's how the NPR story framed it: "Talk to combatants in the long and sometimes nasty debate over the crime bill 20 years ago, and another item on the table back then looks different in hindsight too: a concept known as midnight basketball." The piece went on to interview Bobby Scott, a Virginia congressman who had voted against the bill because he believed it didn't do enough to support prevention programs. After twenty years, he still talked about midnight basketball as representing the better, more effective and more cost-efficient approach. And what is even more revealing is that the story concludes by explaining how "ideas like midnight basketball" are also "winning support from Republican governors who have branded their approach as 'right on crime'—taking money away from prisons and putting it into social programs."

Obviously, we have been down this road before. It is, as the late Yogi Berra might have said, déjà vu all over again. In the right contexts, with sufficient resources, and a proper understanding, sport-based interventions such as midnight basketball can play a positive, productive role in the lives of young people of color living in otherwise marginalized, disadvantaged situations. But in the context of all the complexity and history I have documented in this book, it is incumbent on us to be cautious and skeptical about these visions and claims and all the baggage that goes along with them. It is essential, for example, to recognize that sport-based intervention of any sort—whether oriented toward crime prevention or social intervention or youth development—is never easy or automatic; indeed, it tends to be far more expensive, expansive, and complicated than is usually realized or expected. Moreover, whatever sport-based social intervention programs may have to contribute to improving the lives of urban youth, we must be careful not to expect too much from them—not to treat them as a magic bullet or miracle elixir. Crime prevention and social intervention are complex and challenging enterprises even under the best of circumstances and even with abundant resources and using the most comprehensive and advanced modes of engagement and programming. Given their typically limited resources and scheduling, sport-based programs by themselves, even when brilliantly conceived and properly implemented, will not always succeed. They will fail more often than not. To believe anything else not only overestimates the social force of sport, but it underestimates the difficulties of meaningful social intervention and change.

And what is so dangerous about such misunderstandings is not only the potential failure of these programs themselves; it is also their broader symbolic function and political significance, especially with respect to public policies pertaining to race and crime and social assistance more generally. A failure to understand these realities and the limitations of sport-based programs like midnight basketball can actually serve to reinforce and exacerbate the problems faced by at-risk urban youth by deflecting public attention away from deeper social sources of their problems. There may be no more important and ambitious and unappreciated point of the study of midnight basketball and its past history than this one. Here, let me quote once again, the sport sociologist Jay Coakley (2002, 23): "If we are not cautious," as he has put it, sport-based social intervention programs like midnight basketball "may unwittingly reaffirm ideological positions that identify young people, especially young people of color as 'problems' and then forget that the real problems are deindustrialization, unemployment, underemployment, poverty, racism and at least twenty years of defunding social programs that have traditionally been used to foster community development in ways that positively impact the lives of young people."

Far better, I believe, to focus on the lives and aspirations and needs of the youth and young men of color themselves, the young people who these programs are so typically designed to "target." And rather than thinking of these young people as threats and these programs as solutions to their problems, perhaps we would do better to think of these young folks as not being so different from us, and just try to ensure that they've got some of the basic resources and opportunities that many of us simply take for granted. This larger, more humanist approach to social policy for young African American men and their communities extends far further than sport obviously. But in this context, we would do well to remember that some of the most important benefits of sport-based programming for target are not about intervention and resocialization, but about providing opportunities for recreation and fitness and leisure for populations and communities that are not well served by our usual market-based, profit-driven systems for provision. The most basic benefits, in other words, may be about health and fitness, recreation and leisure, even just sport for itself.

I have not emphasized athletic participation and sport provision itself as much as I could have in this book. In fact, in the early chapters, I was fairly critical of sports practitioners and scholars who saw problems-based sports programming as a solution to the problems of access and provision in poor, urban communities of color. But as the fieldwork presented in the final chapter should have made clear, this is indeed one of the biggest and most basic benefits of any sport-based, athletically oriented programming. And we certainly cannot and should not take the provision of athletic opportunities and services for granted. In fact, of all the challenges and limitations faced by American youth sports programs in this, the first quarter of the new millennium (danger and safety issues; overuse and burnout; the decline of school-based sports and physical education classes; the lack of free, open-play opportunities; specialization and the increasingly competitive and hierarchical sports structure; see LA '84 Foundation [2015], Aspen Institute [2015]), the problems of limited and unequal access along class and race lines remain among the biggest and least appreciated of all (Hartmann and Manning, fothcoming). And too often, when Americans do think about athletic access and opportunity for kids of color, it is to channel them into sports where national pride is at stake or large amounts of money stands to be made; it is, in other words, for purposes of exploitation rather than empowerment.

In *Rituals of Blood* (1998), the iconoclastic Harvard race scholar Orlando Patterson argued that at the end of the twentieth century for the first time in American history African American men were positioned to play a leading role in US culture. In Patterson's view, the aesthetic style and cultural practices most closely associated with black men have long stood as a unique alternative to the staid, Puritan ethos of American culture, especially as it applies to American men and masculinity. It is what he talked about as a more creative, "Dionysian" vision of culture, creativity, and human experience, one that provides a more pleasure-oriented, transcendent alternative to our otherwise repressive and rationalistic culture. For centuries this alternative, Dionysian style was trapped behind and contained within a racist culture that marked it as low status and second class. However, with the decline of the most blatant and overt forms of prejudice in the post–Civil Rights era and the concomitant success and visibility of African American men in American popular culture (not to mention the transformations of culture more generally), this alternative Dionysian style of African American men has now been liberated to serve a more positive, socially celebrated alternative cultural aesthetic and function. And what is most important for my purposes here is that athletes were Patterson's primary examples of this transcendence, sports figures such as 1990s stars Michael Jordan and Dennis Rodman. In a way that was not possible prior to the accomplishments of the civil rights movement, Patterson believed, these African American male athletes—because of their excellence, their celebrity, and most of all their style—brought this new vision and possibility to an otherwise stale, workmanlike American culture.

I have long found Patterson's argument and analysis (formulated, as it was, at just the time midnight basketball was most prominent as a policy innovation) provocative, both with respect to the importance it endows to African American athletes as well as to their meaning and significance in the culture as a whole (May 2009). However, it also seems to me that Patterson's treatment was a bit too limited and constraining, unnecessarily focused on elite-level, celebrity athletes. Indeed, I cannot help but think that the Dionysian liminality and repressed pleasure principles Patterson refers to are also well embodied, if for very different, much more personal reasons, by young men such as those who participated in midnight basketball leagues like the Stay Alive program in Minneapolis.

Whatever the aspirations and intentions of policy makers, the youth and young men I have seen playing basketball late at night over the years are generally not being manipulated, contained, or controlled. They are not really there to be educated, empowered, or enabled, nor are they motivated to play basketball for personal gain or some unlikely quest for stardom or sport-aided mobility. More often, they play their games, whether basketball or something else, whether late at night or during the day, simply because it is fun and enjoyable, something that allows them to maintain a certain degree of physical fitness, health, and leisure in a safe, secure environment. Perhaps it is this alternative vision of basketball, and all manner of athletic activity for youth and young adults of color, that can finally have the possibility of getting beyond the racial stereotypes and images that otherwise seem so pervasive and so easy to reproduce in the context of sport-based risk prevention of any sort. Perhaps, in other words, this simple idea of seeing sport and physical activity as ends to themselves for everyone, especially poor, marginalized kids in communities of color, that would be the most radical analytical and political act of all. Surely that would be a fitting, satisfying tribute to the legacy of midnight basketball and all the youth and young men whose lives it has touched.

The Notion of an Emergent Case Study

In the social sciences, a methodological appendix is usually the place where a researcher will discuss the processes by which he or she collected and analyzed the empirical material that is the foundation of the project at hand. In this vein, someone in my position might use this forum to review the techniques my research collaborators and I used to compile an extensive, representative sample of newspaper and magazine articles on the crime bill debates analyzed in chapter 5, and then discuss the theory and method that guided us in subjecting this data to systematic analysis and/or interpretation. Or, in the case of the ethnographic fieldwork that is the basis of the final three chapters of the study, I might explain how I gained access to various basketball-based programs and established rapport with subjects, how long I was in the field, the kinds of activities I was involved in or observed, and how I recorded and analyzed all this material. I won't do those kinds of methodological expositions here. After all, this book is based on and constructed out of a series of smaller research projects and papers, and my hope is that that the data and methods that constitute each element of this project—and thus the backbone of many individual chapters—are appropriately spelled out along the way, in the notes and main body of the text itself. Instead, my intention is to offer a few brief observations and comments about the properties and general characteristics of the larger, meta-methodological conception and design of this project taken as a whole—the analytic strategy I referred to in the introduction as an "emergent case study."

These reflections will not be extensive. I will restrict myself to two main, meta-methodological points—one having to do with the general, analytic logic or "design" of the project taken as a whole, the other with the centrality of the writing process itself in this approach—and a larger overview of the origins of the project, the semistructured, somewhat organic ways in which this project took shape or "emerged." My hope is that these reflections will help capture and convey the "method" behind the laborious, sometimes chaotic, and surprisingly idiosyncratic research and writing process that resulted in this book.

How the Project Took Shape

While my choice of midnight basketball as an object of study was, as I said in the introduction, shaped by a general theoretical interest in the intersections of race, sport, risk, crime, and social intervention, it was the political intrigue surrounding midnight basketball that really got me thinking of this phenomenon as a potential research project in the first place and drove the initial phases of my research. I am speaking specifically of the controversy that emerged in the context of the 1994 crime bill debates. When I reflected back on that several years after the fact, it was impossible *not* to be struck by how much national attention midnight basketball received. I also started to puzzle over why conservative legislators and pundits had suddenly attacked a program that had been a signature piece for a sitting Republican president only two short years before. Informed by critical race theory and the work of social scientists like Martin Gilens, Tali Mendelberg, and Jill Quadagno on the racial dimensions of late twentieth-century American politics and public policy, I also came to believe that race was at the center of it all, and that an in-depth analysis would demonstrate the profound legislative and public policy consequences of sport and race in American culture.

To test these theories, I read up on the legislative proceedings that produced the landmark bill and assembled transcripts of congressional hearings on the law. With research assistants, I also began to gather samples of the media coverage and commentary on the outcome and entire process. Close textual reading of these documents appeared to confirm my initial, impressionistic suspicions: midnight basketball was inordinately prominent in the legislative discussion and appeared to frame the congressional debate at key moments therein. To further substantiate these ideas and figure out just what it was about midnight basketball that marked it as so significant, I began, in partnership with Darren Wheelock (then a Minnesota graduate student, now a professor of sociology at Marquette University and coauthor of chapter 7), constructing a large, representative sample of media coverage and commentary on the crime bill that would allow formal content analysis of the racial meanings, messages, and impacts I believed were implicit in the debate (these results are summarized and elaborated in chapter 5).

As Wheelock and I worked through this material (and began to make presentations on our preliminary analyses of the legislative debates and media coverage), I found myself thinking back to my earlier, on-the-ground experiences with midnight basketball. Two sets of questions came to preoccupy me. At a foundational level, I wanted to know more about the actual structure and operation of official midnight basketball leagues. How were these programs actually funded and operated? How many were there? Who operated them and for what purposes? And perhaps most of all, was midnight basketball really an effective tool for social outreach and intervention? These questions jumped out at me both because they were the questions people kept asking me and because I didn't really know the answers to them. After all, I had been around a few of these programs early in their development, but I hadn't really observed any from the inside, nor had I taken a larger, global view of the full range of programs and sites that composed the midnight basketball movement.

These questions about the operation and effectiveness of actual basketball-based programs gave rise to a second, more scholarly line of questions about the much broader historical and theoretical issues embedded in the whole midnight basketball case. Was the concept as new and innovative and popular as it had initially appeared? Who had championed it? Why had critique come from the Right, rather than the Left? And what broader, more systemic policies and developments did it respond to (and, perhaps, end up constrained by)? Here, the harsh criticisms of midnight basketball raised in the context of the 1994 crime bill debates made it difficult to understand how there could have been so much enthusiasm and bipartisan support for the concept when it was first introduced, much less whether there was any reason to believe that midnight basketball or any other sport-based program had any real chance of bringing about any kind of meaningful social reform, intervention, or change.

Addressing both of these sets of questions seemed to me essential to unpacking the full social significance embodied in the case of midnight basketball. Yet data and extant analysis proved difficult to come by. Despite the fact that the concept was by then almost ten years old and despite having received remarkable attention (both positive and negative), most of what was "known" about midnight basketball came from journalistic sources that tended to be essentially anecdotal and incomplete.[1] Almost before I knew it, I found myself back on the research trail.

Eventually, Wheelock and I got involved with a basketball-based crime prevention program in the Twin Cities. As described in chapters 7 and 8, the GBA / Stay Alive project was not an official midnight basketball affiliate, but a copycat version that mirrored and mimicked all the key elements of the original official programs. Thus, it served my purposes well. My research team and I spent two full "seasons" observing and working with this program and were afforded incredible access and ethnographic understanding of both the administrative aspects of program operation and the experiences and understandings of participants themselves.

As this fieldwork unfolded, I went back to the library archives and media databases for more information on midnight basketball and the social context in which it emerged. I got on the phone (and later the Internet) and searched for more information about midnight basketball's inception, initial reception, and subsequent evolution. I interviewed program organizers, collected their documents and media clippings, and assembled a small archive of grant applications, administrative documents and reports, and program evaluations from the period. I read all I could about the involvement of key public figures like Jack Kemp, Rush Limbaugh, and Bill Clinton and started looking more carefully at their views on sport, especially with respect to its connections with race. I began reviewing and rethinking research on the history of sport as social intervention as well as on the more recent transformations in both youth sports programming and urban social policies in general. I even started looking into the availability of larger data sets and samples in the hope of testing out theories of effectiveness on a larger, more generalizable scale.

These excursions were unpredictable and time consuming (the fieldwork alone took over two years). They often required me to work with research techniques and types of data with which I had previously had only textbook knowledge or that required me to wait several years until better, more comprehensive histories of political processes or policy shifts emerged. I pressed on, however, driven by Howard Becker's clarion call in *Tricks of the Trade* (1998) for open-ended, question-driven social science. I was also inspired by Pierre Bourdieu's classic exposition of the "general principle of method" in his path-making "Program for a Sociology of Sport" ([1982] 1988) as well as his call for theoretically heterodox, mixed method social scientific research (1988). So it was for me with midnight basketball. I was convinced that midnight basketball was an empirical case pregnant with meaning and significance—and that all the various pieces would eventually coalesce into a meaningful, synthetic whole.

Slowly but surely, my faith was rewarded. An assortment of reports, working papers, presentations, and journal articles began to appear, each adding new depth and dimension to my understanding of midnight basketball and what it represented with respect to the intersections of race, sports, and risk in contemporary American society. And as this happened, the core content and broader, synthetic logic of a book began to take shape in my mind and on the page. This process was organic and based on a great deal of ongoing reflection as well as some intuitive trust, but all of this was far from fully planned and deliberately designed. It was what, in a word, "emerged."

Analytical Logic and Process

Taken as a whole—and I am, again, speaking about the whole of the project here—an emergent case study like this one is the kind of research project where a set of social facts and big, general ideas and conclusions grow out of an intensive, multifaceted, and long-term engagement with a particular empirical object or case, in this instance midnight basketball. In the manner of a detective following a complicated and multidimensional trail of clues, I was constantly trying to figure out how each of the various pieces of the midnight basketball puzzle fit together and what the synthetic, collective whole told us about sports, race, risk, and social intervention, each individually conceived as well as in terms of their various relationships and interactions.

Drawing out such deeper meanings and broader connections requires acts of insight and creativity on the part of the researcher-analyst, but this process is not nearly so haphazard or mystical as I might have made it sound so far, or as it may sound to social scientists who only ask specific empirical questions or operate in more positivistic traditions. For one thing, each piece of the project is inspired by concrete empirical questions framed by the scholarly and theoretical literatures and guided by specific standards and established techniques. More generally, the guiding analytic logic and method behind case-based, emergent inquiry involves an understanding of the relationships between case and context, between the general and the particular, and between theory and practice. These relationships are developed in and through an ongoing, iterative process wherein case and context are each revealed and informed by the other—that is, where the social and theoretical contexts help us grasp the unique features of the case, and then as we develop our understanding of the particularities of the case, this contributes back to our understanding of its role and place in society, and thus of the context more generally.

The art—and, like Robert Alford (1998), I think it is as much art as it science—of grasping and conveying the proper, iterative dialogue between case and context, between particularities and generalities, is one of the greatest methodological challenges of a project like this. Fortunately it is a familiar process and exercise for case studies, and a great deal has been written about these issues in the social sciences (cf. Tavory and Timmermans 2009). Michael Burawoy's extended case method (1998, 2009)—to which my emergent framing is closely related and obviously indebted—was a frequent point of reference for me. Burawoy's original formulations of the extended case method actually offer two different ways to frame and draw out the larger social and theoretical significance of the empirical case material. One of those involves the back-and-forth, iterative dialogue between general theory and the particular case that I have just described. The other is to situate the ethnographic case in its broader social context (urban and capitalist dynamics in his first collaborative volume [1991], global social processes in others [2009]). For me, this would have been neoliberal social policy, shifts in thinking about crime prevention and the politics of race, and the whole history of sport-based social intervention. In both respects, according to Burawoy's depictions and illustrations, there is a constant iterative process, a back-and-forth between theory and data, between the concrete empirical information that is collected and the more abstract, general theories one can use to frame it or implications that can be drawn from that case material.

At least three different features distinguish my particular application and understanding of case-based methods in this project and thus account for my particular, idiosyncratic choice of the label "emergent."

With the more open-ended notion of "emergent," I mean to call attention, first of all, to the multiple methods and miniresearch projects that have driven it. Most case studies are based in a certain type of data and data collection and operate within the techniques and traditions of one research methodology or another—historical comparative, for example, or ethnographic fieldwork. Real research, of course, is almost always more complicated than this—that is, it draws on and is informed by data and analytic insights that extend beyond the formal methods and theories ritualistically rehearsed to establish the research's rigor, reliability, and validity—but this usually is downplayed or hidden in the final production and product. This project takes the opposite approach, and not just for presentation's sake. Throughout, it was far more diverse and multifaceted in terms of data collected and analytical techniques employed. Indeed at certain moments, for certain key empirical questions, I realized the need to formalize and systematize my data collection and the analytic techniques that I was using, and to continue to push to figure out how all these various pieces and parts held together. All of this was kept in check by a rather relentless, dogged commitment to and focus on the empirical material of the midnight basketball case itself. More abstract, general concepts, theories, and forces may have been used to frame and focus the material, and I often tried to draw larger, more general inferences and conclusions from these studies, but the focus of the research, analysis, and presentation all always came back to the case itself. This is one of the reasons I find myself so frequently returning to and reminding myself of Bourdieu's classic description of case selection as a "general principle of method." In this formulation, the theoretical significance derives out of the case, not the other way around.

A second feature of the present research project that contributes to my understanding of the emergent method it employs has to do with the long-term, open-ended, and ever-evolving engagement with the case and case material it required. I chose midnight basketball because I had an interest in the intersections of sport, race, risk, and public policy, but it still wasn't quite clear for quite some time what midnight basketball was a case of. For a while, I thought it was a case of race, sport, and crime—but the further I got from the 1994 crime bill debates, the more I realized that midnight basketball was not only just about crime. It was about intervention, outreach, education, and development in and through sport, and it was also as much about sport's role in politics and public policy as it was about sport itself. After this, I got convinced—convinced myself, I guess—that what I really had was a case study in the racialized neoliberal social programming and policy of the contemporary United States. Midnight basketball was such a case, of course—and the significance of this formulation only increased as time passed and the contours of American social policy began to evolve and shift. However, I eventually realized that this framing was actually a bit too broad on its own terms and that I really lacked the knowledge, expertise, and authority to make a definitive contribution to work in this area. Indeed, one of the real breakthroughs of the book was coming back to my own activist and intellectual roots and realizing that what I really had with midnight basketball was a case of sport-based social intervention, and then situating midnight basketball squarely within the legacy, literature, and ideology of sport as social intervention. This gave me a framework and focus for the project as a whole that also allowed me the ability to speak to issues of racial reproduction, sport policy, and the paradoxical place of sport in culture and politics.

What is important to realize here is that the broader research questions and framing and theoretical conclusions I have just described took a great deal of time to emerge and develop, and thus required taking a rather long, historical view of both the project and the phenomenon in question. For many reasons both within my control and beyond it, this book took a lot longer than it was supposed to, at least a half a dozen years longer. In a certain sense, this is a familiar if unfortunate academic story: by the time someone like me has figured out what I know and have to say about a phenomenon, it almost seems too late. The moment has passed; the audience has moved on. Fortunately, there is also a bright side in this case, several silver linings of sorts. The more positive aspect of the situation (or, perhaps, the more positive way to view these developments) is that the additional time provides perspective and context for one's study—how, in this case, midnight basketball was structured and developed and all that it represented socially and theoretically. It allowed me to see what had changed and what hadn't, what was fashionable and what aspects of youth sport were more entrenched and systemic, as well as understand what midnight basketball gave rise to, what its unique role in all of this had been. It has also forced me to think about and articulate the larger, more general lessons and implications of the midnight basketball case—for sport policy, for social intervention in and through sport, and for how sport fit into the whole racialized neoliberal social policy regime. In other words, this extra time and perspective helped me make some of the larger analytic points and enduring socio-institutional structures more obvious and explicit, and draw out the general social and theoretical insights and implications, the "significance" of the research and the history of midnight basketball.

As foreshadowed in the introduction and implemented throughout the text, these were not all planned but instead emerged in the course of my engagement with midnight basketball—collecting data on various aspects of it, trying to analyze this data and write about it, and trying to publish and present these findings to various scholarly and public audiences. This is a key point and, in my view, another distinguishing feature of emergent, case-based research. The true nature of a project of this sort is not fully fleshed out or understood at the beginning of the project but actually emerges over time, in and through the research and writing process. Which brings me to a third and final distinctive aspect of the emergent case approach: writing itself, the mode of presentation and delivery of the project, what I called in the introductory chapter the "research narrative."

Writing and the Research Process

The first academic article I ever wrote on midnight basketball was published in 2001. It rehearsed many of the historical and analytic themes that appeared in the first and second chapters of this book (indeed, it contained some of the same evidence and formulations I used in those pages), and laid out, in many ways, the research questions that chartered the course for much of the work that I have undertaken over the past decade plus. In the years that followed, I gave a number of talks and presentations on the findings and ideas about different dimensions of midnight basketball and composed conference papers, keynote lectures, reports, and several book chapters on the politics that have surrounded midnight basketball, the theories about sport-based intervention that have been formulated and refined, points of emphasis that have been retained, and those that have been dropped. Some of these pieces were more polished than others, and some got finished while others didn't. But enough of them got published for me to make headway on the project (and get tenure), and it all seemed like more than enough for the book that I told myself (and everyone else) that was really the focal point and objective of all this work.

Still, there was work left to be done. Much of that labor involved shifting my focus as a researcher from original data collection and concrete analysis to a more general, synthetic kind of work—thinking about how various pieces of the puzzle fit together, and how the whole history of the case and its lessons could be framed and told. And this is where writing takes center stage as a central methodological component of this emergent case method.

One writing task was making sure all the different pieces of research, data, and theory found their way into the correct places in the narrative and text. This required constant revision and reorganization, especially as different research questions began to emerge, new papers took shape, or alternative theoretical framings presented themselves. Another came in trying to keep up with the burgeoning (and essential) social scientific literatures and research—on race and neoliberalism, welfare and crime, sport, sport policy, and development as well as earlier work on the idea of a risk society and the whole history of sport as social intervention—that continued to appear. Reading this work raised exciting new questions about the scale, scope, and focus of my project, but also forced me to think about the specifics of the case and what I could or should say about its implications for public policy, political discourse and American culture, or sport-based social intervention more generally. And then there was the challenge of deciding, once and for all, how to write the damn thing—where to let findings and events simply speak for themselves, and when to step back and explain things or put them in context; how to bring the story and lived experience and consequence of midnight basketball to life; and, most of all, what language, style, and voice would best convey my findings, analyses, and interpretations.

Eventually, of course, as I described above and with the input, assistance, and support of innumerable friends, students, and colleagues, the project came together. I settled on a conceptual frame for the project, sorted through what material to include and what to leave out, and finally decided

I had done as much as I could do. And this has been it, presented in narrative form.

I derive this idea of a research narrative, in large part, from the term "research essay" which my one-time teacher Joseph Gusfield used to introduce his classic and still underappreciated book on drinking-driving and public problems, *The Culture of Public Problems* (1981). The research essay, according to Gusfield, is "a book of general ideas developed and expressed in the context of a particular subject matter and experience." With the word "research," Gusfield meant to "call attention to the grounding of ideas in the experience of performing a detailed analysis and description of a specific body of data on a particular issue"; "essay," for its part, signaled the "effort to create a theoretical perspective, grounded in the particular phenomenon of the empirical research." Overall, a research essay is "less bound by the data than in the research report [and] more constrained by them then in the essay of abstract theory" (1981, 2).

I believe that we social scientists would do well to try to produce more books that adopt the rhetorical structure and frame of Gusfield's "research essay." Part of the reason is that I think such presentations are more accessible and engaging for general, nonscholarly readers than standard academic fare. This is why I tried to use individuals such as Jack Kemp and Larry Hawkins or Frank Cauldwell and Raphael Garcia in the text. Because I either knew figures like these well or had particularly rich data and information on them given their public visibility, they were useful figures both for elaborating particular ideas and insights as well as endowing these analyses with a certain personality and narrative. But this writing format and style is more substantive than just creating an engaging presentation. I think that such book-length essays are particularly useful in terms of generating the kind of broad, synthetic thinking and critical analysis that sociologists are uniquely prepared to produce and expected to deliver. Indeed, it is the sensibility that I think C. Wright Mills had in mind when he talked about the "sociological imagination."[2]

Good writing, as my colleague Chris Uggen and I were fond of saying when we edited the American Sociological Association's public outreach publication *Contexts*, is more than just proper punctuation or grammar. It isn't just stringing together words that convey ideas in more accessible, poetic, or clever ways. Good writing is the actual accomplishment and physical embodiment of clear thinking and strong analysis; it is the most basic and fundamental tool of the sociological enterprise, or, as Monte Bute (2008) has put it, "the first method" of the social sciences. And the research essay is one of the ways this can be accomplished.

The chief difference between my writing in this book and Gusfield's no-tion of a research essay is that I have tried to write the book as a narrative of the research process itself—and to make myself and my process of inquiry and discovery part of the story. There were several reasons for this. One was essentially stylistic or presentational and had to do with providing an over-arching story line or narrative for the project as a whole, a thread to make the material meaningful, accessible, and engaging for readers. To do this, I adopted the convention of putting myself and my analytic process—from the initial challenges of data collection and information gathering, to the struggle to interpret and make sense of information and events, to figuring out how they all fit together—more at the center of the book than would usually be the case for social scientific writing.

Writing in this fashion has the virtue of providing something of a story line to integrate and synthesize what otherwise might be a collection of relatively disconnected and disparate pieces. Of course, this approach can also have the consequence of exposing what is often the fairly messy, un-comfortable back stage of the research process itself. We social scientists tend to prefer to keep this to ourselves (and the community of like-minded and similarly trained scholars); we would rather just tell or present our find-ings rather than work through the processes and techniques that yielded them. In this case, I think this particular approach was warranted because it has the virtue of showing how the knowledge and insight of this project was constructed; it lets readers, both scholars and laypeople, engage in this enterprise and evaluate its effectiveness and believability for themselves.

This brings me to a final, more substantive reason for why I decided to construct a research narrative and put myself and my research process at the center of it: to openly acknowledge, if not highlight, the constructed nature of the narrative and research process itself. In writing this book as a research narrative, I want my readers to know how this research and its various findings, interpretations, and claims were constructed and made by me, the researcher and analyst. For those who believe in the absolute author-ity of research and science, this can be off-putting and disconcerting since it can be seen to undermine the credibility and authority of the research process and its findings and claims. I don't think like this. I believe that all knowledge and understanding is contextual and to some extent a social con-struction, and thus prefer to know how claims are constructed and findings are made. In fact, the more that I know about the research process—what data is collected and how it is collected, the manner in which it is analyzed and interpreted—the more I am able to understand and assess the relative strength and power of the claims and findings that are offered.

That being said, I must also admit that the overarching narrative of the chapters in this book did not always follow the actual logic and unfolding of data collection and analysis itself. Much as I aimed to make transparent the backstage analytical construction and architecture of the work (rather than hide and obscure it as is so often the case in conventional social scientific work, obsessed as it is with objectivity, authority, and certainty), the research and writing process is rarely as linear and ordered as one might like, and a straight reporting of it certainly does not make the best reading or clearest analysis. To compensate for this, the book offers a more or less linear narrative which traces the history of the midnight basketball phenomenon, along with my own practical and scholarly engagement with it, across the last decade of the twentieth century into the new millennium.

This is where the writing and presentation of the book needs to be distinguished from the data collection, discovery, and analysis aspects of the research. One of the tricks of writing in my emergent approach was to figure out how explicit and self-conscious to be about my own narrative and analysis—where to let events and data and findings speak for themselves, where to step in and show the research process unfolding, where to contextualize, where to speculate or interpret, and where to draw out larger generalizations and implications. This is the rhetoric of research and writing; it happens in all research—we are just more aware of it in some forms and formats (and for some kinds of questions) than others.

Writing, Reality, and Research

In saying all of this—about writing, about the constructed nature of the research project, and about the central if idiosyncratic role of the researcher—I should also make clear that I do not mean to suggest that research is only a social construction, or that this work is strictly a work of my own imagination and unique creativity (or lack thereof). In this context, it is perhaps worth noting that in one of the earlier versions of this manuscript, I used the word "realities" in the title of the work.

Several friendly readers and reviewers raised serious concerns about this word choice and framing. At the crux of these complaints—all of which came from scholars favoring constructivist, cultural approaches to social science—was that they took the title to suggest that I believed the book held the indisputable facts and true meanings of problems-based athletic initiatives. My erstwhile critics not only dismissed this implicit appeal ("true meanings," as one reviewer put it, "are elusive if not impossible to discover"); they believed that the implied claim violated the cultural, ethnographic, and pluralist sensibilities that were otherwise prominent in the work. They also seemed to think that I should know better.

I actually agreed with the constructivist and culturalist commitments that inspired these concerns—that facts are socially constructed, often multifaceted, that we social scientists help make them, and that our comprehension of them is always and necessarily incomplete. Nevertheless, I was extremely reluctant to completely give up the reference to "the real" (as distinct from the "true" or the "certain"). Influenced by thinkers ranging from Émile Durkheim and Craig Calhoun to Roy Bhaskar, Patricia Hill Collins, and Bruno Latour, I am convinced that we live in a real, material world where social facts do exist and, moreover, that these facts shape human lives in decisive and consequential ways. Indeed, one of the most basic contributions and social obligations of the social scientist is to help people better comprehend these realities and their consequences, particularly in instances when their impacts are undesirable, inequitable, and unjust as is so often the case with the realities of race in the modern world.

This challenge is particularly acute for scholars working on race, on the one hand, and deep play cultural forms like sport, on the other. On the latter front, part of the problem is that it is difficult to get scholars and other elites to take the popular practices of the sporting world seriously as a social force. On the race side, the facts and realities that are the focus of our analyses typically do not fit the materialist, class-based models from which so much critical social theory and analysis has developed; they are subtler, more subjective, ideological, and symbolic. Nevertheless, the fact that some of the most important and misunderstood social facts of this sort are ideas and understandings—ideological conceptions and ways of thinking that shape our lives and experiences in decisive ways—or that they are constructed and conveyed in and through popular practices and forms makes them no less factual or real. To the contrary, their invisibility or taken-for-granted-ness can make them even more powerful (if insidious).

Too often, however, the constructivist-culturalist response to the dominant cultural discourse and conventional empiricist methods about what is real has been to retreat to our own "safe" intellectual spaces and specialties, to write and talk only to those who are inclined to understand (and agree with) what we have to say, or to give up on reality claims altogether. But reality claims need not be reduced to positivism, or set in opposition to a representational and contextual vision of knowledge. Instead, the central task and challenge for critically oriented, culturalist social scientists is to stake a claim to "the real" as it exists in the cultural common sense and is represented with mainstream, empiricist social scientific methods and techniques.

Fortunately, in recent years a small but growing cadre of critically oriented sport scholars have tried to do just that, adopting the language of realism in ways that wouldn't have been imaginable to their mentors and advisors a generation earlier. David Andrews's (1996) pathbreaking description and analysis of the "facts" of Michael Jordan's blackness is a prime example. Another is David Leonard's (2004) paper on the complexity of the color-blind rhetoric that surrounded coverage and commentary of Kobe Bryant's arrest on rape charges, a piece that set the stage for his landmark study of the infamous NBA melee in Detroit, *After Artest* (2011). Leonard says that his project "challenges those commentators and everyday citizens who dismiss the realities of race and deny the use of racial lens/frames to interpret their everyday life." (2004, 285). I believe Leonard, Andrews, and others like them are on the right track, but whether their challenge is successful relies not only on asserting these realities but on using the tools and techniques of the social scientist—critical thinking, empirical data, innovative techniques—to engage and convince those who would think otherwise.

Again, it is my conviction (and hopefully my contribution to the enterprise) that we will be most successful and effective in this struggle when we put the data and analytic processes and biases that go into the production of our knowledge claims front and center—which is what I feel the notion of an emergent case study has to offer and why I have made myself and my research process so central and transparent in this project. Perhaps that's just me. Once again, however, and as always, I must ultimately leave it to readers and fellow reality makers to judge.

NOTES

CHAPTER ONE

1. Sport scholars here include Cole and King (1998); King and Springwood (2001); Hoberman (1997); Cole (1996); Cole and Andrews (1996); on the race side, see Dyson (1993); Goldberg (1998); hooks (1994); Mercer (1994); Patterson (1998); see also Kellner (1996).

2. To the extent there are exceptions to this pattern (for examples, see Markowitz 2011; Reeves and Campbell 1994), the scholars who see athletes and athletics as having a powerful role in the construction of race and criminal justice policies tend to be critical theorists and cultural studies scholars whose work remains on the margins of mainstream social science. Reeves and Campbell's *Cracked Coverage* (1994), for example, included an in-depth treatment of basketball star Len Bias's death by cocaine overdose and its impact on public discourse about crime. Many of the works on O. J. Simpson that appeared in the late 1990s often displayed similar analytic sensibilities and understandings, though not always as explicitly. See, for examples, Crenshaw (1997); L. Johnson and Roediger (2000); Lipsitz (1998, chaps. 5 and 6); Reed (1997); L. Williams (2001).

3. My own contributions to this chorus focused on sport's normative ideals, color blindness, and whiteness. For example, I used the last chapter of my book on the 1968 Olympic protests and their aftermath (Hartmann 2003a)—its narrative ended in the late 1980s, just as midnight basketball was starting to emerge—to analyze how Tommie Smith and John Carlos were made over in the mainstream media from black power extremists representing the worst excesses of the 1960s to civil rights idealists, heroes, and role models to be emulated by activists, athletes, and young people alike by the end of the 1980s. I also wrote papers on Michael Jordan's paradoxical racial status in American culture (Hartmann 2006) and the media coverage and commentary surrounding Rush Limbaugh's infamous attack on Philadelphia Eagles quarterback Donovan McNabb for being overrated because he was African American (Hartmann 2007).

CHAPTER TWO

1. There is actually a whole literature on pickup basketball, both in the black community and elsewhere. For a book-length treatment, see T. McLaughlin (2008); see also Anderson and Millman (1998); DeLand (2013, 2012); Jimmerson (1999, 1996).

2. US Department of Housing and Urban Development (1994). See also "National Association of Midnight Basketball Leagues, Inc.," undated document faxed to me, March 6, 2003. One issue in researching the history of Standifer's official midnight basketball organization is the chaos that the agency underwent in the wake of his untimely death in the 1990s. Basically, there were arguments and disagreements between Standifer's son and various of Standifer's collaborators and affiliates, which not only fragmented the operation but left record keeping and historical documentation a mess. My understanding of these events and reconstruction of the history are informed both by my collection of media treatments and other documents and by my conversations with a number of different individuals exercising some leadership and administrative roles over the years; Roy Jordan and Barbara Edmiston were especially helpful. Vivian Carter's (1998) dissertation on midnight basketball was also informative and generative.

3. See also Capuzzi and Gross (1994); Collingwood (1997); Lovell and Pope (1993); Schultz, Crompton, and Witt (1995); Witt and Crompton (1996b).

4. For more on American sport policy, see Chalip and Johnson (1996). For additional comments on the tensions between market-driven and community-based sports, see Hartmann (2005). For an even more general theoretical statement of the organization of sport as a social system, see Chalip (1988).

5. "The Funding Crisis in High School Athletics: Causes and Solutions" conference summary, 1992, Los Angeles Amateur Athletics Foundation archives.

6. The rise of neoliberal policy transformations on sporting policy and provision and their implications have been even more well documented and analyzed on the international level. See, for examples, Henry (2001) or Houlihan (1997).

7. For more on youth soccer and its place in the turn-of-the-millennium American sporting landscape, see D. L. Andrews (1999); D. L. Andrews et al. (2003).

8. The samples are from "Midnight Basketball Idea Scores," *Chicago Tribune*, December 5, 1989, and "Good Sense Scores a Point," *Chicago Sun-Times*, December 3, 1989.

9. CHA cover letter and proposal submitted to US Department of Housing and Urban Development Secretary's Fund, October 13, 1989. In research files collected by the author from correspondence with various program leaders in the late 1990s and early 2000s.

10. Midnight Basketball Leagues Inc., "The Alternative" (media packet), n.d. This item is also in research files collected in the late 1990s and early 2000s.

11. The structure and funding of the San Diego program was similar to those in Maryland and Chicago. It received one-third of its funding ($50,000) from a state assembly grant and the bulk of the rest from the Junior Seau Foundation (Junior Seau was a San Diego Chargers football player), and its advisory committee included a number of prominent local leaders and two legislators, Dede Alpert and Tom Connolly. The league consisted of sixteen teams with ten players each and played a fourteen-week season. After each game, there were also required classes with guest speakers on topics such as drug abuse, AIDS, relationships, and crime. Nichols: "This league is going to be run right and with quality. We're not going to be stressed because it's underfunded. We're not going to let these kids down" (*San Diego Union Tribune*, March 5, 1994).

12. One possible exception to this general cultural orientation and pattern is the early 1970s, when a "sport-for-all ethos" appeared in America in response to the athletic activism and unrest of the early part of the period. See Hartmann (2003a, chap. 6).

13. There were definitely costs and consequences to different frames and understandings of "the problems" midnight basketball was intended to address. The High Five

group in San Diego learned this the hard way. Although the organization was mainly interested in moral uplift and addiction prevention, the fact that its program was located in neighborhoods plagued by gang violence and ongoing turf wars meant that High Five actually had to create separate gyms and leagues to avoid provocation and conflict. As program director Nichols told the *San Diego Union Tribune*, August 25, 1994: "We certainly have to respect that it's a somewhat volatile area and respect the dynamics of it. . . . There's going to be conflict. But I've been impressed with how they work out their own problems. We're not looking at just gang kids. To me, they are all young people who need some hope. I don't care if he's in a gang or not." "In my mind there is no place for fear. We don't know someone is going to get hurt. Not one incident has been reported from other leagues around the country. If we do our job, I can't anticipate anything happening. At the same time, the league will be highly disciplined. We're doing this for the kids."

14. See also Sampson, Morenhoff, and Earls (1999); Sampson and Raudenbush (1999); Sampson, Raudenbush, and Earls (1997); for a subsequent reassessment and confirmation, see Peterson and Krivo (2005).

15. Contemporaneous scholarship and its public reception exhibited this ongoing ambiguity and confusion as well. For example, in his now classic work, William Julius Wilson (1987) introduced the concepts of social isolation and structural dislocation in an attempt to bridge and transcend these polarized analyses and approaches. Unfortunately, the terms tended to be interpreted and mobilized in a way that minimized some of these structural dimensions and reinforced the more culturally oriented analysis and proposed solutions. Similarly, as rich and contextualized as Elijah Anderson's evocative depiction of the lifeworlds and worldviews of inner-city African American men may have been, his research was often read and interpreted in a structural vacuum, one that seemed to place the responsibility and blame for social problems on the culture and behavior of African American men rather than on the nearly intractable societal conditions in which they found themselves. For a work that has received less attention but strikes a reasonable balance, see Young (2004).

16. This new definition of "risk" is used to organize, justify, and normalize both the provision of social services and social service reforms under the neoliberal label. Soss and Kindervater (unpublished ms., n.d.) further clarify the concept but situate it in contrast to its figural opposite: the entrepreneurial self as an "assemblage of possessions in the form of capacities, credentials, and other capital investments" or, in other words, the supposedly rational, autonomous, free, and responsible citizen-subject. This helps clarify that the risks that at-risk youth supposedly pose are not only to themselves (as in their failure to develop) but to others and society as a whole. They are dangerous, disorderly, a threat to us all. On the rise and predominance in youth policy and intervention contexts of the "risk and resiliency" framework whose ostensible goals are to assess for patterns of risk factors and then develop interventions focused on the reduction of these cumulative risks, see P. Kelly (2003); Hawkins, Catalano, and Miller (1992).

17. See also Atencio and Wright (2008); Buffington and Fraley (2011); Jackson (2007); Leonard (2010); May (2009); Tucker (2003).

CHAPTER THREE

1. Just weeks after the original Chicago program wrapped up its first year of operation, Gil Walker complained that participants in the program hadn't taken advantage of a jobs initiative that was part of it. "It's unfortunate," Walker told the *Chicago Reporter*

(May 1990), "but you can't overcome years of denial with a few months of basket-ball. Many of these guys don't believe in themselves. They're not used to being given opportunities. And some aren't ready for a job that isn't hustling on the streets." According to a commander from the Harrison police district, the program had no discernable impact on the community crime rate in these homes or neighborhoods. Even worse, violent battles over drug turf had erupted around Henry Horner Homes according to the district commander there: "I don't want to belittle midnight bas-ketball because it could help fence-sitters, the guys trying to stay out of trouble. But since the basketball started, three gangs . . . have started a narcotics war around Henry Horner. It's hard to argue that midnight basketball will affect gang activity one way or the other" (*Chicago Reporter*, May 1990).

2. Some clarity has begun to emerge in recent years, but many questions remain. For re-views, see Farb and Matjasko (2012); Hartmann (2008). For even more critical reviews see Shields and Bredemeier (1995).

3. Midnight Basketball Inc. met with some infighting and indecision among Standifer's associates and sons who were all involved with the organization. This eventually led to a regional-based organizational and oversight scheme, where directors in different parts of the country were given authority and responsibility for overseeing midnight basketball affiliates in their respective regions. There was also a great deal of frustra-tion about not having received any funding from Congress despite all the publicity and controversy in 1994. The various programs continued to prosper for many years, and some still do today.

4. Gallup Organization, telephone survey of 1,011 respondents in a national adult sample conducted for CNN and *USA Today* on August 16, 1994, and released on August 19, 1994. The question asked respondents whether they were supportive or not supportive about "providing local communities with federal tax money to provide social pro-grams and activities for low-income children such as *Midnight Basketball*" (emphasis in original survey wording).

5. As political reporter Michael Lewis wrote of Kemp when covering his ill-fated 1996 presidential campaign: "Kemp claims a special affinity to blacks from his experience of playing ball with them." Michael Lewis, "The Quarterback," *New Republic*, Octo-ber 14, 1996.

6. Though he may have fancied himself an intellectual, Kemp had a deep, emotional at-tachment to this basic set of core principles—just one of the reasons I think he made such a compelling, if ultimately unsuccessful, political candidate.

7. In retrospect, many of these points seem pretty obvious to me. However, one of the challenges of developing this analysis is that sport scholars (including myself) have often been critical of such idealistic, even utopian conceptions of development, in-tervention, and change through athletic participation. On the one hand, they have tried to point out that the social and developmental benefits of simple sports par-ticipation are not nearly as universal or automatic as is often implied or assumed by sports idealists. More than this, scholars have emphasized that the history books and the sports pages are replete with stories that belie any easy or automatic or inevi-table relationship between sport and positive social outcomes. Indeed, one of my favorite lines from the sociology of sport is that sport actually produces *characters* as much as character. Another, from Jay Coakley, alludes to the fact that all the dis-cipline and conformity required in the world of sport is actually a kind of deviance itself—"deviance through over-conformity," as R. Hughes and Coakley (1991) put it. So the analytic trick or challenge for this project was to hold on to these critical

insights and yet also acknowledge what is too often forgotten by sport critics: namely, that these idealistic visions of sport exert an immediate, intuitive hold in the culture and on many Americans.

8. For a discussion of the parallels and mutually reproductive overlaps between sport's social ideals and Reagan's vision of political theory, civil rights, and appropriate race relations, see Hartmann (2003a, chap. 8).

9. In fact, as one friendly reader of an earlier draft of this chapter reminded me, poverty politics have tended to be one of the few exceptions to the extreme partisan politics of the past twenty years.

10. "Midnight Basketball: How to Give Young People a Chance," c. early 1990s, planning document cosponsored by Midnight Basketball Inc. and Drug Information and Strategy Clearinghouse, obtained by the author from a noncirculating library archival service at the University of Minnesota, filed under the tab "Maps and Government Information, Government Pamphlets. U.S. Housing and Urban Development, Department of"; *Chicago Reporter*, May 1990.

11. "Taking the Air out of Midnight Basketball," *Chicago Reporter*, May 1990, retrieved June 19, 2003, http://www.chicagoreporter.com/1990/05-90.

12. Chicago Housing Authority to the Housing and Urban Development office, "Midnight Basketball Proposal," n.d. In research files collected by the author from correspondence with various program leaders in the late 1990s and early 2000s. See also Carter (1998).

13. The crisis was not the one about the exploitation of third-world labor Nike has grappled with in more recent years. Instead, the crisis of the early nineties was brought on by three developments, according to Cole: public outrage about youth "sneaker crimes;" Operation Push's proposed boycott of the company; and the backlash against Spike Lee's "racial tolerance" ads. One could easily see it as even more self-serving than this, in my view—that is, as part of a deliberate strategy to nurture and expand consumer demand for athletic footwear. After all, everyone who plays sports needs shoes to play in, and declining sports participation rates among youth and adolescents at the time posed a serious concern for everyone in the sports apparel industry.

14. For more on Jordan and race, see Hartmann (2007); D. L. Andrews (2001).

15. In terms of empirically validating Cole's claims about the differential racial structure and application of the PLAY campaign and youth sport more generally, I can say that the comparative work of David Andrews and his colleagues (Andrews et al. 2003; see also Andrews 1999) on urban sport systems, especially the contrasts with suburban soccer, is indispensable.

16. This was part of a larger politics of race for Clinton and the New Democrats. Other memorable, if not entirely commendable, moments of his campaign that hinged on this racialized politics of culture include Clinton's flight to Arkansas to oversee the execution of a mentally challenged African American prisoner named Ricky Ray Rector, his public reprimand of Jesse Jackson for cozying up to rapper Sister Souljah, and his pledge to "end welfare as we know it."

17. The gendered dimensions of Progressive Era adolescent reforms are revealed in many different respects but come out most clearly in the implementation of juvenile curfew laws and the creation of juvenile courts. Yet, as Abrams has pointed out, juvenile courts treated "wayward girls" both differently and far more harshly than boys. Abrams (2000, 440) explains in her discussion of the juvenile justice system: "Girls who transgressed were much more likely to be removed from their homes, given stricter sentences, and a longer probationary period. The courts frequently sentenced

young women to reformatories or training schools. These institutions sought to re-form wayward females through re-socialization in traditional female codes of con-duct and often detained girls until they were of a marriageable age of 21 or older."

18. Indeed, in researching the protests about race and sport in the late 1960s, I learned that there were other, more recent instances and illustrations of sport as surveillance and containment as well. For example, the NCAA's vaunted National Youth Sports Program (NYSP) (still in existence today) grew out of then Vice President Hubert Humphrey's vision of using parks and recreation facilities to provide alternative spaces and activities to distract and discourage young, inner-city groups from unrest, violence, and crime.

CHAPTER FOUR

1. The political dynamics and processes that Soss and his colleagues describe are obvi-ously far more complicated than I have implied here. For one thing, other issues did not provide the same initial wedge opportunity for Republicans that poverty policy did, or the same opportunity to unite the wings of their coalition. And once dam-aged by the Republican offensive in a domain that they had traditionally dominated, Democrats were obligated to respond on this terrain. Political legacies, alliances, and roles were all somewhat reversed with respect to crime and criminal justice policy.

2. In the early part of the new millennium, leaders from the international Olympic community campaigned to secure a Nobel Peace Prize for longtime IOC president Juan Antonio Samaranch of Spain. In a general sense, the campaign revolved around the claim that the Olympic movement has been a leader in the struggle for human rights, cross-cultural understanding, and international peace in the modern, global world. But the IOC also pointed to several specific moments of global intervention including, most powerfully and importantly, the committee's role in promoting racial reunification in South Africa. Some of this argument was and is familiar. In the standard IOC narrative, the Olympics played a leading (but underappreciated) role in helping dismantle apartheid and reunify South Africans through sports boycotts and embargoes. The idea that South Africans were as moved to transform their racial policies by their exclusion from international sporting competitions as by other eco-nomic or political bans or restrictions is certainly one aspect of the story, and it played a role in IOC posturing and politicking. But far more important in the IOC campaign was a much more concrete and direct role in negotiating, facilitating, and brokering the deal between Nelson Mandela and de Klerk. Under the auspices of and in the confines of the Olympic Studies Center in Lausanne, Switzerland, the IOC actually provided a place for de Klerk and Mandela to meet and begin to work out the details of the agreement that ultimately ended apartheid. Under the cover of sport, the IOC and its president had actually played an active role in this historic agreement. A uni-fied team was fielded at the Barcelona Olympics in 1992 in advance of the formal constitutional reunification of the nation, thus the tremendous pomp and ceremony of South Africans at the games. See Mbaye (1995).

CHAPTER FIVE

1. The sequence of events outlined in this chapter is derived from an extensive reading of political coverage and commentary from the period. The reporting of Holly Idel-son and her colleagues at the *Congressional Quarterly Weekly* was especially useful. In addition, see Jacob Weisberg, "The Guns of August," *New York*, September 12, 1994,

30–32; *Time*, August 22, 1994, 30–37; *Time*, August 29, 1994, 31–35; Rich Loury, "Central Problem," *National Review*, September 26, 1994, 21–24.

2. My discussion of the NRA ad against Chuck Schumer is based on *New Yorker*, May 9, 1994, 42–45. The ad ran under the headline "How to Defeat the Criminal's Best Friend in Congress," and it was derived from a television ad that the NRA had produced and tried to air on CNN. The television ad was sixty seconds long and created by CrimeStrike, an NRA publicity vehicle. It showed a picture of Schumer with the words "Criminals have a friend in Congress named Charles Schumer." The spot ended with the punchline "Stop Schumer. Call your congressman now. Tell him you want Schumer to build prisons, not friendships with criminals."

3. Kellyanne Fitzpatrick, a pollster with Luntz Research Companies (consultant for the NRA), says she did "interviews for a month" after its poll showing 48 percent opposition to midnight basketball came out. Also, Scott Hodge, a fellow at the Heritage Foundation, estimated he did seventy-five radio and television interviews during the furor over the crime bill. Stephen Moore, director of fiscal affairs at the Cato Institute, claimed he did fifty to one hundred.

4. Cong. Rec. S20,425 (daily ed. August 9, 1994).

5. Here, it is important to make manifest the absolute absence of factual information and knowledge about midnight basketball that formed and informed the debates about it. Although partisans on both sides of the aisle issued numerous assertions about the pros and cons of midnight basketball as social policy, these were based on nothing more than personal, anecdotal information (and most were based on much less). Thorough reviews of both the social scientific and applied literatures of the period reveal that no published studies of midnight basketball were available. That is to say, there was no empirical information, scholarly or otherwise, publicly available on midnight basketball at the time.

6. William J. Clinton, "The President's Radio Address," April 16, 1994, The American Presidency Project, by Gerhard Peters and John T. Woolley, retrieved October 5, 2015, http://www.presidency.ucsb.edu/ws/index.php?pid=49989&st=midnight+basketball &st1=.

7. Bob Inglis quoted in Associated Press, Greensville, SC, August 22, 1994. Of course, one irony here is that midnight basketball was part of the larger Clinton/Gore "reinvention of government" initiative which was supposed to diminish classic top-down federal bureaucracy and policy.

8. For a sampling of such comments, see *US News and World Report*, August 19, 1994; *Business Week*, September 5, 1994; *National Review*, September 26, 1994; *Time*, August 22, 1994; *Time*, August 20, 1994; *New Yorker*, September 12, 1994. Interestingly, the most optimistic scenario was reported in *US News*, which offered the unattributed claim that housing projects with Boys and Girls Clubs reported 13 percent fewer juvenile crimes and 25 percent less crack cocaine. Criminologist Jeffrey Roth of the Urban Institute was quoted as saying that midnight basketball "could be a great big experiment" and that "wide testing was justified . . . because things that work in one place may not work elsewhere" (*US News and World Report*, August 19, 1994, 29).

9. Cong. Rec. H21,557 (daily ed. August 11, 1994). As he went on, Everett exposed some of the stereotypes lurking: "My constituents are tired of this kind of waltzing with criminals. They are tired of their hard-earned tax dollars supporting criminals in jail lifting weights and watching color television."

10. Cong. Rec. H21,555 (daily ed. August 11, 1994).

11. As a first step, we coded each article with a reference to midnight basketball (there were 374 in all) according to its expressed political ideology or affiliation (liberal or Democratic, conservative or Republican, or neutral) and its position on midnight basketball (for, against, or neutral). The resulting cross tabulations were striking. When midnight basketball was discussed in a negative light, 98.2 percent of the time the reference came from a conservative/Republican critic; conversely, when midnight basketball was defended as a positive, proactive strategy, 97.9 percent of the time this came from an identifiably liberal/Democratic source.

12. This sample was drawn from *The Reader's Guide to Periodical Literature* which provides a fairly representative collection of magazine and journal articles available to the mainstream, general public. It includes all articles listed under the heading "crime bill" written between March 1 and October 31, 1994, the period of the most intensive crime bill debates and media coverage. In addition, we also included articles under "crime prevention" and "criminal law" if they had more than one substantive paragraph involving the crime bill itself.

13. See also Alan Vanneman, "Anatomy of a Mugging: How the Right Wing Made Midnight Basketball the Willie Horton of the Crime Bill," *Youth Today*, November/December 1994. Clients included the American Conservative Union, the National Rifle Association, and the Law Enforcement Association of America.

14. David Steinhart, "Midnight Basketball Survives Congress, Opens Session," *Youth Today*, November/December 1994, 33 (obtained from http://www.nra.org/pub/ila/Public_Balks_on_Crime_Bill). A hard copy is in the research files of the author.

15. Cong. Rec. S22,055 and S20,425 (daily ed. August 12, 1994) (statements of Sen. Dole).

16. Cong. Rec. H22,516 (daily ed. August 12, 1994) (statement of Rep. Hyde).

17. Charles Schumer quoted in *New Yorker*, May 9, 1994, 44.

18. Cong. Rec. H20,900 (daily ed. August 10, 1994).

19. Cong. Rec. H22,517 (daily ed. August 16, 1994).

20. We generated these estimates conservatively from media coverage at the time. The *Congressional Quarterly Weekly* was particularly useful in this regard; see especially May 7, August 27, and December 10, 1994.

21. The only exception that I could find to this was a poll conducted by Luntz Research Companies reported by the NRA on August 10, 1994. According to Luntz, only one in five Americans (20 percent) felt that Congress should pass the crime bill in early August, with 36 percent preferring that Congress "put the brakes" on passing this "hasty legislation." Described as the first scientific poll of registered voters on the current crime bill (1,000 registered voters surveyed nationwide from August 4 to August 9), the poll reported that those surveyed favored "strong punishment" over "social programs" by a margin of 57 percent to 36 percent. Luntz also reported that 50 percent of voters described the $100 million for dancing lessons and arts programs as "a complete waste of money"; 48 percent characterized midnight basketball in those terms as well. Key "findings" read into the House Record on August 11, 1994, by Representative DeLay (Cong. Rec. H21,565).

22. Gallup Organization Poll conducted for CNN and *USA Today* (survey date August 16, 1994; release date August 19, 1994; telephone survey of 1,011 respondents in a national adult sample). It is worth noting that this level of support held across most demographic groups in the country. There were no discernable gender differences, and there was stronger support among black and Hispanic respondents (82 and 87 percent, respectively) than whites (although 62 percent of whites supported the programs). No regional variations or variations by level of income emerged either. The primary

variations came in three main demographic areas. One had to do with political ideologies and affiliations: Democrats supported the programs by a solid three-quarters majority (75 percent), while just over half of self-identified Republicans (54 percent) supported the programs—independents sat right in the middle at 67 percent. Similarly, self-identified liberals and moderates supported such initiatives at rates of 78 and 74 percent, respectively, while conservatives only offered 53 percent support. The second involved income. Support for the initiatives declined with rising income brackets as well, but not as significantly as one might expect: earners between $15,000 and $19,000 supported at 72 percent, while those over $75,000 gave 62 percent support. The other set of cleavages involved age. Support for midnight basketball–type programs declined steadily and significantly with age from a high of 81 percent among eighteen- to twenty-nine-year-olds to a low of 47 percent for those seventy and over. We were unable to locate any polls that would have allowed us to compare shifts in attitudes toward midnight basketball programs over time on these dimensions or any others.

23. Our selection of these six issues was based on our reading of media coverage, the congressional hearings, and subsequent scholarly analysis and commentary on the bill (cf. Platt 1994).

24. Our analysis of a large, representative sample of national print media coverage of the crime bill (over 2,000 articles) made clear that midnight basketball occupied a central symbolic role in the crime bill debates. Of the articles collected in our sample (N = 2,274), 374—or some 16.4 percent—contained direct and explicit references to (if not more extensive treatments of) midnight basketball. The percentage of articles which made reference to midnight basketball in this particular sample was, of course, not quite as striking as the 40 percent found in our smaller, initial collection of national magazine articles. Nevertheless, the fact that almost one-fifth of the articles on and about the 1994 crime bill make reference to this very small, previously unknown and uncontroversial sport-based program is clearly significant, as is the fact that the vast majority of the references to midnight basketball came in the crucial weeks of the legislative process—the second, third, and fourth weeks of August (with 85, 136, and 68 references, respectively). No other weeks were even close. To control for the possibility that references to midnight basketball increased simply because reporting on the crime bill itself increased, we calculated the number of articles that contained midnight basketball references as a percentage of the total for each week. This procedure not only validated the initial pattern, but it showed that the percentage of crime bill articles that contained midnight basketball references peaked at three of the crucial junctures in the legislative process.

25. William J. Clinton, "Remarks to the Community at Robert Taylor Homes in Chicago," July 17, 1994, The American Presidency Project, by Gerhard Peters and John T. Woolley, retrieved October 5, 2015, www.presidency.ucsb.edu/ws/index.php?pid=50349 &st=midnight+basketball&st.1=; William J. Clinton, "Exchange with Reporters on Anticrime Legislation in St. Louis," June 24, 1994, The American Presidency Project, by Gerhard Peters and John T. Woolley, retrieved October 5, 2015, www.presidency .ucsb.edu/ws/index.php?pid=50388&st=midnight+basketball&st1=.

26. Cong. Rec. H21,560 (daily ed. August 11, 1994).

27. Cong. Rec. S22,127 (daily ed. August 12, 1994).

28. Cong. Rec. H22,517 (daily ed. August 16, 1994).

29. Cong. Rec. H23,161 (daily ed. August 18, 1994).

30. Cong. Rec. H22,519 (daily ed. August 16, 1994); Cong. Rec. H23,070 (daily ed. August 18, 1994).

31. Cong. Rec. H22892 (daily ed. August 17, 1994).

32. Rush Limbaugh quoted in *Time*, January 23, 1995. Limbaugh, it is worth noting, would long remain obsessed, asking "What's going to happen to midnight basketball?" again in 1996 when Clinton supported teen curfews (*Washington Times*, June 3, 1996, A9).

33. For a fuller discussion of the concepts and literature on which this argument is based, see Green and Hartmann (2014). An alternative interpretation or dimension of this process might also highlight the way in which it is sport itself which is seen as a special cultural place, a somehow sacred space above and beyond the messy mundanity of everyday politics and problems. As I discussed in previous chapters, Americans want to have their cake and eat it too when it comes to sport: on the one hand, they want to believe that it is a pure and powerful social force, an arena of opportunity and mobility, an arena of justice and fair play that can be a leader in the quest for racial equality and social justice; on the other hand, they also haven't wanted their safe, smug ideals about sport to be complicated or contested by actual, ongoing social struggles and challenges. The result, then, is that sport is fairly if not entirely a conservative force—one that reinforces and reproduces the prevailing, liberal democratic status quo. Although I think this notion is often a factor, I don't believe it played as significant a role in this case because no one was really trying to defend sport—either on its own terms or in relation to the cultural status of politics and policy.

34. One additional insight that my research into the media coverage and commentary of the Rush Limbaugh/Donovan McNabb controversy revealed involved the ways in which the mainstream media was actually complicit with Limbaugh's racialized worldview, even in spite of its ostensible outrage and condemnation of him. When I looked closer at the coverage and commentary that was supposed to put Limbaugh in his place, I found that many of the views contained underlying assumptions about sport and race that actually overlapped with and reinforced Limbaugh's own worldview and assumptions. This was because the dominant way of criticizing Limbaugh was to suggest that sport was not racist but in fact color-blind and above the fray of any and all political commentary whatsoever. Though meant to reject the obvious racialism and racism embedded in Limbaugh's ostensibly "color-blind" analysis, this orientation ignores and thus reinforces all the ways in which racial ideologies, images, and inequalities are embedded in the discourse and cultural practice of many sporting forms, especially one like midnight basketball. This is just one more illustration of the peculiar and yet powerful ways in which we both see and celebrate the racial character and progress of sport, and yet refuse to acknowledge its complicated dimensions and consequential societal effects.

CHAPTER SIX

1. I referred previously to the confusion and discord that engulfed the national midnight basketball association in the wake of G. Van Standifer's death in 1992. Eric Standifer, the eldest son of G. Van, had been a warehouse broker. After the death of his father, Eric assumed the presidency of the national midnight basketball organization and moved the headquarters (along with the national director's office) to Oakland, California. Another of G. Van's sons, Nelson, took over the day-to-day operation of the Glenarden program. Suffice it to say, it was never an entirely coordinated or satisfactory arrangement for the parties involved.

2. "Oakland Midnight Basketball—Men's Program Executive Summary," research file document, dated January 1999, collected from Barbara Edmiston, program manager of the Oakland site, 1520 Lakeside Drive, Oakland, CA 94612.

3. Undated document on after-school programs released by the National Youth Violence Prevention Resource Center, which operated out of Rockville, Maryland.

4. Antoni Tang, while still an undergraduate at the University of Minnesota, served as my research assistant on this section, collecting much of the data and information as well as helping to sketch out the presentation and analysis.

5. This section adapts and illustrates ideas from Hartmann (2012b).

6. As mentioned in the introduction, I worked for Hawkins and his organization full-time in various capacities for a year and a half after my graduation from college and before my move to California to begin PhD work in sociology. Over the 1990s, I maintained fairly regular contact with Hawkins. I attended several of the conferences and symposia he organized, returned to spend two full summers working with the organization in Chicago, made several shorter visits, and called fairly regularly. During this period, I took field notes, conducted a series of interviews with Hawkins and many folks associated with his organization, and had full access to his large but unorganized personal files. All this work and its results are presented in Hartmann (2003b), from which these points are drawn.

CHAPTER SEVEN

1. For a defense of the cultural studies approach and a counterattack against MacAloon's ethnographic, comparative method, see Hargreaves and Tomlinson (1992); for a later commentary on the exchange—albeit one which ultimately sides with MacAloon— see Morgan (1994).

2. Although we have identified the program by name, we have taken measures to maintain the confidentiality of those public figures who ran and operated the league— administrators, staff, and players alike. Names of people have been changed to protect anonymity and some minor changes have been made to dates and details to ensure the privacy of individuals who participated in the program. It should be noted, however, that those who ran the program were all well aware of and consented to be involved in our study, and cooperation with our research and evaluation were a condition of participation in the league.

3. Garcia reframed the racial background question as "What is your culture?" This elicited many different responses, such as "hip-hop culture" and "American culture," that, for programmatic assessment, were more or less useless. Garcia eventually relented in the year of our involvement, allowing specific questions about participants' racial background, but his change of heart came with some reluctance and consternation. While these peculiar decisions annoyed Klausmeyer, the agency's in-house analyst, they reveal the dubious and complicated role race played in Garcia's understanding of the program.

4. To fulfill our evaluation functions and responsibilities, we wrote and submitted a formal evaluation report for Garcia and the Department of Health and Family Support; we also wrote an article for the Center for Urban and Regional Affairs (CURA) at the University of Minnesota (Hartmann and Wheelock 2002). Our evaluations had little to say about actual outcomes and effectiveness and focused almost exclusively on implementation. Even so, we never heard a lot back from the city folks on these reports and had only sporadic interactions after they came out. We did, however, maintain much stronger ties with Cauldwell and Witters over the next few years, helping them write several grant proposals, though both moved around and, eventually, moved on with their lives and lifework.

5. While they never fully took blame (or accepted responsibility) for this shortcoming, it is impossible to overstate the importance of these shortcomings for sport

instrumentalists like Garcia and his staff. Their vision of sport as violence prevention required the development and implementation of this nonsport programming. Anything less, in their view, meant not only that sport might fail to achieve its positive promises, but that it could actually serve to reproduce or reinforce problematic preexisting behaviors and social networks. And what we saw was not just "anything less," but a lot less. (Conversely, the absence of successful nonsport elements was *not* a problem for folks like Cauldwell and Witters whose primary objective was simply providing a competitive summer basketball league.)

CHAPTER EIGHT

1. As mentioned above, we conducted formal interviews with fifteen program participants, including a representative from at least one of each of the eight teams at the site in South Minneapolis. The interview protocol, developed in close consultation with program administrators, was structured in a way so as to emphasize how each interviewee got involved in the program and to focus especially on its crime prevention aspects—the life skills components especially. Sample questions included "What did you think about the life skills components [of the program]?"; "Do you feel like you have a good understanding of the program's goals?"; and "Do you feel that the program helped you in any way make positive changes in your life situation?" We secured interviews by approaching individual players with whom we had established relationships and rapport over the course of the summer and also by asking for referrals from team coaches or site organizers from those teams for whom we had no earlier personal contact. However, all interview subjects knew and recognized us as part of the research and evaluation team.

2. It is worth noting that attendance at these games was obviously gendered, composed primarily of wives, girlfriends, and kids of league players. This reflects the larger gendered dynamic of the entire league which was dominated in every way (from the playing of the games to operational procedures to staffing) by men and an overt masculine ethos. The one woman formally involved—staff evaluator Annie Klausmeyer—was marginalized and ineffective simply because the young men who ran the program didn't respect her or take her seriously. They did what she wanted only when Garcia stepped in; most ignored her altogether. She herself talked of feeling "completely out of context"; she thought she was perceived as the "white girl with the clipboard" and was not respected as a legitimate voice in program development (field notes, April 4, 2000). The only time we saw a woman taken seriously as more than a spectator in the project was in a development meeting where a woman of color (a Latina friend of Garcia's) who was a grant writer and a fund-raiser offered a series of suggestions to organizers.

CHAPTER NINE

1. Nick Kenney, "Five Teens Shot after Midnight Basketball Tournament," June 24, 2014, Action News 5, retrieved September 5, 2014, http://www.wmcactionnews5.com/story/25850437/five-teens-shot-after-midnight-basketball-tournament.

METHODOLOGICAL APPENDIX

1. Those few scholarly works that did exist (Mendal 1995; Farrell et al. 1995; Derezotes 1995) were essentially short-term, evaluative descriptions of individual midnight basketball leagues, driven as much by the expectations of funding agents as by the concerns of policy evaluation or social scientific knowledge. The literature on sports-

and-recreation-based social interventions—what Pitter and Andrews (1997) called the "social problems industry" in urban sport provision (see also Schultz, Crompton, and Witt 1995)—was beginning to appear and offered some insights on midnight basketball; however, a coherent theoretical framework was not yet in place and its findings with respect to effectiveness were uneven and inconclusive at best. The only sustained treatment of midnight basketball I could find was a dissertation that used interviews with key political elites and program administrators to construct a basic history of the origin and early evolution of the initiative (Carter 1998).

2. For a basic explication of Mills's sociological imagination, see Hartmann (2009).

REFERENCES

Abrams, Laura S. 2000. "Guardians of Virtue: The Social Reformers and the 'Girl Problem,' 1890–1920." *Social Service Review* 74 (3): 436–52.

Acland, Charles R. 1995. *Youth, Murder, Spectacle: The Cultural Politics of "Youth in Crisis."* Boulder, CO: Westview Press.

Alexander, Michelle. 2012. *The New Jim Crow: Mass Incarceration in an Age of Colorblindness.* New York: The New Press.

Alford, Robert R. 1998. *The Craft of Inquiry: Theory, Methods, Evidence.* New York: Oxford University Press.

Anderson, Elijah. 2000. *Code of the Street: Decency, Violence, and the Moral Life of the Inner City.* New York: W.W. Norton.

———. 2013. *Streetwise: Race, Class, and Change in an Urban Community.* Chicago: University of Chicago Press.

Anderson, Lars, and Chad Millman. 1998. *Pickup Artists: Street Basketball in America.* New York: Verso.

Andrews, David L. 1996. "The Fact(s) of Michael Jordan's Blackness: Excavating a Floating Racial Signifier." *Sociology of Sport Journal* 13:125–58.

———. 1999. "Contextualizing Suburban Soccer: Consumer Culture, Lifestyle Differentiation and Suburban America." *Culture, Sport, Society* 1:31–53.

———, ed. 2001. *Michael Jordan, Inc.: Corporate Sport, Media Culture, and Late Modern America.* Ithaca, NY: SUNY Press.

Andrews, David L., Robert Pitter, Detlev Zwick, and Darren Ambrose. 2003. "Soccer, Race, and Suburban Space." In *Sporting Dystopias: The Making and Meanings of Urban Sport Cultures,* edited by Ralph C. Wilcox, David L. Andrews, Robert Pitter, and Richard L. Irwin, 197–220. Albany, NY: SUNY Press.

Andrews, David L., and Michael L. Silk. 2010 "Basketball's Ghettocentric Logic." *American Behavioral Scientist* 53 (11):1626–44.

Andrews, Vernon L. 1996. "Black Bodies—White Control: The Contested Terrain of Sportsmanlike Conduct." *Journal of African American Men* 2 (1): 33–59.

———. 1998 "African American Player Codes on Celebration, Taunting, and Sportsmanlike Conduct." In *African Americans in Sport,* edited by Gary Sailes, 145–80. New Brunswick, NJ: Transaction Press.

Aspen Institute. 2015. *Sport for All | Play for Life: A Playbook to Get Every Kid in the Game.* Washington, DC: Aspen Institute, Project Play. http://aspenprojectplay.org/sites/default/files/Aspen%20Institute%20Project%20Play%20Report.pdf.

Astbury, R., B. Knight, and G. Nichols. 2005. "The Contribution of Sport Related Interventions to the Long-Term Development of Disaffected Young People: An Evaluation of the Fairbridge Program." *Journal of Park and Recreation Administration* 23(3): 82–98.

Atencio, Matthew, and Jan Wright. 2008. "'We Be Killin' Them': Hierarchies of Black Masculinity in Urban Basketball Spaces." *Sociology of Sport Journal* 25 (2): 263–80.

Axthelm, Pete. 1970. *The City Game: Basketball from the Garden to the Playgrounds.* New York: Penguin.

Baldwin, C. K. 2000. "Theory, Program and Outcomes: Assessing the Challenges of Evaluating At-Risk Youth Recreation Programs." *Journal of Park and Recreation Administration* 18 (1): 19–33.

Barnes-Josiah, Debora, Beth Ansari, and Douglas S. Kress. 1996. "Minneapolis Youth Homicide Study: Victims and Charges, 1994–1995." Minneapolis Department of Health and Family Support, Minneapolis, MN, April.

Baum, Dan. 1996. *Smoke and Mirrors: The War on Drugs and the Politics of Failure.* New York: Little, Brown.

BBC. 1999. "Education Scheme Offers Change of Court." BBC News, May 4. http://news.bbc.co.uk/2/hi/uk_news/education/334933.stm.

Beck, Ulrich. 1992. *Risk Society: Towards a New Modernity.* London: Sage.

———. 1999. *World Risk Society.* Malden, MA: Blackwell.

Becker, Howard S. 1998. *Tricks of the Trade: How to Think about Your Research While You're Doing It.* Chicago: University of Chicago Press.

Beckett, Katherine, and Bruce Western. 2001 "Governing Social Marginality: Welfare, Incarceration, and the Transformation of State Policy." *Punishment & Society* 3 (1): 43–59.

Bell, Joyce M., and Douglas Hartmann. 2007. "Diversity in Everyday Discourse: The Cultural Ambiguities and Consequences of 'Happy Talk.'" *American Sociological Review* 72 (6): 895–914.

Benedict, Jeff. 1998. *Public Heroes, Private Felons: Athletes and Crimes against Women.* Boston, MA: Northeastern University Press.

Berry, Bonnie, and Earl Smith. 2000. "Race, Sport, and Crime: The Misrepresentation of African Americans in Team Sports and Crime." *Sociology of Sport Journal* 17 (2): 171–97.

Berrey, Ellen. 2015. *The Enigma of Diversity: The Language of Race and the Limits of Racial Justice.* Chicago: University of Chicago Press.

Birrell, Susan, and Mary G. McDonald. 2000. *Reading Sport: Critical Essays on Power and Representation.* Boston: Northeastern University Press.

Bobo, Lawrence D., and Camille Z. Charles. 2009. "Race in the American Mind: From the Moynihan Report to the Obama Candidacy." *Annals of the American Academy of Political and Social Science* 621 (1): 243–59.

Bonilla-Silva, Eduardo. 2010. *Racism without Racists: Color-Blind Racism and the Persistence of Racial Inequality in the United States.* Lanham, MD: Rowman & Littlefield.

Bourdieu, Pierre. [1982] 1988. "Program for a Sociology of Sport." *Sociology of Sport Journal* 5:153–61.

———. 1988. "Vive la Crise! For Heterodoxy in Social Science." *Theory and Society* 17:773–87.

———. 1998. *Practical Reason: On the Theory of Action.* Redwood City, CA: Stanford University Press.

Boyd, Todd. 1997. ". . . The Day the Niggaz Took Over: Basketball, Commodity Culture, and Black Masculinity." In *Out of Bounds: Sports, Media and the Politics of Identity*, edited by Aaron Baker and Todd Boyd, 123–44. Bloomington: Indiana University Press.

———. 2003. *Young, Black, Rich, and Famous: The Rise of the NBA, the Hip Hop Invasion, and the Transformation of American Culture*. New York: Doubleday.

Boyd, Todd, and Kenneth L. Shropshire. 2000. *Basketball Jones: America above the Rim*. New York: New York University Press.

Boyer, Peter J. 1994. "Whip Cracker." *New Yorker*, September 5, 38–54.

Brenner, Neil, and Nik Theodore, eds. 2002. *Spaces of Neoliberalism: Urban Restructuring in North America and Western Europe*. Malden, MA: Blackwell.

Brooks, Scott N. 2009. *Black Men Can't Shoot*. Chicago: University of Chicago Press.

———. 2008. "Fighting Like a Basketball Player: Basketball as a Strategy against Social Disorganization." In *Against the Wall: Poor, Young, Black, and Male*, edited by Elijah Anderson, 147–64. Philadelphia: University of Pennsylvania Press.

Brown, Hana E. 2013. "Racialized Conflict and Policy Spillover Effects: The Role of Race in the Contemporary US Welfare State." *American Journal of Sociology* 119 (2): 394–443.

Brown, Michael K. 1999. *Race, Money and the American Welfare State*. Ithaca, NY: Cornell University Press.

Brown, Timothy. 2005. "Allen Iverson as America's Most Wanted: Black Masculinity as a Cultural Site of Struggle." *Journal of Intercultural Communication Research* 34 (1): 65–87.

Brown, Wendy. 2006. "American Nightmare: Neoliberalism, Neo-conservativism, and De-democratization." *Political Theory* 34 (6): 690–714.

Buffington, Daniel, and Todd Fraley. 2011. "Racetalk and Sport: The Color Consciousness of Contemporary Discourse on Basketball." *Sociological Inquiry* 81(3): 333–52.

Burawoy, Michael. 1991. *Ethnography Unbound: Power and Resistance in the Modern Metropolis*. Oakland: University of California Press.

———. 1998. "The Extended Case Method." *Sociological Theory* 16:4–33.

———. 2009. *The Extended Case Method: Four Countries, Four Decades, Four Great Transformations, and One Theoretical Tradition*. Oakland,. University of California Press.

Burke, Meghan. 2012. *Racial Ambivalence in Diverse Communities: Whiteness and the Power of Color-Blind Ideologies*. Lanham, MD: Lexington Books.

Bute, Monte. 2008. "Writing to Be Read." *Contexts* 7 (2): 70–71.

Cameron, Margaret, and Colin MacDougall. 2000. *Crime Prevention through Sport and Physical Activity*. Trends and Issues in Crime and Criminal Justice, no. 165. Australian Institute of Criminology, Canberra, Australia, September.

Caponi-Tabery, Gena. 2002. "Jump for Joy: Jump Blues, Dance, and Basketball in 1930s African America." In *Sports Matters: Race, Recreation, and Culture*, edited by John Bloom and Michael Nevin Willard, 39–74. New York University Press.

Capuzzi, Dave, and Douglas R. Gross. 1994. *Youth at Risk: Targeting in on Prevention*. Reston, VA: American Association for Leisure and Recreation.

Carr, Leslie G. 1997. *Colorblind Racism*. Thousand Oaks, CA: Sage Publications.

Carrington, Ben. 1998. "Sport, Masculinity and Black Cultural Resistance." *Journal of Sport and Social Issues* 22 (3): 275–98.

———. 2010. *Race, Sport and Politics: The Sporting Black Diaspora*. London: Sage.

Carrington, Ben, and Ian McDonald, eds. 2009. *Marxism, Cultural Studies, and Sport*. London: Routledge.

Carter, Vivian Louise. 1998. "From the Neighborhood to the Nation: The Social History of Midnight Basketball." PhD diss., University of Oklahoma.

Cashmore, Ellis. 2005. *Tyson: Nurture of the Beast*. Cambridge: Polity Press.

Cavallo, Dominick. 1981. *Muscles and Morals: Organized Playgrounds and Urban Reform, 1880–1920*. Philadelphia: University of Pennsylvania Press.

Chalip, Laurence. 1988. "The Framing of Policy: Explaining the Transformation of American Sport." PhD diss., University of Chicago.

Chalip, Laurence, and Arthur Johnson. 1996. "Sports Policy in the United States." In *National Sports Policies: An International Handbook*, edited by Laurence Chalip, Arthur Johnson, and Lisa Stachura, 404–30. Westport, CN: Greenwood Press.

Chambliss, William. 1995. "Crime Control and Ethnic Minorities: Legitimizing Racial Oppression by Creating Moral Panics." In *Ethnicity, Race and Crime: Perspectives across Time and Place*, edited by Darnell F. Hawkins, 235–58. Albany, NY: SUNY Press.

Clark, Michael A. 2003. "Researching Youth Sports Programs in a Metropolitan Setting: Essentials of, Barriers to, and Policy for Achieving a Comprehensive Program." In *Sporting Dystopias*, edited by Ralph C. Wilcox, David L. Andrews, Robert Pitter, and Richard L. Irwin, 179–96. Albany, NY: SUNY Press.

Coakley, Jay. 2002. "Using Sports to Control Deviance and Violence among Youths: Let's Be Critical and Cautious." In *Paradoxes of Youth and Sport*, edited by Margaret Gatz, Michael A. Messner, and Sandra J. Ball-Rokeach, 13–30. Albany, NY: SUNY Press.

———. 2011. "Youth Sports: What Counts as 'Positive Development'?" *Journal of Sport and Social Issues* 35 (3): 306–24.

Coalter, Fred. 2007. *A Wider Social Role for Sport: Who's Keeping the Score?* New York: Routledge.

———. 2009. "Sport-In-Development: Accountability or Development?" In *Sport and International Development*, edited by R. Levermore and A. Beacom, 55–75. Hampshire, England: Palgrave Macmillan.

———. 2010. "The Politics of Sport-for-Development: Limited Focus Programmes and Broad Gauge Problems?" *International Review for the Sociology of Sport* 45 (3): 295–314.

Cole, Cheryl L. 1996. "American Jordan: P.L.A.Y., Consensus and Punishment." *Sociology of Sport Journal* 13:366–97.

Cole, Cheryl L., and David L. Andrews. 1996. "Look—It's NBA Showtime! Visions of Race in the Popular Imagery." *Cultural Studies Annual* 1:141–81.

Cole, Cheryl L., and Harry Denny III. 1994. "Visualizing Deviance in Post-Reagan America: Magic Johnson, AIDS and the Promiscuous World of Professional Sport." *Critical Sociology* 20 (3): 123–47.

Cole, Cheryl L., and Samantha King. 1998. "Representing Black Masculinity and Urban Possibilities: Racism, Realism, and Hoop Dreams." In *Sport and Postmodern Times*, edited by Geneviève Rail, 49–86. Albany, NY: SUNY Press.

Coleman, James S. 1963. *The Adolescent Society: The Social Life of the Teenager and Its Impact on Education*. New York: Free Press.

———. 1991. "Sport as an Educational Tool." *School Sports and Education*, National Conference Issue, Institute for Athletics and Education, 3–5.

Collingwood, Thomas R. 1997. "Providing Physical Fitness Programs to At-Risk Youth." *Quest* 49:67–84.

Collins, Jane, and Victoria Meyer. 2010. *Both Hands Tied: Welfare Reform and the Race to the Bottom of the Low Wage Labor Market*. Chicago: University of Chicago Press.

Correira, Mark E. 1997. "Boot Camps, Exercise and Delinquency: An Analytical Critique of the Use of Physical Exercise to Facilitate Decreases in Delinquent Behavior." *Journal of Contemporary Criminal Justice* 13 (2): 94–113.

Crapanzano, Vincent. 1986. "Hermes' Dilemma: The Masking of Subversion in Ethnographic Description." In *Writing Culture: The Poetics and Politics of Ethnography*, edited by James Clifford and George E. Marcus, 51–76. Oakland, CA: University of California Press.

Crenshaw, Kimberle W. 1997. "Color-Blind Dreams and Racial Nightmares: Reconfiguring Racism in the Post–Civil Rights Era." In *Birth of a Nation'hood: Gaze, Script and Spectacle in the O. J. Simpson Case*, edited by Toni Morrison, 97–168. New York: Random House.

Crompton, John L. 1998. "Forces Underlying the Emergence of Privatization in Parks and Recreation." *Journal of Park and Recreation Administration* 16 (2): 88–101.

Crompton, John L., and Andrew T. Kaczynski. 2003. "Trends in Local Park and Recreation Department Finances and Staffing from 1964–65 to 1999–2000." *Journal of Park and Recreation Administration* 24 (4): 124–44.

Crompton, John L., and B. McGregor. 1994. "Trends in the Financing and Staffing of Local Government Park and Recreation Services." *Journal of Park and Recreation Administration* 12 (3): 19–37.

Crompton, John L., and B. E. Wicks. 1988. "Implementing a Preference Equity Model for the Delivery of Leisure Services in the United States Context." *Leisure Studies* 7 (3): 287–304.

Cunningham, Phillip. 2009. "'Please Don't Fine Me Again!': Black Athletic Defiance in the NBA and NFL." *Journal of Sport and Social Issues* 33 (1): 39–58.

Danish, Steven J., and V. C. Nellen. 1997. "New Roles for Sport Psychologists: Teaching Life Skills through Sport to At-Risk Youth." *Quest* 49 (1): 100–113.

Danziger, Sheldon, and Peter Gottschalk, eds. 1993. *Uneven Tides: Rising Inequality in America*. New York: Russell Sage Foundation.

Darnell, Simon C. 2007. "Playing with Race: Right to Play and the Production of Whiteness in 'Development through Sport.'" *Sport in Society* 1 (4): 560–79.

DeLand, Michael. 2012. "Suspending Narrative Engagements: The Case of Pick-Up Basketball." *Annals of the American Academy of Political and Social Science* 642:96–108.

———. 2013. "Basketball in the Key of Law: The Significance of Disputing in Pick-Up Basketball." *Law & Society Review* 47 (3): 653–84.

Dennis, Christopher, Marshall H. Medoff, and Michele N. Gagnier. 1998. "The Impact of Racially Disproportionate Outcomes on Public Policy: The U.S. Senate and the Death Penalty." *Social Science Journal* 35 (2):169–81.

Derezotes, David. 1995. "Evaluation of the Late Nite Basketball Project." *Child and Adolescent Social Work Journal* 12 (1): 33–50.

Dyson, Eric Michael. 1993. "Be Like Mike? Michael Jordan and the Pedagogy of Desire." In *Reflecting Black: African-American Cultural Criticism*, 64–75. Minneapolis, MN: University of Minnesota Press.

Early, Gerald. 2011. *A Level Playing Field: African American Athletes and the Republic of Sports*. Cambridge, MA: Harvard University Press.

Edelman, Murray. 1964. *The Symbolic Uses of Politics*. Urbana: University of Illinois Press.

Edsall, Thomas Byrne, and Mary D. Edsall. 1991. *Chain Reaction: The Impact of Race, Rights and Taxes on American Politics*. New York: Norton.

Edwards, Harry. 2000. "Crisis of Black Athletes on the Eve of the 21st Century." *Society* 37 (3): 9–13.

Eliasoph, Nina. 1999. "'Everyday Racism' in a Culture of Political Avoidance: Civil Society, Speech, and Taboo." *Social Problems* 46 (4): 479–502.

———. 2011. *Making Volunteers: Civic Life after Welfare's End*. Princeton, NJ: Princeton University Press.

Entman, Robert M., and Andrew Rojecki. 2000. *The Black Image in the White Mind: Media and Race in America*. Chicago: University of Chicago Press.

Farb, Amy Feldman, and Jennifer L. Matjasko. 2012. "Recent Advances in Research on School-Based Extracurricular Activities and Adolescent Development." *Developmental Review* 32:1–48.

Farrell, Walter C., Jr., James H. Johnson Jr., Marty Sapp, Roger M. Pumphrey, and Shirley Freeman. 1995. "Redirecting the Lives of Urban Black Males: An Assessment of Milwaukee's Midnight Basketball League." *Journal of Community Practice* 2 (4): 91–107.

Feagin, Joe, and Hernan Vera. 1995. *White Racism: The Basics*. New York: Routledge.

Feeley, Malcolm, and Jonathan Simon. 1992. "The New Penology: Notes on the Emerging Strategy of Corrections and Its Implications." *Criminology* 30:449–74.

Fine, Gary Alan. 1987. *Little League Baseball and Preadolescent Culture*. University of Chicago Press.

Foster, Karen Rebecca, and Dale Spencer. 2011. "At Risk of What? Possibilities over Probabilities in the Study of Young Lives." *Journal of Youth Studies* 14 (1): 125–43.

Fox, James Alan, and Sanford A. Newman. 1997. "After-School Crime or After-School Programs? Tuning in to the Prime Time for Violent Juvenile Crime and Implications for National Policy." A Report to the United States Attorney General. Accessed October 13, 2015. http://files.eric.ed.gov/fulltext/ED412319.pdf.

Franklin, Jane, ed. 1998. *The Politics of Risk Society*. Malden, MA: Blackwell.

Gambone, Michelle Alberti, and Amy J. A. Arbreton. 1997. "Safe Havens: The Contributions of Youth Organizations to Healthy Adolescent Development." Public/Private Ventures Report, Philadelphia, PA, April.

Gans, Herbert. 1995. *The War against the Poor*. New York: Basic Books.

Garland, David. 2002. *The Culture of Control: Crime and Social Order in Contemporary Society*. Chicago: University of Chicago Press.

Geertz, Clifford. 1973. "Deep Play: Notes on the Balinese Cockfight." In *Interpretation of Cultures*, edited by Clifford Geertz, 412–54. New York: Basic Books.

George, Nelson. 1992. *Elevating the Game: Black Men and Basketball*. New York: HarperCollins.

Gilens, Martin. 1995. "Racial Attitudes and Opposition to Welfare." *Journal of Politics* 57 (4): 994–1014.

———. 1999. *Why Americans Hate Welfare*. Chicago: University of Chicago Press.

Giulianotti, Richard. 2004. "Human Rights, Globalization and Sentimental Education: The Case of Sport." *Sport in Society* 7 (3): 355–69.

———. 2009. "Risk and Sport: An Analysis of Sociological Theories and Research Agendas." *Sociology of Sport Journal* 26 (4): 540–56.

———. 2011. "Sport, Peacemaking and Conflict Resolution: A Contextual Analysis and Modelling of the Sport, Development and Peace Sector." *Ethnic and Racial Studies* 34 (2): 207–28.

Goldberg, David Theo. 1998. "Call and Response: Talk Radio and the Death of Democracy." *Journal of Sport and Social Issues* 22 (2): 212–23.

———. 2008. *The Threat of Race: Reflections on Racial Neoliberalism*. New York: Wiley-Blackwell.

Gottfredson, Denise C. 1986. "An Empirical Test of School-Based Environmental and Individual Interventions to Reduce the Risk of Delinquent Behavior." *Criminology* 24 (4): 705–31.

Green, Kyle, and Douglas Hartmann. 2014. "Politics and Sports: Strange, Secret Bedfellows." In *The Social Side of Politics*, edited by Douglas Hartmann and Christopher Uggen, 87–102. New York: W.W. Norton.

Gruneau, Richard S. 1983. *Class, Sport and Social Development*. Boston: University of Massachusetts Press.

Gusfield, Joseph. [1963] 1986. *Symbolic Crusade: Status Politics and the American Temperance Movement*. Urbana: University of Illinois Press.

———. 1981. *The Culture of Public Problems: Drinking-Driving and the Symbolic Order*. Chicago: University of Chicago Press.

Hall, Stuart, Chas Critcher, Tony Jefferson, John Clarke, and Brian Roberts. 1978. *Policing the Crisis: Mugging, the State and Law and Order*. New York: Holmes and Meier Publishers.

Handler, Joel F. 2004. *Social Citizenship and Workfare in the United States and Western Europe: The Paradox of Inclusion*. Cambridge: Cambridge University Press.

Hardy, Stephen, and Alan Ingham. 1983. "Games, Structures, and Agency: Historians on the American Play Movement." *Journal of Social History* 17:285–302.

Hargreaves, John. 1986. *Sport, Power and Culture*. London: Polity Press.

Hargreaves, John, and Alan Tomlinson. 1992. "Getting There: Cultural Theory and the Sociological Analysis of Sport in Britain." *Sociology of Sport Journal* 9:207–19.

Hartmann, Douglas. 1996. "The Politics of Race and Sport: Resistance and Domination in the 1968 African American Olympic Protest Movement." *Ethnic and Racial Studies* 19 (3): 548–66.

———. 2000. "Golden Ghettos and Contested Terrain: Rethinking the Relationships between Race and Sport in American Culture." *Sociology of Sport Journal* 17:229–53.

———. 2001. "Notes on Midnight Basketball and the Cultural Politics of Recreation, Race and At-Risk Urban Youth." *Journal of Sport and Social Issues* 25 (4): 339–71.

———. 2003a. *Race, Culture, and the Revolt of the Black Athlete: The 1968 Olympic Protests and Their Aftermath*. Chicago: University of Chicago Press, 2003.

———. 2003b. "Theorizing Sport as Social Intervention: A View from the Grassroots." *Quest* 55 (2):118–40.

———. 2003c. "What Can We Learn from Sport if We Take Sport Seriously as a Racial Force? Lessons from C. L. R. James's *Beyond a Boundary*." *Ethnic and Racial Studies* 26 (3): 451–83.

———. 2005. "Community." In *Berkshire Encyclopedia of World Sport*, edited by David Levinson and Karen Christensen, 359–65. Great Barrington, MA: Berkshire Publishing.

———. 2006. "Bound by Blackness or Above It? Michael Jordan and the Paradoxes of Post–Civil Rights American Race Relations." In *Out of the Shadows*, edited by David K. Wiggins, 301–24. Fayetteville: University of Arkansas Press.

———. 2007. "Rush Limbaugh, Donovan McNabb, and 'A Little Social Concern': Reflections on the Problems of Whiteness in Contemporary American Sport." *Journal of Sport and Social Issues* 31 (1): 45–60.

———. 2008. "High School Sports Participation and Educational Attainment: Recognizing, Assessing, and Exploiting the Relationship." Report prepared for the LA '84 Foundation, Los Angeles, CA, January.

———. 2009. "Re-Claiming the Sociological Imagination: A Brief Overview and Guide." In *Bureaucratic Culture and Basic Social Problems: Advancing the Sociological Imagination*, edited by Bernard Phillips and J. David Knottnerus, 25–38. Boulder, CO: Paradigm.

———. 2012a. "Beyond the Sporting Boundary: The Racial Significance of Midnight Basketball." *Ethnic and Racial Studies* 35 (6): 1007–22.

———. 2012b. "Rethinking Community-Based Crime Prevention through Sports." In *Sport for Development, Peace, and Social Justice*, edited by Richard Schinke and Stephanie J. Hanrahan, 73–87. Morgantown, WV: Fitness Information Technology.

———. 2015. "Sport and Social Intervention." In *Sociology of Sport Handbook*, edited by Richard Giulianotti, 335–44. London / New York: Routledge.

Hartmann, Douglas, and Brooks Depro. 2006 "Re-thinking Sports-Based Community Crime Prevention: A Preliminary Analysis of the Relationships between Midnight Basketball and Urban Crime Rates." *Journal of Sport and Social Issues* 30:180–96.

Hartmann, Douglas, and Christina Kwauk. 2011. "Sport and Development: An Overview, Critique, and Reconstruction." *Journal of Sport and Social Issues* 35 (3): 284–305.

Hartmann, Douglas, and Alex Manning. Forthcoming. "Kids of Color in the American Sporting Landscape: Limited, Concentrated, and Controlled." In *Child's Play*, edited by Michael Messner and Michaela Musto. New Brunswick, NJ: Rutgers University Press.

Hartmann, Douglas, and Darren Wheelock. 2002. "Sport as Prevention? Minneapolis's Experiment with Late-Night Basketball." *CURA* [Center for Urban and Regional Affairs] *Reporter* 32 (3): 13–17.

Harvey, David. 2005. *A Brief History of Neoliberalism*. London: Oxford University Press.

Hawkins, J. David, Richard F. Catalano, and Janet Y. Miller. 1992. "Risk and Protective Factors for Alcohol and Other Drug Problems in Adolescence and Early Adulthood: Implications for Substance Abuse Prevention." *Psychological Bulletin* 112 (1): 64–105.

Hays, Sharon. 2003. *Flat Broke with Children: Women in the Age of Welfare Reform*. Oxford: Oxford University Press.

Heclo, Hugh. 2001. "The Politics of Welfare Reform." In *The New World of Welfare*, edited by Rebecca Blank and Ron Haskins, 169–200. Washington, DC: Brookings Institute.

Henry, Ian P. 2001. *The Politics of Leisure Policy*. London: Macmillan.

Hoberman, John M. 1984. *Sport and Political Ideology*. Austin: University of Texas Press.

———. 1997. *Darwin's Athletes: How Sport Has Damaged Black America and Preserved the Myth of Race*. New York: Houghton Mifflin.

hooks, bell. 1994. *Teaching to Transgress: Education as the Practice of Freedom*. New York: Routledge.

Houlihan, Barrie. 1997. *Sport, Policy, and Politics: A Comparative Analysis*. New York, Routledge.

Howell, James C., ed. 1995. *Guide for Implementing the Comprehensive Strategy for Serious, Violent and Chronic Juvenile Offenders*. Washington, DC: US Department of Justice, Office of Juvenile Justice and Delinquency Prevention.

Hughes, Glyn. 2004. "Managing Black Guys: Representation, Corporate Culture, and the NBA." *Sociology of Sport Journal* 21 (2) 163–84.

Hughes, R, and Jay Coakley. 1991. "Positive Deviance among Athletes: The Implications of Overconformity to the Sport Ethic." *Sociology of Sport Journal* 8:307–25.

Hunt, Darnell M. 1999. *O. J. Simpson Facts and Fictions: New Rituals in the Construction of Reality*. Cambridge: Cambridge University Press.

Idelson, Holly. 1994. "Provisions: Crime Bill Provisions." With David Masci. *Congressional Quarterly Weekly*, December.

Ingham, Alan G. 1985. "From Public Issue to Personal Trouble: Well-Being and the Fiscal Crisis of the State." *Sociology of Sport Journal* 2 (1): 43–55.

Jackson, Bernard, Jr. 2007. "Hoop Dreams, Blacktop Realities: Basketball's Role in the Social Construction of Black Manhood." In *Basketball and Philosophy: Thinking Outside the Paint*, edited by Jerry Walls and Gregory Bassham, 158–67. Lexington: University of Kentucky Press.

James, C. L. R. [1963] 1983. *Beyond a Boundary*. Durham, NC: Duke University Press.

Jimerson, Jason. 1996. "Good Times and Good Games How Pickup Basketball Players Use Wealth-Maximizing Norms." *Journal of Contemporary Ethnography* 25 (3): 353–71.

———. 1999. "'Who Has Next?' The Symbolic, Rational, and Methodical Use of Norms in Pickup Basketball." *Social Psychology Quarterly* 62 (2): 136–56.

Johnson, Leola, and David Roediger. 2000. "Hertz, Don't It? Becoming Colorless and Staying Black in the Crossover of OJ Simpson." In *Reading Sport: Critical Essays on Power and Representation*, edited by S. Birrell and M. G. McDonald, 40–73. Boston: Northeastern University Press.

Johnson, Shane D., and Kate J. Bowers. 2003. "Opportunity is in the Eye of the Beholder: The Role of Publicity in Crime Prevention." *Criminology and Public Policy* 2 (3): 363–96.

Kappeler, Victor E., and Peter B. Kraska. 1997. "Militarizing American Police: The Rise and Normalization of Paramilitary Units." *Social Problems* 44:1–18.

Katz, Michael B. 1989. *The Undeserving Poor: From the War on Poverty to the War on Welfare.* New York: Pantheon Books.

Kearney, Jeremy, and Cahterine Donovan, eds. 2013. *Constructing Risky Identities in Policy and Practice.* Basingstroke, UK: Palgrave Macmillan.

Kelley, Robin D. G. 1997a. "Playing for Keeps: Pleasure and Profit on the Postindustrial Playground." In *The House That Race Built*, edited by Wahneema Lubiano, 195–231. New York: Pantheon.

———. 1997b. *Yo' Mama's Disfunktional! Fighting the Culture Wars in Urban America.* New York: Beacon.

Kellner, Douglas. 1996. "Sports, Media Culture, and Race—Some Reflections on Michael Jordan." *Sociology of Sport Journal* 13:458–67.

Kelly, Laura. 2011. "'Social Inclusion' through Sports-Based Interventions?" *Critical Social Policy* 31 (1): 126–50.

———. 2013. "Sports-Based Interventions and the Local Governance of Youth Crime and Antisocial Behavior." *Journal of Sport and Social Issues* 37 (3): 261–83.

Kelly, Peter. 2000. "The Dangerousness of Youth-at-Risk: The Possibilities of Surveillance and Intervention in Uncertain Times." *Journal of Adolescence* 23:463–76.

———. 2003. "Growing Up as Risky Business? Risks, Surveillance and the Institutionalized Mistrust of Youth." *Journal of Youth Studies* 6 (2): 165–80.

Kett, Joseph F. 1977. *Rites of Passage: Adolescence in America, 1790 to the Present.* New York: Basic Books.

Kettl, Donald F. 2002. *The Transformation of Governance: Public Administration for 21st Century America.* Baltimore, MD: Johns Hopkins University Press.

Kidd, Bruce. 2008. "A New Social Movement: Sport for Development and Peace." *Sport in Society* 11 (4): 370–80.

Kinder, Donald, and Lynn M. Sanders. 1996. *Divided by Color: Racial Politics and Democratic Ideals.* Chicago: University of Chicago Press.

King, C. Richard, and Charles Springwood. 2001. *Beyond the Cheers: Race as Spectacle in College Sports.* Albany: SUNY Press.

Kingdon, John. 2003. *Agendas, Alternatives, and Public Policies.* New York: Longman.

Korpi, Walter, and Joakim Palme. 1998. "The Paradox of Redistribution and Strategies of Equality: Welfare State Institutions, Inequality, and Poverty in the Western Countries." *American Sociological Review* 63:661–87.

Kozol, Jonathan. 1992. *Savage Inequalities: Children in America's Schools.* New York: Harper Perennial.

———. 2000. *Ordinary Resurrections: Children in the Years of Hope.* New York: Crown Publishers.

Kpo, Wolanyo. 1990. "Summary Evaluation Report: Midnight Basketball League Program 1989–90 Pilot." Windows of Opportunity, Inc. / Chicago State University, December.

Kramer, Ronald, and Raymond Michalowski. 1995. "The Iron Fist and the Velvet Tongue: Crime Control Polices in the Clinton Administration." *Social Justice* 22 (2): 87–100.

LA '84 Foundation. 2015. *Reforming Youth Sports: 3rd Annual Summit Report, October 9, 2014, Los Angeles, California*. Los Angeles: LA '84 Foundation. http://library.la84.org/9arr/Research Reports/LA84_2014_Summit.pdf.

LaFrance, Marc, and Genevieve Rail. 2001. "Excursions into Otherness: Understanding Dennis Rodman and the Limits of Subversive Agency." In *Sports Stars: The Cultural Politics of Sports Celebrity*, edited by Andrews and Jackson, 35–50. New York: Routledge.

Lapchick, Richard. 2003. "Crime and Athletes: The New Racial Stereotypes of the 1990s." *Sports Business Journal*. Retrieved September 8, 2008. www.bus.ucf.edu.

Leonard, David J. 2004 "The Next MJ or the Next OJ? Kobe Bryant, Race, and the Absurdity of Colorblind Rhetoric." *Journal of Sport and Social Issues* 29:284–313.

———. 2006. "The Real Color of Money: Controlling Black Bodies in the NBA." *Journal of Sport and Social Issues* 30 (2): 158–79.

———. 2010. "Jumping the Gun: Sporting Cultures and the Criminalization of Black Masculinity." *Journal of Sport and Social Issues* 34 (2): 252–62.

———. 2011. *After Artest: The NBA and the Assault on Blackness*. Albany, NY: SUNY Press.

Levermore, Roger. 2009. "Sport-In-International Development: Theoretical Frameworks." In *Sport and International Development*, edited by R. Levermore and A. Beacom, 26–54. Hampshire, England: Palgrave Macmillan.

Levermore, Roger, and Aaron Beacom. 2009. "Sport and Development: Mapping the Field." In *Sport and International Development*, edited by R. Levermore and A. Beacom, 1–25. Hampshire, England: Palgrave Macmillan.

———. 2013. "International Relations and Sport." In *Social Sciences in Sport*, edited by Joseph Maguire, 219–46. Champaign, IL: Human Kinetics.

Leviton, Laura C., and Russell G. Schuh. 1991. "Evaluation of Outreach as a Project Element." *Evaluation Review* 15 (4): 420–40.

Lewis, A. E. 2004. "'What Group?' Studying Whites and Whiteness in the Era of 'Color-Blindness.'" *Sociological Theory* 22:623–46.

Lieberman, Robert C. 1998. *Shifting the Color Line: Race and the American Welfare State*. Cambridge, MA: Harvard University Press.

Lipsitz, George. 1998. *The Possessive Investment in Whiteness: How White People Profit from Identity Politics*. Philadelphia, PA: Temple University Press.

Lipsyte, Robert. 1975. *Sports World: An American Dreamland*. New York: Quadrangle / New York Times Book Co.

Lott, Eric. 2013. *Love and Theft: Blackface Minstrelsy and the American Working Class*. With a foreword by Greil Marcus. New York: Oxford University Press.

Lovell, Rick, and Carl E. Pope. 1993. "Recreational Interventions." In *The Gang Intervention Handbook*, edited by Arnold P. Goldstein and C. Ronald Huff, 319–32. Champaign, IL: Research Press.

Luker, Kristen. 1996. *Dubious Conceptions: The Politics of Teenage Pregnancy*. Cambridge, MA: Harvard University Press.

Lusane, Clarence. 1991. *Pipe Dream Blues: Racism and the War on Drugs*. Boston, MA: South End Press.

MacAloon, John J. 1981. *This Great Symbol: Pierre de Coubertin and the Origins of the Modern Olympic Games*. Chicago: University of Chicago Press.

———. 1984. "Olympic Games and the Theory of Spectacle in Modern Societies." In *Rite, Drama, Festival, Spectacle: Rehearsals Toward a Theory of Cultural Performance*, edited by John J. MacAloon, 241–80. Philadelphia: Institute for Study of Human Issues.

———. 1987. "Missing Stories: American Politics and Olympic Discourse." *Gannett Center Journal* (Columbia University) 1 (2): 111–42.

———. 1992. "The Ethnographic Imperative in Comparative Olympic Research." *Sociology of Sport Journal* 9:104–30.

———. 1995. "Interval Training." In *Choreographing History*, edited by S. L. Foster, 32–53. Bloomington: Indiana University Press.

———. 1998. "Double Visions: Olympic Games and American Culture." In *The Olympic Games in Transition*, edited by Jeffrey O. Segrave and Donald Chu, 279–94. Champagne, IL: Human Kinetics.

Mackenzie, Doris Layton. 1990. "Boot Camp Prisons: Components, Evaluations, and Empirical Issues." *Federal Probation* 54:44–52.

———. 1993. "Boot Camp Prisons in 1993." *National Institute of Justice Journal* 227:21–28.

Mackenzie, Doris Layton, and James W. Shaw. 1990. "Inmate Adjustment and Change during Shock Incarceration: The Impact of Correctional Boot Camp Programs." *Justice Quarterly* 7 (1): 125–50.

Macleod, David I. 1983. *Building Character in the American Boy: The Boy Scouts, YMCA, and Their Forerunners, 1870–1920*. Madison: University of Wisconsin Press.

Mangan, J. A. 2000. *Athleticism in the Victorian and Edwardian Public School: The Emergence and Consolidation of an Educational Ideology*. London: Frank Cass.

Manza, Jeff. 2000. "Race and the Underdevelopment of the Welfare State: A Review Essay." *Theory and Society* 29:819–32.

Markowitz, Jonathan. 2011. *Racial Spectacles: Explorations in Media, Race, and Justice*. New York: Routledge.

Martinek, Thomas J., and Donald R. Hellison. 1997. "Fostering Resiliency in Underserved Youth through Physical Activity." *Quest* 49:34–49.

Mauer, Marc, and The Sentencing Project. 1999. *Race to Incarcerate*. New York: The New Press.

May, Reuben. 2008. *Living through the Hoop*. New York: New York University Press.

———. 2009. "The Good and Bad of It All: Professional Black Males Basketball Players as Role Models for Young Black Male Basketball Players." *Sociology of Sport Journal* 26 (3): 443–61.

Mbaye, Keba. 1995. *The International Olympic Committee and South Africa: Analysis and Illustration of a Humanist Sports Policy*. Lausanne, Switz.: International Olympic Committee.

McCann, Rebecca, and Cynthia D. Peters. 1996. "At-Risk Youth: the Phoenix Phenomenon." *Journal of Physical Education, Recreation, and Dance* 6 (2): 38–40.

McLaughlin, Milbrey W., Mertia A. Irby, and Julie Langman. 1994. *Urban Sanctuaries: Neighborhood Organizations in the Lives and Futures of Inner-City Youth*. San Francisco: Jossey-Bass.

McLaughlin, Thomas. 2008. *Give and Go: Basketball as a Cultural Practice*. Albany, NY: SUNY Press.

Mead, Lawrence. 1997. *The New Paternalism: Supervisory Approaches to Poverty*. Washington, DC: Brookings Institute.

Mendel, Richard A. 1995. "Prevention or Pork? A Hard-Headed Look at Youth-Oriented Anti-Crime Programs." Evaluative/feasibility report, American Youth Policy Forum, Washington, DC.

Mendelberg, Tali. 1997. "Executing Hortons: Racial Crime in the 1988 Presidential Campaign." *Public Opinion Quarterly* 61:134–57.

———. 2001. *The Race Card*. Princeton, NJ: Princeton University Press.

Mercer, Kobina. 1994. *Welcome to the Jungle: New Positions in Black Cultural Studies*. London: Routledge.

Midnight Basketball Australia Ltd. 2007. "Project Overview: Redfern Waterloo Midnight Basketball League." Crows Nest: Midnight Basketball Australia Ltd.

Midnight Basketball Zürich. 2007. "Sponsoring." Retrieved and archived by the author January 29, 2007. http://midnight-basketball.ch/sponsoring.php?id_location=.

Miller, Jerome G. 1996. *Search and Destroy: African-American Males in the Criminal Justice System*. Cambridge: Cambridge University Press.

Miller, Kathleen E., Merril J. Melnick, Grace M. Barnes, Don Sabo, and Michael P. Farrell. 2007. "Athletic Involvement and Juvenile Delinquency." *Journal of Youth and Adolescence* 36:711–23.

Morgan, William J. 1994. "Hegemony Theory, Social Domination, and Sport: The Mac-Aloon and Hargreaves-Tomlinson Debate Revisited." *Sociology of Sport Journal* 11:309–29.

Murray, Charles. 1984. *Losing Ground: American Social Policy, 1950–1980*. New York: Basic Books.

Myerscough, Keith. 1995. "The Game with No Name: The Invention of Basketball." *International Journal of Sport History* 12(1): 137–52.

National Playing Field Association. 2001. "November 2001: National Midnight Basketball Tournament in Mansfield" [press release]. Retrieved and archived by the author February 12, 2007. http://www.npfa.co.uk/content/newsarticle/36/index.html.

Newman, Joshua I., and Michael D. Giardina. 2011. *Sport, Spectacle, and NASCAR Nation: Consumption and the Cultural Politics of Neoliberalism*. New York: Palgrave MacMillan.

Nichols, Geoff. 1997. "A Consideration of Why Active Participation in Sport and Leisure Might Reduce Criminal Behaviour." *Sport, Education and Society* 2 (2): 181–90.

———. 2004. "Crime and Punishment and Sports Development." *Leisure Studies* 23 (2): 177–94.

———. 2010. *Sport and Crime Reduction: The Role of Sports in Tackling Youth Crime*. New York: Routledge.

Nichols, Geoff, and Iain Crow. 2004. "Measuring the Impact of Crime Reduction Interventions Involving Sports Activities for Young People." *Howard Journal of Criminal Justice* 43 (3): 267–83.

Novak, Michael. 1976. *The Joy of Sports: End Zones, Bases, Baskets, Ball and the Consecration of the American Spirit*. New York: Basic Books.

Omi, Michael, and Howard Winant. 1994. *Racial Formation in the United States: From the 1960s to the 1990s*. 2nd ed. New York: Routledge.

Oriard, Michael. 1991. *Sporting with the Gods: The Rhetoric of Play and Game in American Culture*. Cambridge: Cambridge University Press.

Pager, Devah. 2007. *Marked: Race, Crime, and Finding Work in an Era of Mass Incarceration*. Chicago: University of Chicago Press.

Patterson, Orlando. 1998. *Rituals of Blood: Consequences of Slavery in Two American Centuries*. New York: Basic Books.

Peck, Jamie, and Adam Tickell. 2002. "Neoliberalizing Space." *Antipode* 34 (3): 380–404.

Peterson, Ruth D., and Lauren J. Krivo. 2005. "Macrostructural Analyses of Race, Ethnicity, and Violent Crime: Recent Lessons and New Directions for Research." *Annual Review of Sociology* 31:331–56.

Pierson, Paul. 1994. *Dismantling the Welfare State? Reagan, Thatcher and the Politics of Retrenchment*. Cambridge: Cambridge University Press.

Pitter, Robert, and David L. Andrews. 1997. "Serving America's Underserved Youth: Reflections on Sport and Recreation in an Emerging Social Problems Industry." *Quest* 49:85–99.

Platt, Anthony M. 1994. "The Politics of Law and Order." *Social Justice* 21 (3): 3–13.

Pope, Steven Wayne. 1997. *Patriotic Games: Sporting Traditions in the American Imagination, 1876–1926*. New York: Oxford University Press.

Quadagno, Jill. 1994. *The Color of Welfare: How Racism Undermined the War on Poverty.* Oxford: Oxford University Press.

Rauner, Diana Mendley, L. Stanton, and J. Wynn. 1994. "Sports and Recreation for Chicago Youth: Existing Services, Opportunities for Improvement." Discussion Paper Number 51, Chapin Hall Center for Children, University of Chicago, January.

Reed, Issac. 1997. "Bigger and OJ." In *Birth of a Nation'hood: Gaze, Script and Spectacle in the O. J. Simpson Case,* edited by Toni Morrison, 169–96. New York: Random House.

Reeves, J. L., and R. Campbell. 1994. *Cracked Coverage: Television News, the Anti-Cocaine Crusade, and the Reagan Legacy.* Durham, NC: Duke University Press.

Riley, Alexander. 2010. *Impure Play: Sacredness, Transgression, and the Tragic in Popular Culture.* Lanham, MD: Lexington Books.

Rios, Victor M. 2011. *Punished: Policing the Lives of Black and Latino Boys.* New York: NYU Press.

Roberts, Dorothy E. 1997. *Killing the Black Body: Race, Reproduction and the Meaning of Liberty.* New York: Pantheon Books.

Roediger, David. 1997. "White Workers, New Democrats, and Affirmative Action." In *The House That Race Built,* edited by Wahneema Lubiano, 48–65. New York: Pantheon.

Russell, Katheryn K. 1998. *The Color of Crime: Racial Hoaxes, White Fear, Black Protectionism, Police Harassment and Other Macroaggressions.* New York: New York University Press.

Sampson, Robert J., Jeffrey D. Morenhoff, and Felton Earls. 1999. "Beyond Social Capital: Spatial Dynamics of Collective Efficacy for Children." *American Sociological Review* 64:633–60.

Sampson, Robert J., and Stephen W. Raudenbush. 1999. "Systematic Social Observation of Public Spaces: A New Look at Disorder in Urban Neighborhoods." *American Journal of Sociology* 105:603–51.

Sampson, Robert J., Stephen W. Raudenbush, and Felton Earls. 1997. "Neighborhoods and Violent Crime: A Multilevel Study of Collective Efficacy." *Science* 227:918–24.

Sampson, Robert J., and William Julius Wilson. 1995. "Toward a Theory of Race, Crime, and Urban Inequality." In *Crime and Inequality,* edited by John Hagan and Ruth D. Peterson, 37–54. Stanford, CA: Stanford University Press.

Sandford, Rachel A., Kathleen M. Armour, and Paul C. Warmington. 2006. "Re-Engaging Disaffected Youth through Physical Activity Programmes." *British Educational Research Journal* 32 (2): 251–71.

Savic, Enes. 2003. "Gewaltprävention durch Sport zur Verhinderung von Jugendkriminalität in sozialen Brennpunkten - dargestellt am Beispiel des Projektes 'Midnight-Basketball' in Hamburg - Rahlstedt." Retrieved and archived by the author March 13, 2007. http://www.streetlife.net/html/mbb.html. The archived version cited here contains summary points in English from which the quotations in the text were drawn.

Schultz, Lorina Espericueta, John L. Crompton, and Peter A. Witt. 1995. "A National Profile of the Status of Public Recreation Services for At-Risk Children and Youth." *Journal of Park and Recreation Administration* 13 (3): 1–25.

Schuman, Howard, Charlotte Steeh, and Lawrence Bobo. 1985. *Racial Attitudes in America: Trends and Interpretations.* Cambridge, MA: Harvard University Press.

Scott, Daryl Michael. 1997. *Contempt and Pity: Social Policy and the Image of the Damaged Black Psyche, 1880–1996.* Chapel Hill: University of North Carolina Press.

Segrave, Jeffrey O. 1980. "Delinquency and Athletics: Review and Reformulation." *Sport Psychology Today* 2:82–89.

Sherman, Lawrence W. 1997. "The Effectiveness of Local Crime Prevention Funding." In *Preventing Crime: What Works, What Doesn't, What's Promising,* edited by Lawrence W.

Sherman, Denise Gottfredson, Doris Mackenzie, John Eck, Paul Reuter, and Shawn D. Bushway, 68–89. Collingdale, PA: Diane Publishing Co.

Sherman, Lawrence W., Denise C. Gottfredson, Doris L. MacMenzie, John Eck, Peter Reuter, and Shawn D. Bushway. 1998. "Preventing Crime: What Works, What Doesn't, What's Promising." *National Institutes of Justice Research in Brief*, July.

Shields, David Lyle Light, and Brenda Jo Light Bredemeier. 1995. *Character Development and Physical Activity*. Champaign, IL: Human Kinetics.

Shivers, Jay S., and Joseph W. Halper. 1981. *The Crisis in Urban Recreational Services*. East Brunswick, NJ: Associated University Presses.

Simon, Jonathan. 2007. *Governing through Crime: How the War on Crime Transformed American Democracy and Created a Culture of Fear*. New York: Oxford University Press.

Skocpol, Theda. 1995. *Social Policy in the United States: Future Possibilities in Historical Perspective*. Princeton, NJ: Princeton University Press.

Smith, Robert C. 1995. *Racism in the Post–Civil Rights Era: Now You See It, Now You Don't*. Albany, NY: SUNY Press.

Snyder, Howard N., and Melissa Sickmund. 1999. *Juvenile Offenders and Victims: 1999 National Report*. OJJDP Statistical Briefing Book. Office of Juvenile Justice and Delinquency Prevention, Washington, DC, September 30.

Sommerfeld, Peter, Edgar Baumgartner, Roland Baur, Regina Klemenz, Silke Müller, and Edith Maud Piller. 2006. "Evaluation 'Midnight Basketball' Projekte Bericht im Auftrag der Gesundheitsförderung Schweiz." Basel, Switz.: Fachhochschule Nordwestschweiz, Hochschule für Soziale Arbeit.

Soss, Joe, Richard C. Fording, and Sanford F. Schram. 2011. *Disciplining the Poor: Neoliberal Paternalism and the Persistent Power of Race*. Chicago: University of Chicago Press.

Soss, Joe, and Garnet Kindervater. n.d. "At-Risk Youth and the Governance of Social Marginality." Hubert H. Humphrey School for Public Affairs, University of Minnesota, Minneapolis, MN. Unpublished manuscript.

Soss, Joe, Sanford F. Schram, and Richard C. Fording. 2008. "Neoliberal Poverty Governance: Race, Place and the Punitive Turn in U.S. Welfare Policy." *Cambridge Journal of Regions, Economy and Society* 1 (1):17–36.

Soss, Joe, Sanford Schram, Richard Fording, and Linda Houser. 2009. "Deciding to Discipline: Race, Choice, and Punishment at the Frontlines of Welfare Reform." *American Sociological Review* 74 (3): 398–422.

Spaaij, Ramon. 2009a. "The Glue That Holds the Community Together? Sport and Sustainability in Rural Australia." *Sports in Society* 12:1132–2246.

———. 2009b. "The Social Impact of Sport: Diversities, Complexities and Contexts." *Sport in Society* 12:1109–17.

Stanfield, Rochelle L. 1996. "Talking around 'Race.'" *National Journal*, September 28, 2059–62.

Swadener, Beth Blue, and Sally Lubeck, eds. 1995. *Children and Families "At Promise": Deconstructing the Discourse of Risk*. Ithaca, NY: SUNY Press.

Swartz, Teresa Toguchi, and Douglas Hartmann. 2007. "The New Adulthood? The Transition to Adulthood from the Perspective of Transitioning Young Adults." In *Constructing Adulthood: Agency and Subjectivity in the Life Course*, edited by Ross Macmillan, 255–89. Advances in Life Course Research, vol. 11. Elsevier/JAI Press.

Tavory, Iddo, and Stefan Timmermans. 2009. "Two Cases of Ethnography: Grounded Theory and the Extended Case Method." *Ethnography* 10 (3): 243–63.

Telander, Rick. 1976. *Heaven Is a Playground*. New York: Simon and Schuster.

Thomas, Damion L. 2012. *Globetrotting: African American Athletes and Cold War Politics*. Champaign: University of Illinois Press.

Thurman, Quint C., Andrew L. Giacomazzi, Michael D. Reisig, and David G. Mueller. 1996. "Community-Based Gang Prevention and Intervention: An Evaluation of the Neutral Zone." *Crime and Delinquency* 42 (2): 279–95.

Tierney, Joseph, P., and Jean Baldwin Grossman, with Nancy L. Resch. 1995. *Making a Difference: An Impact Study of Big Brothers/Big Sisters*. Philadelphia, PA: Public/Private Ventures.

Tindall, B. Allan. 1995. "Beyond 'Fun and Games': Emerging Roles of Public Recreation." *Journal of Park and Recreation Administration* 30 (3): 86–93.

Tucker, Linda. 2003. "Blackballed: Basketball and Representations of the Black Male Athlete." *American Behavioral Scientist* 47 (3): 306–28.

Uggen, Christopher, and Suzy McElrath. 2014. "Six Social Sources of the U.S. Crime Drop." In *Crime and the Punished*, edited by Douglas Hartmann and Christopher Uggen, 3–20. New York: W. W. Norton.

US Department of Housing and Urban Development. 1994. *Midnight Basketball: How to Give Young People a Chance*. Washington, DC: US Government Drug Information and Strategy Clearinghouse.

Venkatesh, Sudhir Alladi. 2000. *American Project: The Rise and Fall of a Modern Ghetto*. Cambridge, MA: Harvard University Press.

Wacquant, Loïc. 2004. *Body and Soul: Notebooks of an Apprentice Boxer*. Oxford: Oxford University Press.

———. 2008a. "Racial Stigma in the Making of the Punitive State." In *Race, Incarceration, and American Values*, edited by Glenn Loury et al., 59–70. Cambridge, MA: MIT Press.

———. 2008b. *Urban Outcasts: A Comparative Sociology of Advanced Marginality*. Cambridge: Polity Press.

———. 2009. *Punishing the Poor: The Neoliberal Government of Social Inequality*. Durham, NC: Duke University Press.

Wacquant, Loïc, and William Julius Wilson. 1989. "Poverty, Joblessness and the Social Transformation of the Inner City." In *Welfare Policy for the 1990s*, edited by Cottingham and Ellwood, 70–102. Cambridge, MA: Harvard University Press.

Weisburd, David, and John E. Eck. 2004. "What Can Police Do to Reduce Crime, Disorder, and Fear?" *Annals of the American Academy of Political and Social Science* 593 (1): 42–65.

Wheelock, Darren, and Douglas Hartmann. 2007. "Midnight Basketball and the 1994 Crime Bill Debates: The Operation of a Racial Code." *Sociological Quarterly* 48:315–42.

Wideman, John Edgar. 2001. *Hoop Roots*. New York: Houghton Mifflin/Mariner Books.

Wilkins, Nathaniel O. 1996. "Mayor's Night Hoops." In *Recreation Programs That Work for At-Risk Youth: The Challenge of Shaping the Future*, edited by Peter A. Witt and John L. Crompton, 237–44. State College, PA: Venture Publishing.

Williams, Lois. 2001. *Playing the Race Card: Melodramas of Black and White from Uncle Tom to O. J. Simpson*. Princeton, NJ: Princeton University Press.

Wilson, Brian. 1997 "'Good Blacks' and 'Bad Blacks': Media Constructions of African-American Athletes in Canadian Basketball." *International Review for the Sociology of Sport* 32 (2): 177–89.

Wilson, Brian, and Phillip White. 2001. "Tolerance Rules: Identity, Resistance, and Negotiation in an Inner-City Recreation/Drop-In Center." *Journal of Sport and Social Issues* 25 (1): 73–103.

Wilson, John. 1994. *Playing by the Rules: Sport, Society and the State*. Detroit, MI: Wayne State University Press.

Wilson, William J. 1987. *The Truly Disadvantaged: The Inner-City, the Underclass and Public Policy*. Chicago: University of Chicago Press.

Witt, Peter A., and John L. Crompton. eds. 1996a. "The At-Risk Youth Recreation Project." *Journal of Park and Recreation* 14 (3): 1–9.

———. 1996b. *Recreation Programs That Work for At-Risk Youth: The Challenge of Shaping the Future.* State College, PA: Venture Publishing.

———. 1997. "The Protective Factors Framework: A Key to Programming for Benefits and Evaluating for Results." *Journal of Park and Recreation Administration* 15 (3): 1–18.

———. 2003. "Positive Youth Development Practices in Recreation Settings in the United States." *World Leisure Journal* 45 (2): 4–11.

Wixon, Renee Vanman. 1998. "Promising Approaches to Youth Violence Prevention: A Program Planning Guide." Minneapolis Department of Health and Family Support, Minneapolis, MN, December.

Young, Alford A. 2004. *The Minds of Marginalized Black Men: Making Sense of Mobility, Opportunity, and Future Life Chances.* Princeton, NJ: Princeton University Press.